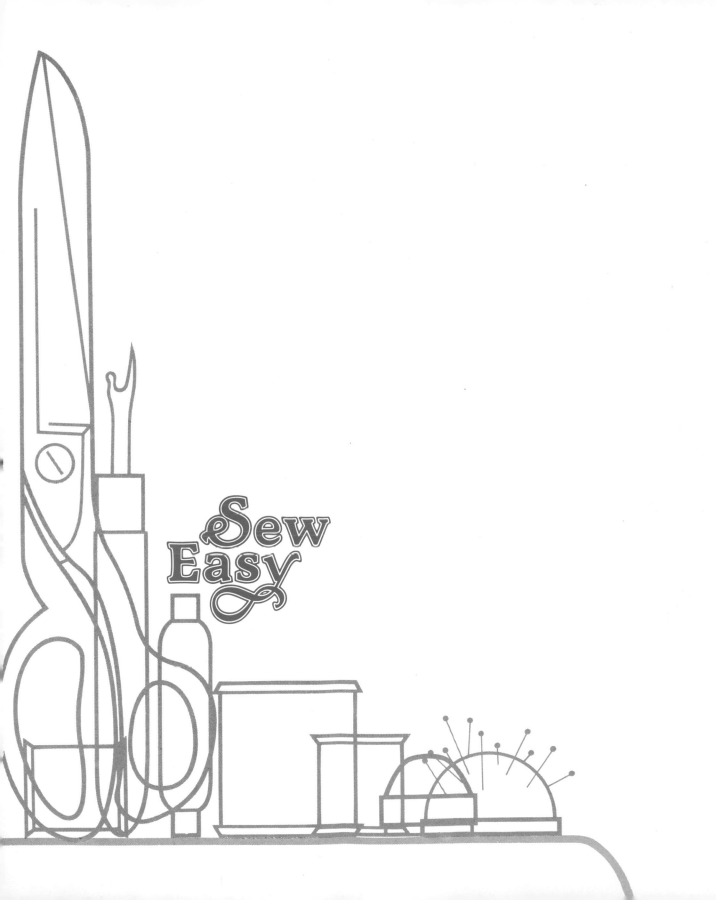

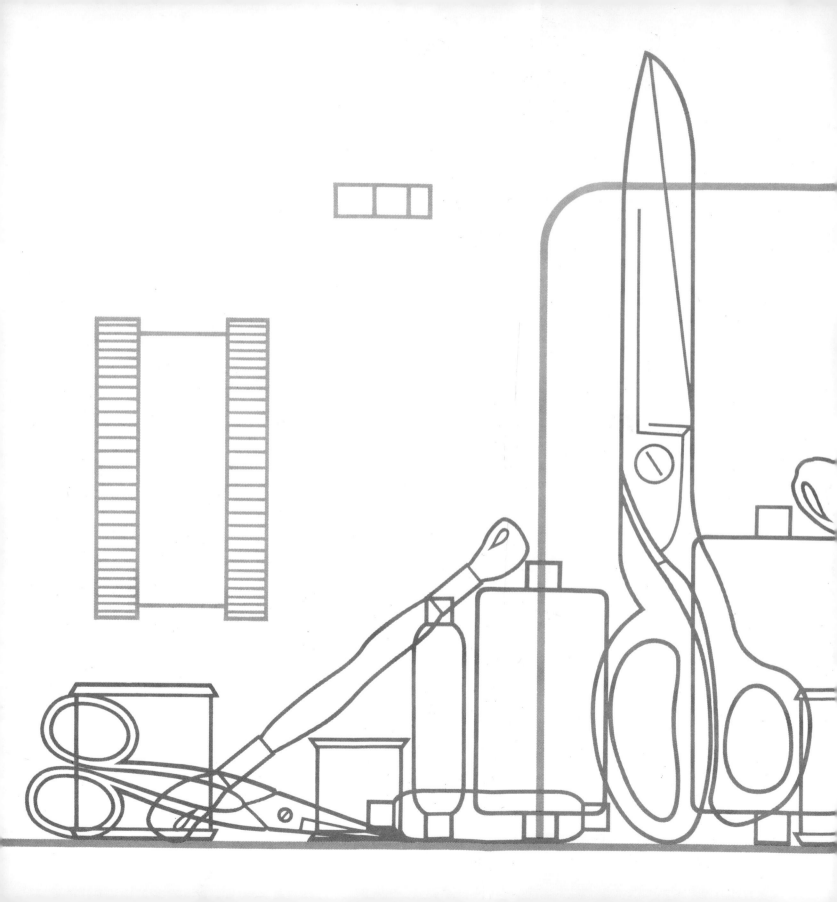

Sew Easy

An
Illustrated Guide by
JANET BARBER

William Luscombe

First published in Great Britain in 1976 by
William Luscombe Publisher Limited
The Mitchell Beazley Group
Artists House, 14 Manette Street
London W1V 5LB

ISBN 0 86002 048 7

Set in Monotype Sabon by
Tradespools Limited, Frome, England
Printed Photolitho in Great Britain by
Ebenezer Baylis & Son, Ltd.,
The Trinity Press, Worcester, and London

Editor Alan Folly
Production Bob Towell
Design Arka Graphics
Art Director Le Roy-Chen
Cover photograph by Harry Scotting

Introduction

SEW EASY is for all of you who, like me, enjoy making your own clothes, and things for your friends, family and home. Who want the satisfaction of working to a good standard without being puritanical about it, and to produce virtually professional results in modern terms. With the superb paper patterns available, sewing machines and other equipment, this is readily possible.

I hope the combination of clear explanation, drawings and photographs co-ordinated in an orderly way from the very first steps – from threading the needle and knotting the thread, right through to pressing the finished article – will be really helpful, and I wish you every success in your sewing.

I should like to thank most appreciatively the Vogue and Butterick Pattern Services for kindly permitting me to reproduce from a Butterick paper pattern and for supplying photographs and other material, and for their general helpfulness in this matter. Grateful acknowledgements and thanks, too, to the Singer Company (U.K.) Ltd., for permission to use photographs and drawings based on Singer sewing machines, and to Elna Sewing Machines Ltd. for photographs and other information, to A. E. Arthur Ltd., for permission to use photographs of their Diana (also shown on the cover) and Trimfit dress forms, and to Scovill-Dritz for use of their 'Superboard' cutting-out board, pressing and other equipment. Also to all other people concerned in SEW EASY – especially the illustrators Julia Hamlyn and Marian Appleton, designer Chensie Le Roy Chen and others at Arka Graphics, photographer Nicholas Wegner, and Helen Broughton and Elizabeth Wegner.

JANET BARBER

Contents

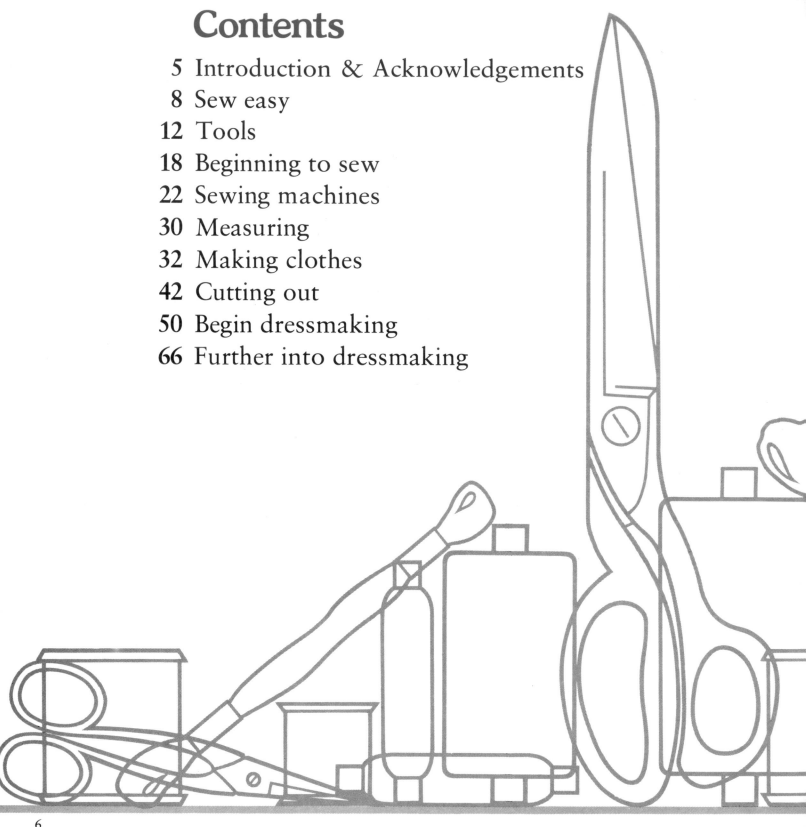

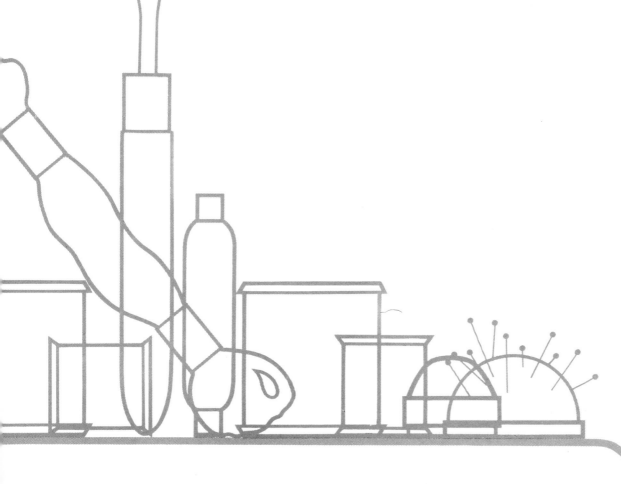

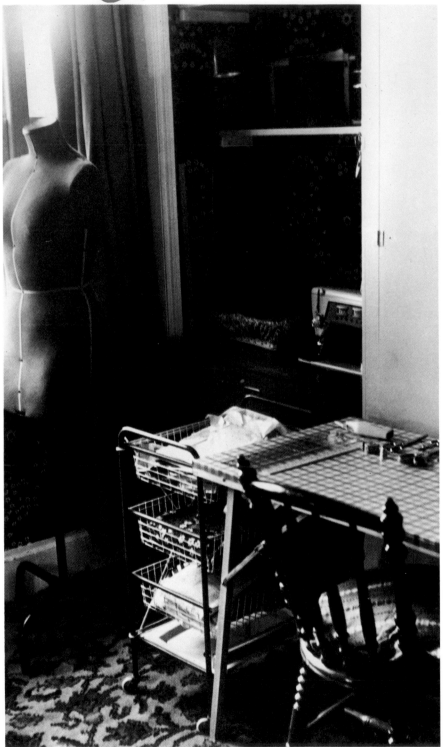

Sewing room corner

A streamlined, simple sewing set-up which works most effectively. The sewing machine in its well-lit alcove has shelves above for thread boxes, needlework basket, sewing books and journals. Scissors hang on a wall rack.

The sewing machine accessories and tool box are kept in the cabinet with the machine instruction book. Rulers, metre or yardstick, and skirt marker nearby.

When not in use, the sewing work-table is folded up and stowed away with the cardboard cutting board in the cupboard. A rack on castors with sewing, paper patterns and other items in use can be wheeled from machine to work-table conveniently.

Sewing notions and materials are stored in a tallboy and paper patterns in a filing cabinet. Pressing equipment, a dressmaker's form, a couple of upright chairs and a wastepaper basket complete a practical arrangement.

Dressmaker's dummy

A dressmaker's dummy, the nickname given to a dress form, is a model made to the dimensions and shape of the figure, with centre and seam guidelines on it, sometimes with a built-in hem marker. It is on a stand adjustable for height and is an invaluable asset when dressmaking.

There are various kinds of dress form available, the familiar elaborate fabric covered padded types, you can adjust to your main measurements, though not to your exact three-dimensional shape. Inexpensive cardboard-like dummies, that can be fitted to you, or plastic-coated wire mesh forms you can shape on your figure, do the job admirably. You can cover them with a thin layer of padding, marked with taped guidelines, if you wish.

These forms are easy to come by. You find them in the home sewing department in a store, or through mail order advertisements in dressmaking magazines and elsewhere, or specialist suppliers.

One tip: don't make the garment skin-tight on the form. It should fit easily with space to spare or it will fit too closely on you later. Leave a seam open too, or you may have difficulty in taking the garment on and off the form, unless it is a flexible type.

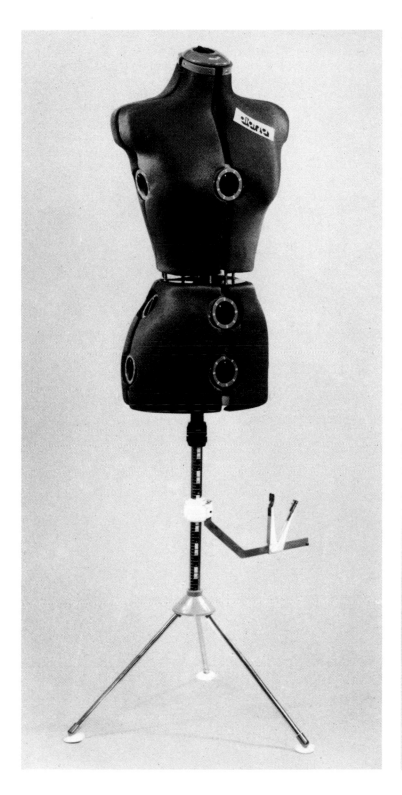
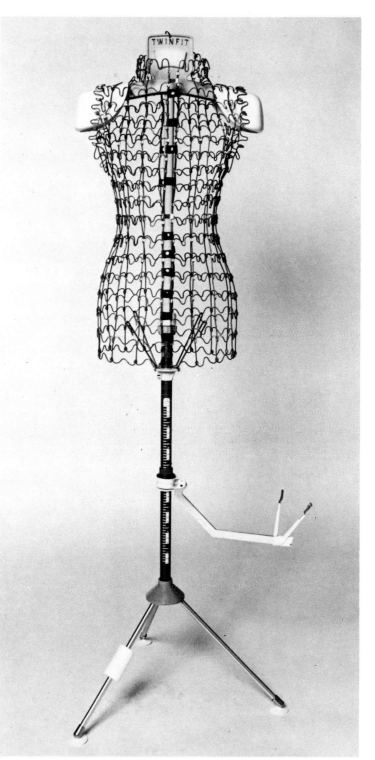

Work table

Sewing, especially dressmaking, requires a large, smooth, clean work surface, for spreading out the material with the pattern pinned on; cutting out and marking it or tacking the garment together. You can be sure the work will be easy to handle and keep free of snags and dust if you have a special table for the purpose.

The dining table is fine, provided you check that it has been dusted clean, and any grease has been removed, which could ruin your material. In any case, this is a table other people want to use.

Large corrugated cardboard cutting boards which fold away are a useful alternative. Marked with centimetres, and sometimes inches as well, they also have straight and bias guidelines. They cost only a few pounds. Two placed side by side, perhaps on the floor, give you a wide clean area for cutting out such problem garments as circular skirts.

Otherwise, the table should ideally be long, fairly wide, steady and smooth, with painted or varnished legs, splinter-free, and a plastic laminated surface, or covered with contact adhesive. You should be able to move all round it, for cutting out and working from both sides, and at the ends, and be able to sit anywhere along the sides for sewing with the work level, to avoid having to move it.

One ingenious solution where space is limited is to use a cheap wallpaper pasting table. Portable and made of lightweight materials, this table folds up to the size of a flat drawings case, with a carrying handle. Opened out, it makes a reasonable stable trestle table rather narrow, but a good length, about 180cm. long × 56cm. wide or 70in. × 22in. A trestle table is also suitable.

Whichever table you use, do paint or varnish it, and cover the top with plastic. If you use

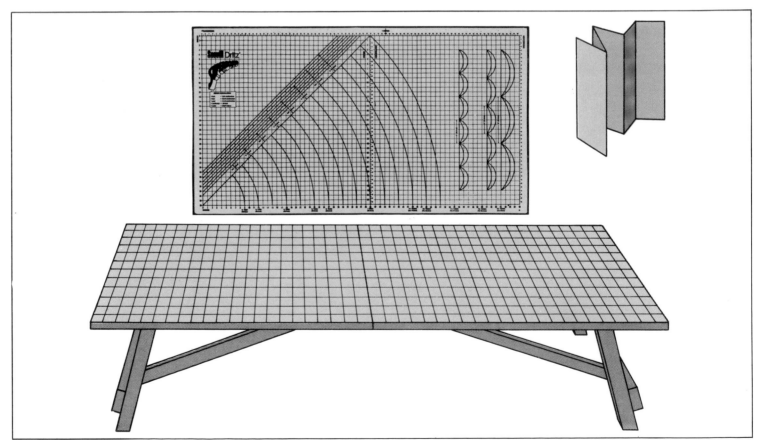

contact adhesive patterned with bold check gingham, carefully aligned at right angles with the help of a T-square, you can provide yourself with length and crosswise guidelines too.

Pressing equipment

As sewing proceeds the word 'press' crops up constantly. At every stage in sewing, careful ironing makes it easier to carry out the next stage from a well-prepared base. Otherwise the material would become steadily more crumpled, shapeless and formless. Final pressing of the finished garment is important also, to give it a good appearance and professional look.

Excellent sets of tailor's ham, pressing roll and press mitt, are obtainable not too expensively from large stores in most cities. These have a drill side and a thicker cloth side to the covers.

1 IRONING BOARD: It should be stable, streamlined and adjustable to the right height, with a stand for the iron. A Milium-coated ironing board cover makes an excellent pressing surface.

2 IRON: A 'dry' iron used with dampened press cloths for steam pressing, or a steam and dry iron. Steam-dry-spray irons are also available. Choose one with thermostatic controls clearly marked with words as well as numbers.

3 TAILOR'S HAMS: Hard, shaped cushions with padded covers, made in different sizes, for pressing the curved shapes of a garment.

4 SLEEVE BOARD: A small-size ironing board for fitting inside sleeves and pressing similar small items.

5 ROLL-SHAPED PRESSER: A padded roll for pressing sleeve and other seams and tailored collar roll lines.

6 PRESSING MITT: A padded covered mitt worn over the hand, the pad over the palm, for pressing gathers and puff sleeves etc.

7 BANGER: A wooden clapper (or you can use a clean brush back) for flattening steamed tailored collars or used over a pad, for tapping down glued leather.

8 VELVET PRESSING MAT: A mat with short wires like bristles, for pressing velvet face down. A homely alternative is a Turkish towel or a pressing cloth of velvet, or a stiff, clean clothes brush.

9 PRESS CLOTHS: A press cloth can be used dry, or damp for steam pressing. Cheese cloth or cotton sheeting press cloths are suitable for light fabrics, damped if need be first by sprinkling the cloth with water and rolling up for a minute or two before ironing. Drill or undyed canvas, or wool, are suited to wool pressing.

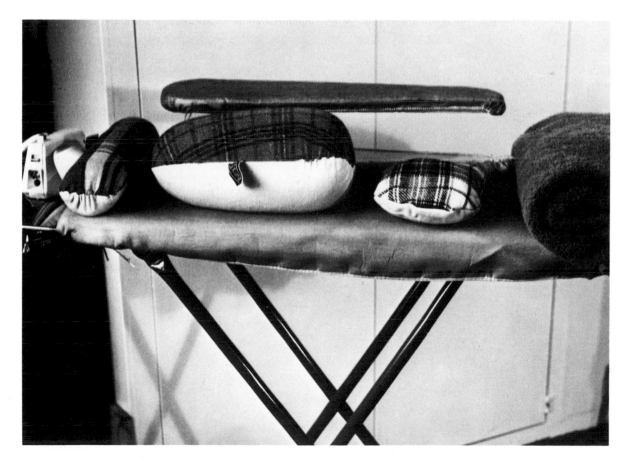

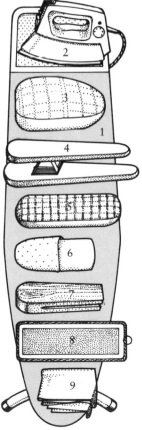

Tools 2

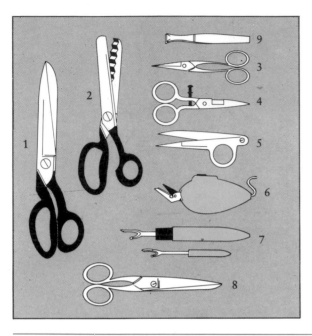

Cutting-out tools

Storing scissors: Scissors can be stored tidily in an easily accessible way on a row of plastic-coated cup hooks fixed to a board, or a metal kitchen tool holder, screwed to the wall in the sewing area. Keep the sharp points of embroidery scissors in a cork when not in use, and carry scissors points down.

1 CUTTING-OUT SHEARS: Large scissors used for cutting out material. Bent-handled shears allow for cutting the material level on the work table.
2 PINKING SHEARS: Scissors with serrated blades for cutting a zig-zag finish to the edge of material.

3 EMBROIDERY SCISSORS: Small pointed scissors, used for fine cutting, snipping thread and trimming.
4 BUTTONHOLE SCISSORS: Scissors with half blades for cutting buttonholes.
5 THREAD CLIP: Spring shears for quick thread snipping.
6 ELECTRIC SCISSORS. Battery operated for cutting material. Labour saving.

7 SEAM RIPPER: Sharp hook for unpicking seams by placing the hook blade under stitches and cutting neatly through the threads.
8 MEDIUM-SIZE SCISSORS: For general use in sewing, including trimming material edges or cutting out small shapes.
9 TWEEZERS: For picking thread out of material.

Marking tools

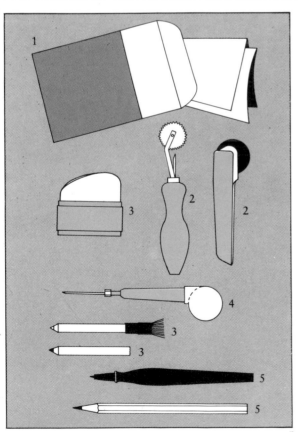

Various marking tools are needed for transferring the dressmaking pattern marks on to the material, as well as for marking any alterations during sewing. They are few, simple and inexpensive, and well worth obtaining (from the haberdashery department in a store or shop).

1 DRESSMAKER'S CARBON PAPER: Non-smudging sheets of special coloured carbon paper which are used for transferring the pattern markings onto the material, in conjunction with a tracing wheel, and with a piece of board under the material.
2 TRACING WHEEL: A small metal or plastic wheel with a serrated edge, fitted to a handle and rolled over the pattern markings and carbon paper, to transfer

them onto the material. A tracing wheel with a plain edge is used to impress marks on fine materials, without carbon paper.
3 TAILOR'S CHALK: Light, firm, compacted chalk, used for drawing pattern markings and alterations on material. It comes in white, blue or pink, in a slender-edged tablet or as powder, as well as in pencil form.
4 TAILOR'S TACKING TOOL: A needle threaded from a small spool in the handle,

which, when jabbed into the pattern markings, makes tailor's tacking stitches, and offers a quick and easy alternative to tailor's tacking by hand. Use in conjunction with a padded board.
5 MARKERS: A pencil and felt-tip pen will be needed not only for making notes when measuring, but for marking pattern alterations where necessary.

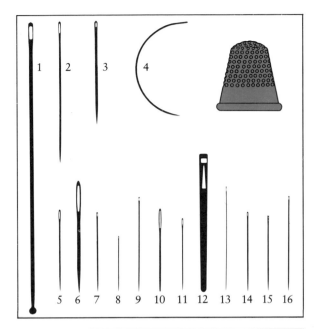

Needles, pins and thimble

There is a wide range of needles to suit every sort of sewing job, from slender little 'betweens' for fine hand sewing, to large double-pointed mattress needles used for making bedding.

A needle should be straight, sharp and completely free of rust, and chosen to suit the type and weight of the material being sewn. For example, when tacking you could use either a fine darner or a milliner's or straw needle, because you need a slightly longer needle for the tacking stitches. For embroidery on fine material, a crewel needle would be best, with its long eye which enables you to thread stranded and embroidery cottons easily. For ordinary everyday sewing, sharps are probably the most useful all-round needles for stitching up a hem or sewing on a button, or other plain sewing.

A list of needles which crop up fairly frequently in sewing is given here with their main applications. To begin with, you could have a large packet of assorted household needles, which would probably include one or two darners and even a needle threader. The lowest number, 1, is for the largest needle. The larger the number, the smaller the needle. Needles are best kept in a felt or flannel needle-book, and just as well in a home-made one.

A thimble is a metal or plastic cover worn when hand sewing, usually on the middle finger of the sewing hand, to protect the finger tip when pressing the end of the needle through layers of fabric. It should be a snug fit, neither slipping up and down nor pinching. Once you become accustomed to sewing wearing a thimble, you will wonder how you ever managed without one, especially when sewing thick or tough materials.

PINS: Pins must be rustless steel for dressmaking. Suit the pin size to the material thickness and durability or delicacy. Glass-headed pins are easy to see and pick up. A magnet is a boon for retrieving dropped pins.

THREADING A SMALL NEEDLE: (a) Trim thread at clean angle. (b) Dampen thread and pass through needle eye.

KNOT IN THREAD: (a) When threaded, pass thread end across needle point. (b) Wind thread round needle twice. (c) Pull needle through and form knot.

USING NEEDLE THREADER: (a) Pass hair-thin loop of wire on needle threader through needle eye. (b) Pass thread through wire. (c) Pull thread in wire loop back through needle eye. Remove thread from threader.

WOOL THREADING: (a) Pinch wool end over tip of large needle. (b) Press pinched wool through eye. Draw through.

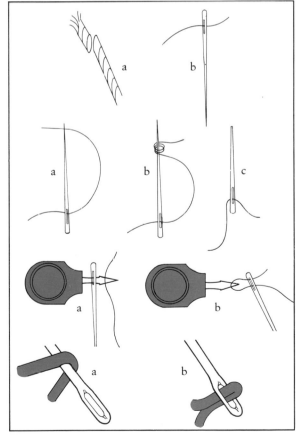

1 LONG BODKIN: For threading elastic, tape etc.
2 DOUBLE LONG DARNER: For heavy-duty darning.
3 CARPET NEEDLE: For sewing carpet.
4 CURVED SPRING NEEDLE: For upholstery sewing.
5 DARNER: For darning and tacking.
6 LARGE EYE WOOL NEEDLE: For sewing with wool.
7 SHARPS: Plain needles for general sewing.
8 BETWEENS: Similar to 'sharps' but shorter. For sewing fine stitches.
9 MILLINER'S OR STRAWS: Long slender needles for tacking and millinery sewing.
10 TAPESTRY: Blunt-tipped needles for canvas or linen embroidery. CHENILLE needles are similar to 'tapestry', but sharp pointed.
11 CREWEL: Embroidery needles.
12 BODKIN: For threading elastic through a hem or casing.
13 BEADING: For sewing on small beads.
14 BALL-POINT NEEDLES: Needles with rounded tips for sewing knit and stretch fabrics.
15 CALYX EYE: Slit through the top for easy threading.
16 GLOVE: Three-sided needle for sewing leather.

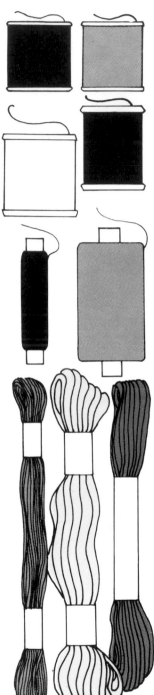

Thread guide

Today thread is made out of synthetic as well as natural fibres, and you should preferably use the type which corresponds with your fabric; to sew synthetic material with synthetic thread, and natural material with natural thread. For example, if perhaps you are sewing synthetic material such as Terylene, choose Terylene thread. For cotton or woollen fabrics, mercerised or plain cotton thread is suitable . . . and so on.

The thickness of the thread is important too, and would need to be appropriate to the weight, that is the density and thickness as well as heaviness, of the material. The thickness of the thread is shown in a number printed on the reel. Thread number 50 is fine, and would be suited to sheer materials; number 40 is a widely used medium thread. Lower numbers still indicate strong thread for sewing tough fabrics such as denim or drill.

Thicker grades of thread on slightly larger reels are now available for machine embroidery. Bear in mind that zig-zag and fancy-stitch patterns tend to use a larger amount of thread, twice as much at least as for straight sewing.

Extra strong threads, made of heavy-duty cotton or linen twist, are the ones to choose for sewing buttons on winter overcoats, or for stitching braid round carpet. Sometimes drawing heavy-duty thread like this through beeswax makes it easier to use and to avoid knots.

The thread guide given here suggests the appropriate needle to use, though there is no hard and fast rule. Different types of needle in the same size and thickness ranges are often interchangeable for different sewing jobs. The needle size would relate to the thickness of the thread, and also to the weight of the material.

Choose a thread colour which matches or is a shade darker than your fabric as it tends to show up when lighter.

Tools: Thread guide

	THREAD	NEEDLES		THREAD	NEEDLES		THREAD	NEEDLES
Tacking thread	Number 60 thread or Gun Basting Thread are light and disposable for tacking.	Fine darner or milliner's (also known as straws).	Machine twist	Number 36 or less. For heavy cotton such as calico, denim. Synthetic: Gütermann 30.	Strong sharps, small darner, strong machine needle.	Soft embroidery cotton	Soft string-like matt yarn for canvas embroidery, and simple decorative stitchery.	Large tapestry or crewel embroidery.
Mercerised machine twist	Number 50 thread. Use for sheer or extra lightweight materials in natural fibre.	Small-size sharps or betweens. Fine machine needle.	Buttonhole twist	Cord-like silk thread for sewing buttonholes.	Larger sharps or betweens, embroidery.	Tapisserie wool	3ply embroidery wool for felt, wool or blanket embroidery, or tapestry or canvas embroidery.	Tapestry, small darner, large crewel or wool needle.
Synthetic thread	Number 50 in polyester, nylon or Dacron or Terylene, or synthetic thread combined with cotton. Also Gütermann 100 Polyester Thread.	Small-size sharps or betweens. Fine machine needle.	Button thread	Extra strong cotton thread for sewing on buttons. Draw through beeswax for easier sewing.	Strong sharps.			
			Carpet thread	Thick linen thread for sewing carpet. Use beeswaxed.	Carpet needle.	Elastic thread	Elastic yarn for elastic shirring.	Large machine needle.
						Bead cord	Nylon thread or fine cord. Use beeswaxed where directed.	Beading needle.
Mercerised machine twist	Number 40 thread. Silky-looking cotton thread used for a wide medium range of natural materials; small buttonholes.	Medium-size sharps or betweens or machine needles.	**EMBROIDERY THREAD**					
			Machine embroidery thread (Mercerised cotton or synthetic)	Number 30. For machine embroidery and buttonholes.	Medium-size machine or twin machine needles.	Darning	Nylon thread, stranded mercerised thread; fine wool and nylon mixture thread for darning. For machine darning use mercerised thread number 50 for fine fabrics; number 40 or 30 for medium fabrics.	Darners and machine needles suited to the material thickness.
				THREAD	NEEDLES			
Silk thread	Fine silk thread used for tacking velvet, sewing silk and fine fabrics.	Fine sharps or betweens, machine needle.	Stranded embroidery cotton	Six-stranded mercerised cotton, in brilliant colours. Use from one to six strands.	Crewel embroidery, chenille.			

Measuring tools

When sewing and dressmaking, you will appreciate having a wide range of measuring tools to hand. Measuring takes place at every stage of sewing, from calculating the size of a simple square cushion cover, to working out the exact position of a double row of buttonholes on a bodice. Each type of measuring tool has its own particular application, whether used occasionally like a hem guide, or constantly like the tape measure. Some could be described as being essential, others optional, though helpful to have if possible.

It is wise to choose your measuring tools with metric markings these days, that is to say, marked in centimetres and millimetres with the metre as the larger unit. A metre is 39.37in. long compared with the 36in. yard. The centimetre is a hundredth part of a metre, and a millimetre a tenth part of a centimetre and a thousandth part of a metre. Machine stitches in metric units

for instance are so many millimetres long, or from 2 to 8 per centimetre rather than from 6 to 20 to the inch.

It is a system which has been in use in most countries in the world for many years, but which has only been officially adopted in the United Kingdom since January, 1975. Some people living in countries which have always had imperial measurements may find it difficult to make the change, though as soon as you become accustomed to working in metric measurements, happily they are discovered to be surprisingly easy to cope with.

As everything is now manufactured in metric measurements, probably the best choice for anyone who still thinks in yards and inches, will be to acquire sewing tools marked with metric units which also carry imperial markings. This way you can make conversions from imperial to metric or vice versa quickly and easily.

1 30CM. (12IN.) AND 46CM. (18IN.) RULERS: For general measuring and for use with the tracing wheel or tailor's chalk when transferring pattern markings.

2 TRANSPARENT 15CM. (6IN.) PLASTIC RULER: Handy for short measurements.

3 TRANSPARENT 'DRESSMAKER'S' RULER: A wide, long ruler with parallel slots for spacing buttonholes etc. Useful instead of a T square. Also Pikaby curved 'Fashion Ruler'.

4 T SQUARE: A T-shaped ruler for aligning the pattern etc.

5 TAPE MEASURE: A flexible measuring tape, reversible and plainly marked, preferably both in inches and centimetres.

6 SPRING SPOOL TAPE MEASURE: Carry when shopping for materials for instant measuring.

7 SEWING GAUGE: A small gauge with a movable marker, for instant repetitive measurement checks.

8 HEM GUIDE: Used for checking hem depth. 'Ezy-Hem' Gauge includes curved and straight edges, right angle and curved corners, and can be used with an iron following manufacturer's directions.

9 'SEE-THRU' SCALLOP GUIDE: For measuring and marking scallops.

10 HEM MARKER: A do-it-yourself version or traditional floor stand skirt marker needing help to use.

11 METRE AND/OR YARDSTICK: A long wooden ruler for making curtains or measuring longer pieces of fabric or items.

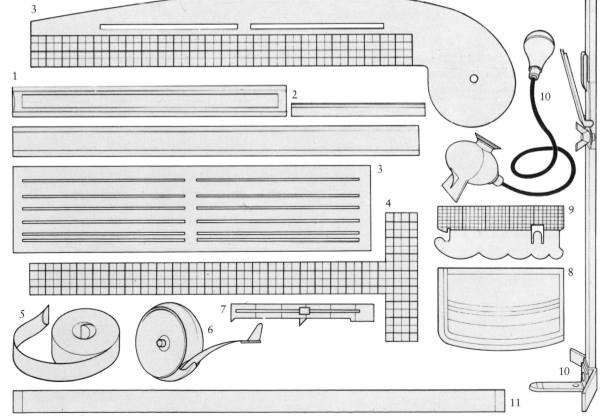

15

Materials section: a patchwork of fabrics

Among the information printed on the pattern envelope, is a suggested choice of suitable fabrics for making up the garment concerned. For instance, for a pattern for a smock coat, the materials include shantung, linen, lightweight wool crepe, and lightweight cashmere. Another pattern for a soft summer dress suggests using crepe, or jersey, or crepe de chine . . . and one for a tailored suit . . . gaberdine, flannel or double knit.

All of these names refer to very distinctive types of fabric, and are just a few among the scores available for you to choose from. It could be all too confusing, yet selecting the most appropriate material for the pattern will give better results in terms of the design.

There are other factors which have a bearing on the sort of material you choose – the way the material is constructed, such as whether it is knitted or woven, or whether the fibres are synthetic, that is, man-made, or from natural sources. Technical terms, which nevertheless do make a difference to your shopping list.

Man-made or natural?

Until about thirty or forty years ago, except for rayon, all textiles were made from natural fibres. Since then, chemically produced from petroleum by-products, synthetic fibres have come on the scene, and now account for over half the world's textile requirements.

Natural fibres

These traditional fibres, still very popular, are all made from raw materials obtained from natural sources. Wool fibres from the sheep; silk from silkworms; cotton from cotton plants; and linen from the strong fibres of the flax plant. Other 'natural' fabrics are made from goat's hair – mohair for one, cashmere for another. Camel hair, usually blended with wool, makes the favourite toffee-coloured material used for overcoats; alpaca, which comes from one of the llama breeds, is often used blended with cotton. Add to these, leather, fur and feathers and you can see the picture.

Man-made fibres

There are six main groups of synthetic fibres at present, world-wide: viscose/rayon; acetate and triacetate; nylon; polyester; acrylics and mod-acrylics; polyolefins (such as polythene). These are mostly only known as the smallprint below a variety of famous trade-names . . . Orlon, Acrilan, Courtelle . . . Terylene, Lycra etc.

Advantages and disadvantages:

NATURAL FIBRES: Though these vary in strength, and not all are soft (think of Harris tweed) they are usually of a comfortable texture for clothing. They 'breathe', and can be warm (wool) or fresh (cotton and linen). They are easy to sew, and handle, and have beauty and quality.

Unless they have been specially treated in the mill, they can be prone to shrink, and sometimes to felt and fray, when washed.

SYNTHETIC FIBRES: These have pronounced hard-wearing advantages; they are easily washable, and drip dry. They do not shrink or attract insects such as moths. Although not naturally absorbent like wool and cotton, the manufacturers have solved this problem, which used to give trouble in the early days, by texturing the fibres, to help the air to circulate through them. Today, synthetic fibres are very comfortable, the weaves and dyes brilliant and subtle.

BLENDS AND MIXTURES: If you have a fabric which is a combination of both man-made and natural fibres, such as Terylene and wool, then you probably have the best of both worlds.

So where does this make a difference to your dressmaking shopping list? Everything needs to harmonise in your sewing materials. If you sew tough synthetic material with cotton thread, this thread, because of its different, softer fibres is likely to fray and wear out more quickly than the garment fabric. Similarly, strong, synthetic thread would be far too abrasive for delicate fabric, like silk. For this you would need to buy silk or at least suitable mercerised thread.

Another important reason for knowing a lot about your fabric, is the lining you choose for it. An all-synthetic garment, man-made material lined with synthetic lining material and stitched with synthetic thread, apart from having the same resistance to wear and tear in all its parts, will be easier to launder or press.

Imagine how you would set about cleaning and pressing a nylon wind-cheater, lined with fine pure wool flannel.

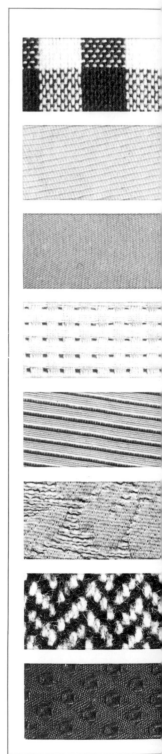

Kinds of weaves:

PLAIN WEAVE: This is the simplest weave, in which weft threads are woven in and out across warp threads, alternately like hand darning.

TWILL WEAVE: The weft threads are woven in steps across the warp threads, and the result is an attractive effect of diagonal patterns in the fabric.

SATIN WEAVE: In satin, the threads cross several of the opposing threads at a time, creating a smooth effect which reflects the light like a mirror.

BASKET WEAVE: Rather like plain weave, but with pairs or more of threads each way, woven in and out of one another alternately.

RIB WEAVE: Woven fabric with a pronounced corded effect, due to weaving thin fibres one way, with thicker fibres the other way.

JACQUARD WEAVE: elaborately woven patterns of roses and other fancy designs, such as brocade.

HERRINGBONE WEAVE: similar to twill weave but with the 'steps' of weaving taken both ways, so that a zig-zag effect is formed.

DOBBY WEAVE: Raised patterns rather like those you see on biscuits, or ice cream cornets, such as you find in waffle pique.

WOVEN OR KNITTED? The biggest effect comes when you begin to sew.

WOVEN MATERIAL: The way the threads are woven in and out can produce very different pattern effects on the fabric surface.

KNITTED MATERIAL: A whole range of know-how has evolved for sewing this successfully, from special stretch stitches on modern sewing machines, to ball-point needles, invented to part the knit when sewing rather than to split it with a sharp point. If you are lining extra-stretchy jersey, you would need to find a fine, firm but stretchy tricot lining material to go with it . . . and one in the right type of fibre.

Fabrics with a difference

FELT: A non-woven fabric formed by compressing fibres industrially. It does not fray, but up till now, the sort you can generally buy in the shops spoils with washing, and is not dye-fast.

LACE: Fabric made of threads knotted and twisted together in patterns, sometimes with ribbon stitched on top, or inter-woven with gold thread.

GOLD AND SILVER FABRIC: Metal- or plastic-coated threads woven or knitted in many fabric variations, with or without a mixture of other fibres. Available in copper, bronze, pewter and colours too.

SEQUIN AND BEADED FABRIC: This fabric is made of net encrusted with beads or sequins or both, and is usually very expensive.

PILE FABRIC: Carpet-like material with little soft bristles all over on a woven or knitted background such as velvet, or fake fur with short or long hairs and patterns to imitate animal fur, or as novelty fabric. *Nap* is the fabric or suede brushed surface.

Fabric treatments

NON-WOVEN BONDED MATERIAL: Fibres fused together with adhesive industrially, i.e. Vilene. Used for interfacing.

LAMINATED MATERIAL: Also known as bonded fabric. Ordinary material with a layer of foam plastic or thin tricot jersey glued over the wrong side, to act instead of underlining, and lining.

CREASE RESISTANT: Fabric treated to prevent it from creasing. To test, crumple a little fabric in the palm of your hand and pinch it. If it holds creases, it is not crease-resisting.

PERMANENT PRESS: Pleats and trouser creases set in place in the factory.

PRE-SHRUNK: *Important:* Natural fibres untreated may shrink. Man-made fibres won't. Look for a pre-shrunk label, or pre-shrink, yourself, before sewing. This applies to cord, tape and binding, too.

DYE OR COLOUR FAST: Dye which has been fixed not to run below a certain temperature. Read maker's instructions.

FLAME RETARDANT: Fabric treated to prevent the spread of flames through it. Important for children's nightwear and net. Teklan, a mod-acrylic, has fire-resistant properties.

OIL OR WATER REPELLENT: Fabric treated to resist penetration by oil or grease; or water, to keep out rain showers.

DRIP DRY: Material which won't need pressing if hung up carefully to dry after washing.

When shopping for dress fabrics:

METRIC SHOPPING FOR FABRICS:
Woven widths of dress fabrics on the bale: *

Metric	Imperial		
70cm.	27in.	127cm.	50in.
90cm.	36in.	140cm.	54in.–56in.
100cm.	39in.	150cm.	60in.
115cm.	45in.	175cm.	68in.–70in.
122cm.	48in.	180cm.	72in.

The smallest amount you can buy as a rule is 10cm. or $\frac{1}{8}$ yard ($4\frac{1}{2}$in.).

* Lining fabrics are available in many of these widths, but interfacing varies.

Dressmaking definitions:

SHEER: Transparent material.

SEMI-SHEER: Semi-transparent.

LIGHTWEIGHT: Lightweight fabric for a particular type of material. (Lightweight wool is heavier than heavy cotton, but very light for wool.)

DRESS WEIGHT: Heavy crepe, but when applied to wool, thin and relatively lightweight. A suitable weight fabric for dresses or dressmaker suits.

SUITING: Strong, fine tweed or worsted flannel, or similar fabrics, used for men's lounge suits and women's tailored costumes.

COAT WEIGHT: Heavy weight fabric for overcoats, from relatively light to very heavy.

Beginning to sew 3

Basic stitches

1 STARTING AND FINISHING: To secure a thread firmly, always begin with a knot or small backstitches on the wrong side of the material. End with two or three small backstitches or oversewing stitches.

2 RUNNING STITCH: Running stitch consists of level, equal-sized stitches and spaces in a line.
Method: (1) Use knotted thread (about 35–40cm. or 14–16in.) or as required for long gathering rows. Push the needle through the material, and bring the point out level a stitch in front. Push the needle through a stitch ahead. Repeat for two or three stitches and draw the needle and thread through. (2) Repeat for the row.

3 TACKING (also called BASTING): Long, easily removed stitches like running stitch.
Method: (1) Use slightly long knotted tacking thread (about 60cm. or 24in. long) and a fine darner or straw needle. (2) Pin the seam or hem or dart in position first. Begin close to the proposed stitch line. (3) Work with the material level and take the tacking through all layers to be joined. Diagonal tacking is for thick turnings and slip basting (see p. 44) worked from the right side. (4) Finish with long crossed backstitches.

4 BACKSTITCH: Backstitch is a line of level stitches which make a sturdy neat join.
Method: (1) Use a 'sharp' needle and not too long thread (about 30cm. or 12in.). Beginning from the right, push the needle through the material from the back, and draw the thread after it. (2) Push the needle in again, on the stitchline, a stitch *back* and bring it out a stitch ahead. (3) Repeat, always putting the needle in at the end of the last stitch. Do not draw the stitches tightly so they pucker the material.

5 OVERSEWING: Oversewing is stitching over the edge of material, or to join two layers.
Method: (1) Use knotted thread, not too long (about 30cm. or 12in.) and a plain sewing or embroidery needle. Push the needle through from the back, just below the edge. (2) Draw the thread right through and take it back over the edge a short stitch to the left or right. (3) Push the needle in again as before. Repeat 1 and 2. Do not pucker material. End with one or two overstitches and tuck the cut thread end between the layers.

6 HEMMING STITCH: Hemming is a plain stitch for fastening down hems or for stitching round

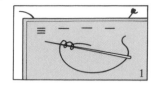
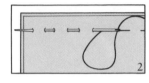
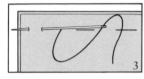
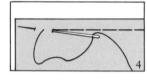
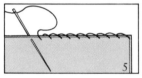
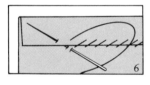
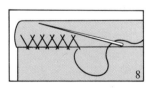
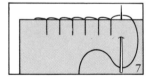
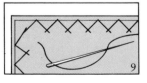

appliqué. For hems the aim is not to let the stitches show too much on the right side of the material. Keep the stitches even.
Method: (1) The hem is turned first (or appliqué tacked in place). Use knotted thread, not too long (about 30cm. or 12in.) and a plain sewing needle. (2) Starting from the right, push the needle into the material under the hem edge, and bring it through. Draw the thread after. (3) Push the needle into the main material a stitch along, close under the hem edge, picking up just two or three of the fabric threads. Repeat. Hem round the appliqué edge in the same way.

7 BLANKET STITCH: Blanket stitch, usually made for fastening down a single turning of thick material, or for decorating an edge. Also closed-up for simple buttonholes.
Method: Start from the left, with the edge of the material at the top, and the right side facing you. Start with a backstitch on the wrong side. (2) Push the needle into the material a stitch length below the edge, in front, and take it point up vertically at the back of the material but in front of the thread. Draw the needle and thread through evenly. (3) Pivot stitches round a corner. A wheel of blanket stitches pivoted from the centre can be used in embroidery.

When stitching a single turning with blanket stitch, work from the wrong side and always put the needle in just below the tacked-down raw edge of the turning.

8 HERRINGBONE STITCH: A flat, decorative stitch used for fastening down a single turning or in interfacing and appliqué. Work from wrong side for single hem, otherwise from right side.
Method: Use not too long knotted thread and a plain sewing needle or embroidery thread and needle. (1) Starting from the left, push the needle through from the back of the material. (2) Draw the thread through and push the needle in again a stitch down to the right diagonally. (For a hem, under the raw edge.) (3) Push the needle in level across the back of the material, a small stitch to the left. (4) Draw the thread through, and push the needle in again a stitch up to the right diagonally. (5) Bring the needle out a small level stitch to the left. (6) Repeat, making level, equal-sized stitches. End with backstitches.

9 CATCH STITCH: An opened out form of Herringbone stitch for sewing on interfacing.

18

Now with a few simple sewing essentials ready, tools, scissors, needles, threads, materials and some basic stitches, you can begin to sew. (If you want to sew some simple item why not make the cushion cover on p. 30.)

Organising the work area is important. The maxim 'Clear as you go' is as important in sewing as it is in cooking. An uncluttered surface on your work table or cutting board in a good light, is a good point to start from.

PREPARING THE MATERIAL: Separate the pieces you will be working on from the rest. Place these flat on the table and smooth them out. Handle them firmly but lightly, matching raw edges and folding them level, with as little picking up and crumpling as is practical. The right side of the material is the brighter, best side; the wrong side is the back of the fabric, the unprinted, dull side, except in reversible fabrics, such as gingham. 'Facing' in this context means placing the right side surfaces together, or the wrong side surfaces, as directed.

PINNING: With the folded or faced together material placed on the work table, try to move it as little as possible when putting in the pins, which are needed to anchor a seam or a dart in place before tacking and sewing begins.

Using the appropriate pins for the material, gently slip your finger and thumb over the edge to hold it firm, then put the pin in firmly through all layers, bringing it out about a centimetre further on. Pin at about every six to eight centimetres or two and a half to three inches, and more frequently for knitted, floaty or slippery fabrics. To secure a seam firmly, especially with springy material, it may be preferable to pin parallel to the stitchline in the seam allowance, but for stretchy, soft knits, or setting a sleeve into an armhole, right angled pinning is more suitable.

THIMBLE: Wear your thimble on the middle finger of your sewing hand, and press the tip of the thimble onto the needle to help you to push it through the material without making your finger sore.

TACKING: With the pinned-together fabric shapes resting flat on the table, try to tack with the material level, merely lifting up the edge as you sew. Tack in a straight line close to the stitch line, or evenly round curves. This helps as an

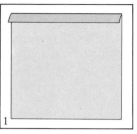

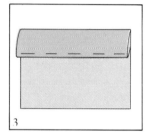

extra seam guide when machining later. When the tacking is complete, remove the pins.

HAND SEWING: For hand sewing you often need to hold the prepared sewing over your hand. Have your threaded needle ready, with not too long a piece of thread, or it may tangle. Hold the part you are going to stitch over the index finger of your non-sewing hand, pinching it between your thumb and middle finger. Begin to stitch evenly, carefully, without hurrying, moving the sewing along as each part is stitched, always anchoring the thread securely at the beginning and end.

It is easier to stitch some wide, light fabric garments with the sewing spread out flat on the work-table. When finished, remove the tacking stitches.

Turning a basic hem is a job which soon arises in sewing. Here is how to set about it.
1 Fold over raw edge 1cm. or $\frac{3}{8}$in. on to wrong side.
2 Fold over a second time to the required hem depth. Pin and tack folded edge.
3 Remove pins and hem.

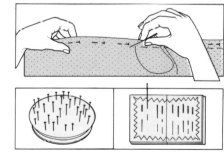
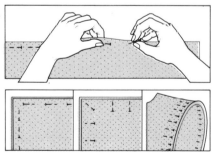

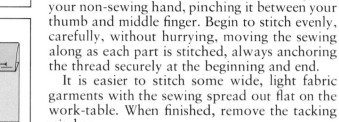

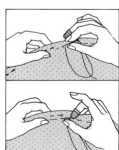
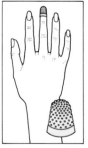

Bias binding

BIAS BINDING is a band of bias cut fabric folded and stitched over the edge of material. It gives a finished edge without taking away any of the material in hem turnings. It is decorative as well as practical and adds a plain brightly-coloured border to outline patterned material, or a pretty patterned edge to plain material. Rather wide bias bindings in stripes or plaid, or check gingham can give a dull outfit considerable sparkle.

It has other uses: as braid stitched flat along both edges; bias binding sewn on this way can act as casing for elastic etc.; for finishing seams, especially the raw edges of armhole seams in unlined coats; as tie strings or rouleau for button loops, folded over and machined along its length; for facing hems.

BIAS: The word 'bias' means that the material has been cut 'on the cross'. If you visualise a square of material with the selvages at each side and the raw edges across above and below, the bias is the diagonal from the top left corner to the lower right corner, or from the upper right corner to the lower left corner. If you were to take these two corners into each hand and tug them, you would be able to stretch the fabric slightly.

For bias binding you need strips of material cut along this diagonal line, so that the binding can be stretched round curved edges. A straight strip of material cut from the straight grain of the material, that is from up and down the material, or one cut across the material, doesn't have any built-in stretch in woven fabrics. It would have to be pleated and tucked and gathered to persuade it to fit round a curved edge, and would be far too bulky. Straight cut strips can only be used to bind or face a straight edge or for shaped facings.

KNITS: With knitted fabrics with built-in stretch the problem is less difficult, but knits tend to be rather thick to handle for binding, and to roll into untidy shapes. Knit binding usually needs an extra row of top stitching to make it stay flat, and to be machined along with zig-zag stitches, or special stretch stitches if it is sewn round stretch material.

COMMERCIAL BIAS BINDING: Bias binding – by the metre or in packets – is obtainable in haberdashery shops and store departments, and a rainbow range of colours. The most common

width is 12mm. or $\frac{1}{2}$in., in fine cotton or nylon, 25mm. or 1in. and 50mm. or 2 in. widths are popular too, the latter more as ready-made hem facing. Unlike home-made bias cut strips, commercial bias binding is turned in along both raw edges, an extra convenience.

MACHINED BIAS BINDING: For advice on sewing on bias binding by the special binding attachment on your sewing machine see page 26.

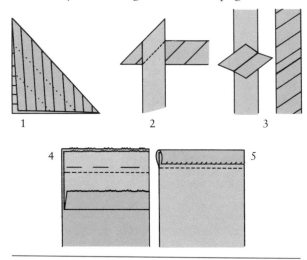

Facing

FACING: Facing is a bias strip of material sewn to the edge of the main material and folded over completely, so it gives a flat, ribbon-like finish along the edge. It can be used either on the right or wrong side of material, such as for lengthening a skirt where the hem allowance is let down to gain extra fabric, when facing is added to tidy the raw edge.

Facings can be shaped too. More about this and those deep turned back facings inside jacket fronts, called 'extended facings', on page 81.

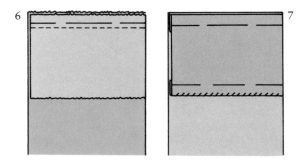

Making your own bias strips (1) With selvages at sides and raw edges top and bottom, mark a diagonal line for the first strip, using chalk, pins or tacking thread marking. Fold material along diagonal line. Cut along fold. Make second fold for strip width. Repeat for other strips, and cut out.

(2) Place ends of bias strips at right angles over one another, right sides facing, and pin them together as shown. Tack. Remove pins and stitch across.

(3) Open out jointed strips, and press seams open. Trim edges of strip level.

BIAS BINDING:
(4) Right sides facing, place raw edge of binding against raw edge of material. Pin binding to material. Tack and remove pins. Backstitch or machine binding to material about 0.5cm. or $\frac{3}{16}$in. from raw edge (in crease of bought bias binding).

(5) Fold binding strip over edge onto wrong side of material. Press. Turn under other raw edge and press (except for already turned bought binding). Pin and tack folded over binding to wrong side of material. Remove pins. Hem in place, just above stitch line. Do not allow stitches to show through to right side of binding.

SEWING ON FACING:
(6) Measure, cut out and join facing strips as for bias binding. A facing strip for a hem would usually be cut to the required hem depth plus the seam allowances. Right sides facing, match the raw edge of the facing

to the raw edge of the material, and pin about 1.25cm. or ½in. from the edge. Tack the facing to the material all round, then remove the pins and machine with straight stitching.

(7) Turn the facing onto the wrong side of the material. Press. Pin. Tack. Remove pins and hem or slip hem the facing to the material along the inner, turned under edge.

CORNER: To mitre is a way of making a neat join at a corner.

(8) A MITRING BIAS BINDING:
(a) Follow previous instructions (4) for sewing on bias binding, but at the corner make a diagonal pleat in it.
(b) Turn the binding over onto the wrong side of the material and turn under the other raw edge. Following the previous instruction for sewing on bias binding (b) pleat the corner on this side also. Oversew these corner pleats if necessary.

(9) MITRING FACING: To face a corner.
(a) Tack the facing to the right side of the material as before. Pleat the facing diagonally at the corner. Stitch right across the diagonal crease of this pleat. (b) Cut away the mitre pleat leaving about 1.25cm. or ½in. seam allowance. Open out this seam allowance and press. Now machine the facing all round the edge close to the tacked stitchline, and taking in the mitred corner.
(c) Turn the facing onto the wrong side and hem. (Facing can also be mitred onto the right side and top-stitched.)

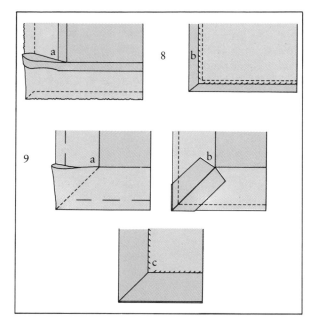

SCALLOPS:
1 Plan the scallops to balance along the facing, and draw (on tissue paper if wished, which can be torn away after the machining). Pin and tack facing right sides together along the scallop edge.
2 Machine or backstitch the facing to the material round the scallop outline. Remove the tacking and paper.
3 Cut away the facing and material outside the scallops, tapering close into the points. Cut little snips into the seam allowance, but not through the stitches, so that the scallops will lie flat when turned.

4 Turn the facing onto the wrong side. Push out and tack round the scallops. Press. Turn in the raw edge. Pin and tack. Remove the pins, press, and slip hem lightly.
5 The pressed, finished scalloped edge should not show any stitches on the right side.
6 Pointed zig-zags can be made in the same way, but substituting triangular shapes for round ones.
7 Zig-zags can also be bound, with mitred corners at the inner and outer angles.

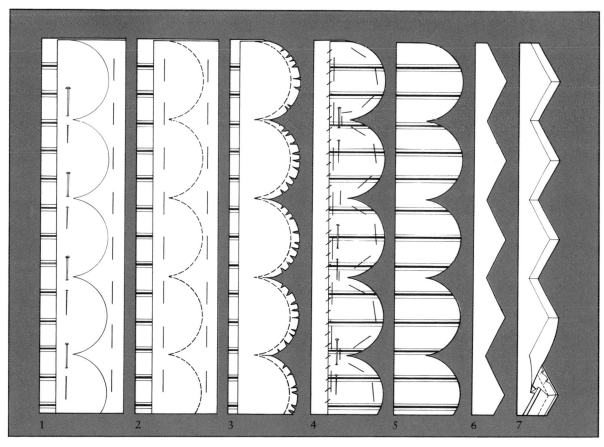

Sewing machines 4

Choice of sewing machines

Probably one of the most worthwhile shopping around exercises is when you set out to buy a sewing machine. Opportunities for buying re-conditioned bargains, or sales drive special offers are frequently available. It is important too, to try and find out all you can about what the many different models offer, so you really do get the best value, and the best one for you.

Hand- or treadle-operated machines, the older type, are still obtainable second-hand and in use in many households. Most sewing machines today, however, are powered by electric motor, from portable, often very versatile, versions the size of a lightweight typewriter, to super-automatic machines in a cabinet.

Types of sewing machines

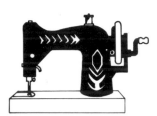

HAND SEWING MACHINES: Operated by turning a hand wheel, this machine will usually sew straight stitches. Modern versions will reverse the stitch line for finishing off, and have a number of attachments for different sewing jobs.

TREADLE MACHINE: A treadle machine has a movable grid underneath pushed up and down by the feet to operate the needle. It is usually a straight stitch machine and has a variety of sewing attachments. You can acquire the knack of operating the treadle, and practising straight stitch rows on lined paper.

ELECTRIC MACHINE: With electricity you merely switch on, press your foot on the foot control, and immediately the needle starts to go up and down at speed, stitching without any effort on your part. Electric sewing machines come in several categories. The simplest is the straight stitch model, with attachments for a variety of sewing jobs. All sewing machines have straight stitch as the basic stitch, but the majority of modern ones also do *zig-zag stitching*, which increases the number of sewing jobs possible.

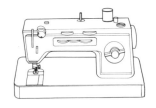

SEMI-AUTOMATIC MACHINES are straight and zig-zag machines, programmed in addition to carry out a limited number of fancy stitch patterns for special stitches for sewing knits, etc.

FULLY AUTOMATIC SEWING MACHINES carry out a wide range of sewing functions automatically. Extra cams or discs can be inserted into the machine to widen its range of stitch patterns and make it possible to carry out practically any sewing job you will encounter by machine.

Some questions you could ask when shopping for your machine. How up-to-date is this model? (You don't want to miss out on any improvements.) Is this a practical machine for you? Have you got space for storing it? Would it be heavy for you to move? Is a carrying case or solid non-wobbly cabinet or table available to house it? If so, how much will they add to your bill? A cabinet should be rock steady with a good work area, and comfortable to work at, and include storage space.

Basically what sort of machine is it? Straight stitch? Plain zig-zag? Semi-automatic, automatic or super-automatic? Are the electricals safe and well thought out and do they conform to lawful standards? Will the machine interfere with television or radio when operating? Is it noisy? What sort of controls has it got? Are they plainly marked and easy to adjust? The same goes for the bobbin. Is it easy to fill, and has it any automatic controls? Has the machine got an adequate range of stitch lengths? Forward and reverse stitching? Does it have a good foot control? An effective non-glare light? Helpful built-in stitch guide lines? Will the machine: blind-stitch? sew on binding? a button? sew elastic or knits with a stretch stitch? Will it overedge a seam? Zig-zag stitch a buttonhole? Fully automatically? Darn? How many embroidery stitches will it do, and what practical applications do these stitches have? Such as multi-stitch zig-zag which looks pretty and is also useful for sewing on elastic. What sort of attachments does it have? Has it got a quilting foot? A zipper foot? A tucking attachment? A roller foot for sewing P.V.C.? A narrow hemmer? Among others. Can other attachments be added when new ones are brought out?

At a more exotic level, will it do free motion darning and embroidery? Sew circular stitching? Smocking? Are additional cams available to increase the range of stitches? Does it have a free arm for tubular sewing?

Maintenance: Is it easy to maintain, backed by good service and spare parts facilities? Does it have a tool kit? Is the instruction book comprehensive, fully illustrated and easy to use not only for sewing with the machine, but for maintaining it? Are any lessons available to help you use the machine when you buy it?

Machine parts

Perhaps you haven't realised the number of jobs a sewing machine will take care of.

It is worth getting to know yours thoroughly, so you can make the fullest use of its versatile applications in dressmaking and home sewing, and as a time- and money-saver.

Although designs vary in detail, all sewing machines have a lot in common, like different makes of motor cars. Why not work your way round this chart, and in the process learn about a sewing machine? Then turn to your own instruction book, and do the same with your own model.

Advanced sewing machines have additional interchangeable discs called 'cams' for a greater variety of stitch patterns. Another spool pin for the second colour thread will be included where twin needle sewing is available.

On the floor the foot control is pressed to operate the needle.

After sewing the machine should be disconnected and the plug taken out of the socket.

MACHINE NEEDLES: A sewing machine needle has a flat side or a long groove to enable you to insert it in the needle bar in its correct position. A minute number is engraved on it. Colour coding helps size selection.

EXTRA-FINE NEEDLE for sewing very fine fabrics.
British size: 9
Continental size: 65
Thread: 60–50
FINE NEEDLE for sewing fine or sheer fabrics such as: lawn, silk, voile, lace, chiffon, light taffeta, organdie, velvet.
British size: 11
Continental size: 70–75
Thread: 50

MEDIUM NEEDLE for sewing medium fabrics such as cotton poplin, brushed rayon, satin, cotton piqué, flannel, heavy crepe, wool and nylon or cotton mixtures, fine jersey.
British size: 14
Continental size: 80–90
Thread: 50–40
HEAVY NEEDLE for sewing tough or rather thicker materials, such as tweed, calico, drill, denim, towelling, sailcloth, double jersey.
British size: 16
Continental size: 100
Thread: 40–36–30 and under

EXTRA HEAVY NEEDLE for sewing weighty, thick bulky fabrics such as winter coating or upholstery.
British size: 18
Continental size: 110
Thread: 36 or under
WEDGE-POINTED NEEDLES for sewing leather, to be used with a longer machine stitch length. Available in varied sizes.
BALL-POINT NEEDLES for sewing knits.
TWIN NEEDLE two-pointed needle for sewing twin rows of stitching.

Machine needle threaders can be purchased separately and are in various designs. Some sewing machines have built-in needle threaders.

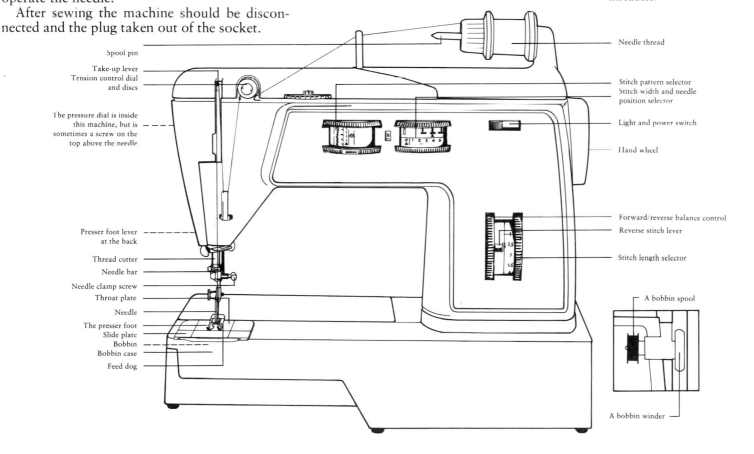

Spool pin
Take-up lever
Tension control dial and discs
The pressure dial is inside this machine, but is sometimes a screw on the top above the needle
Presser foot lever at the back
Thread cutter
Needle bar
Needle clamp screw
Throat plate
Needle
The presser foot
Slide plate
Bobbin
Bobbin case
Feed dog

Needle thread
Stitch pattern selector
Stitch width and needle position selector
Light and power switch
Hand wheel
Forward/reverse balance control
Reverse stitch lever
Stitch length selector
A bobbin spool
A bobbin winder

Threading your machine

REPLACING THE SEWING MACHINE NEEDLE:
Your sewing machine needle will need to be replaced if it shows any signs of being blunt or bent, indicated when the machine begins to sew heavily, or the thread breaks easily. The correct brand of machine needle recommended for your machine should always be used, as well as the right size and type of needle for the material you are sewing, (see charts at the end of the book).

Construction and design details vary for different makes of sewing machine, but the usual procedure for changing the sewing machine needle in the majority of them is as follows: with the presser foot lever up, take hold of the hand wheel and turn it away from you, raising the needle to its highest point. Loosen the needle clamp screw to the right of the needle and remove the old needle. Replace this in the pack if it is in good condition. Throw it away if it is bent or blunt. Rescue the tip of a broken needle from the bobbin case too!

Push the new needle up into the needle bar, the post which holds it, as high as it will go. The needle must be positioned correctly, with the flat or grooved side placed as indicated in your machine instruction book. When the needle is in position, tighten the needle clamp screw again.

WINDING THE BOBBIN SPOOL AND GETTING UP THE BOBBIN THREAD:
The bobbin spool needs to be filled with thread too, and after it has been clipped into its case, you will want to draw the thread up on to the machine surface. On the majority of machines, before the needle is threaded, the small spool is usually clipped into a little bobbin-winding device at the top of the machine, often somewhere close by the hand wheel. First make sure every little piece of thread remaining on it from earlier sewing has been removed. Bobbin spools tend to collect a tangle of thread ends as time goes by, which can make it difficult to wind the new thread smoothly. Do keep spare spools by you for different coloured threads.

(Sewing machines exist in which the bobbin spool is filled automatically while in position in the case from the threaded needle, a patented feature of advanced Singer sewing machines.) Whichever type of machine you have, as always, do refer to your instruction book first before winding the bobbin spool.

THREADING THE SEWING MACHINE NEEDLE
In order for a sewing machine to stitch properly, it must be threaded correctly. Your sewing instruction book is your best guide, but here, broadly, is a countdown of the needle-threading procedure on an average sewing machine.
1 Place the reel of thread on the spool pin.
2 Raise the needle to its highest point. The presser foot should be up.
3 Take the thread through the first wire guide hook.
4 Take the thread round between the metal tension discs sometimes at the back of a tension regulating dial, and sometimes close beside it, and across the wire tension take-up spring on the left.
5 Pass the thread through the hole or slot in the end of the thread take-up lever.
6 Bring the thread back down the end of the machine, passing it through the rest of the guide hooks.
7 Trim and pinch the thread end, and pass it through the machine needle eye from left to right, or from front to back depending on your machine.
8 Draw the thread back between the presser foot, and trim it to about 10cm. to 12cm. ready for stitching.

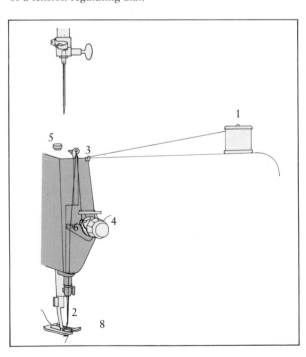

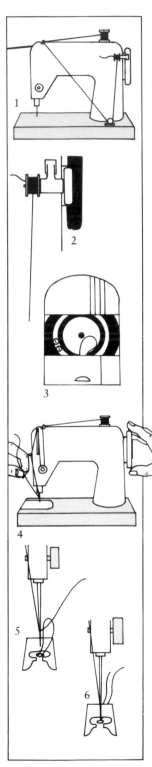

FOR FILLING THE BOBBIN SPOOL: Always use the same thread as for the needle, with one or two exceptions, such as when shirring, when the bobbin spool is wound with elastic thread by hand, or for a different-colour thread, though in similar thickness and fibre.

1 Take the thread round the bobbin thread guides. Wind it two or three times clockwise round the spool, then clip it into the bobbin winder.

2 Stop the needle operating while the bobbin is being wound, as directed. Start the bobbin winder. When the spool is filled, remove the spool winder and turn the screw in the hand wheel again to make the needle operational.

3 In recent machines the bobbin case is usually placed immediately under this slide plate. Older treadle machines often have it tucked away underneath, with a separate case into which the spool is clipped first before being fitted into the machine. As directed for your machine, clip the spool into the bobbin case, and where required, draw the thread end back through a groove in the side of the case. Thread the needle.

4 Draw out a short length of thread from the spool. To draw this thread up onto the machine, with the presser foot raised, take hold of the hand wheel, and holding the needle thread to one side in your left hand, slowly turn the hand wheel towards you to lower the machine needle right down.

5 When you reverse the wheel again by hand, the threaded needle will draw up a loop of thread from the bobbin. Pull this loop up until the thread comes on to the machine surface.

6 Draw both the upper and lower threads back between the presser foot. Trim.

Machine stitching

When making any adjustments to your machine settings, unless otherwise directed, the needle should be up to its highest point, out of the fabric, with the presser foot off the material. Use the same thread in needle and bobbin.

Always make the settings with reference to your machine instruction book. They often have to be taken in sequence.

The way to get the best out of your sewing machine? Lots of practise. Practise the embroidery stitch patterns. Make as many buttonholes as you can. Practise machine sewing on buttons, and using the attachments.

No matter how often you sew, always begin by testing the stitches on a scrap of fabric, and through all layers to be sewn. Suit the needle size to the fabric.

STRAIGHT STITCHING: Straight stitching is a row of straight stitches like backstitch, but equal on both sides of the fabric. It is used for seams, darts and gathers and for topstitching, it can be reversed to finish the stitching.

ZIG-ZAG STITCHING: Zig-zag means that the needle moves to and fro while the stitchline is made.

Zig-zag, used for general machining produces an attractive flat finish. Also for making machine buttonholes and sewing on buttons; for simple embroidery; appliqué; patchwork.

MACHINE SEWING KNITS: Recent zig-zag plus machines include stretch stitches for sewing knits. On straight or simple zig-zag machines, two close parallel rows of small stitches are best for this purpose.

BUILT-IN EMBROIDERY STITCH PATTERNS: When appropriately set the machine automatically produces delightful and practical fancy stitches which double for such jobs as multi-stitch zig-zag for sewing on elastic, or blindstitch for hems.

With all automatic stitch patterns from zig-zag to the more elaborate versions, consult your instruction book before attempting to reverse stitch with them.

TWIN NEEDLE SEWING: For twin needle sewing, the double-pointed needle is inserted in the needle bar. The width stitch is set to correspond with the maximum width apart of these twin needles. Two spools of thread are used.

When you begin to sew, two rows of stitching will appear, exactly parallel. It is possible to use fancy as well as straight stitches with twin needle sewing.

EMBROIDERY DISCS OR CAMS: These are separate discs to increase the range of embroidery stitch patterns available on the machine. The disc is set inside the machine manually.

COMBINATION STITCH PATTERNS: Some sewing machines can be set to make a combination stitch pattern, where the disc and built-in stitch patterns come out as a mix of the two.

ADVANCED EMBROIDERY STITCH CAMS: Stitch not only from side to side but in forward-reverse patterns, which make formerly industrial machine sewing possible, such as an overlocking edge stitch for knit fabrics without any seam allowance.

MACHINE TACKING (or basting): Speeds up tacking. Sometimes machine chain stitch is used for this purpose.

BUTTONS: Using a button foot with a needle slotted in as directed to make a thread shank, the button is sewn on with zig-zag satin stitch set to the exact width of the button's holes. The machine needle then stitches to and fro through them into the fabric.

BUTTONHOLES: Basically a machined buttonhole is a double bar of machined zig-zag, with round or square ends and a hairline space between the stitching which is snipped open meticulously carefully.

FREE-MOTION STITCHING: The feed dog teeth are covered, and a special presser foot added. The fabric stretched taut in an embroidery hoop is slipped under the machine needle. Stitches can then be made in any direction and in varied lengths. For darning or to make varied embroidery shapes such as seraphs and leaves.

CHAIN STITCHING: Chain stitching is a chain of stitches along the surface only, for embroidery and easily removable stitching. Chain stitching has to be sewn off securely because otherwise it unravels easily.

CIRCULAR-MOTION STITCHING: Using a fabric-guiding attachment, the material is moved round in circles, producing circular or semicircular stitch lines for embroidery or scallops.

FREE-ARM MACHINING: Any tubular shape, such as a sleeve, or trouser leg, can be slipped over the machine free arm for free-arm stitching. It is ideal for smocking or embroidery.

Attachments

Every sewing machine, except the most old-fashioned, has at least a few attachments, extra parts to add to the machine which will enable you to carry out specific sewing jobs in one operation. A tucking attachment for making tucks automatically, for example, or a ruffler for shirring and gathering material, useful where long lengths of frill are being ruffled for bed counterpanes or curtains.

On older machines, attachments often look like Heath Robinson contraptions, even though they work well. Today they are simple in design and simple to use . . . and a real help. It is well worth getting to know how to use these time- and labour-saving gadgets. Usually you screw them to the needle bar instead of the general presser foot, but some are screwed into the flat bed of the machine. Your machine instruction book should give you full illustrated directions for using them.

1 GENERAL PRESSER FOOT: The general presser foot is basic to all sewing machines and is used for all general sewing. Sometimes a presser foot is hinged to ride across the tips of pins used for pin basting. The presser foot is screwed in position onto the needle bar.

2 ZIPPER FOOT: The zipper foot is narrow, pared to enable the foot to be taken close against the zipper teeth when sewing. It is also used for sewing cord into piped bias binding and for any machining which requires stitching closely to a raised edge, such as for quilting.

(Quilting is also provided for with a quilting foot, somewhat similar to a zipper foot, but with a guide rod extending from the side to keep the spaces between the quilting stitch lines parallel and equal.)

3 NARROW HEMMER: Easy to use for making narrow hems in one operation, turning and stitching the fabric automatically without tacking. It is best for sewing non-stretch lightweight fabrics such as lawn or voile. The raw edge of the material is folded over the centre of the narrow hemmer, and the hem is stitched for a short distance slowly. With the raw edge steadied in the left hand, evenly fed under the needle, a neat narrow machine-stitched hem is made. Following your instruction book, lace trimming can be stitched under or over the hem at the same time.

4 BINDER: The binder attachment is for sewing bias binding along the edge of material. Commercial bias binding is easy to use with it. The bias binding is trimmed to a point, longest at the folded edge, which is inserted into the scroll of metal on the binder and brought out at the back underneath. The raw edge of the material to be bound is slotted between the sides of the scroll, into the binding crease, then stitched. Rather a tricky business but time saving if you acquire the knack of using this attachment, especially if you are binding round one hundred and fifty aprons for a charity stall.

5 BUTTONHOLE FOOT: A presser foot devised for making machine-stitched buttonholes. Its counterpart, 6 the BUTTON FOOT is a presser foot with a slot in the top into which the needle is slipped, so that

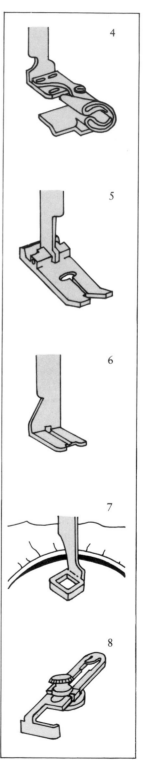

when the button is positioned between the button foot and the machine, and stitched, a thread shank will be formed. Machine sewing on buttons and buttonholes is an encouragement to having multiple rows of buttons on a garment!

7 DARNER AND EMBROIDERY FOOT: The open presser foot enables the fabric to be held lightly while, after appropriate adjustments to the machine, the needle moves freely to and fro in free-motion stitching over material held taut in an embroidery hoop. A throat plate to cover the feed dog called the *feed cover plate* is used with it.

For satin stitch a special embroidery foot with a raised centre is used, to accommodate the thick stitch row.

8 SEAM GUIDE: Attached by a screw into a screw thread socket in the machine bed, the end of the guide is aligned to the outside edge of the material, which has been adjusted to the required distance from the needle. When stitching, the material edge is kept against the end of the guide steadily, producing a level, even stitchline an equal distance from the material edge. Other guides include a blind-stitch hem guide, and on some machines an adjustable hemmer and attachment for circular stitching.

Singer's Even Feed Foot keeps plaid, knits and slippery fabrics perfectly aligned.

Machine sewing

Sit comfortably at the sewing machine. Check that the presser foot is up (lifted by raising the presser foot lever), and the needle is at its highest point.

If necessary, before switching on the light and power, you may want to change the needle for size, to suit your material, and if required, possibly the presser foot and throat plate too. Your sewing machine instruction book will tell you when to do this.

Add any attachment to the machine you want to use; make your stitch length, width and pattern selections. Check over the sequence of adjustments to make sure you haven't overlooked anything before you begin sewing, such as when straight stitching on a zig-zag machine, returning the stitch width to zero.

Simple straight stitching or zig-zag stitching can easily be carried out in a few operations you will soon know by heart. Built-in embroidery procedures are equally simple. With more complicated machine sewing, however, such as non-automatic buttonhole making or using alternative embroidery discs, which may require a fairly elaborate series of adjustments, a second count-down with the instruction book in hand is always wise.

TESTING THE STITCHES: Always make it a rule to begin by testing the stitches on a spare piece of the fabric. Are they even, and do they look equal and perfect on both sides of the material? If there are any problems with them, you could consult pages 28 and 29 and then make the necessary adjustments. Switch off the power between sewing.

BEGIN TO SEW: With the needle up, place the material with the beginning of the proposed stitch line exactly in position under the needle. At the same time, align the seam or hem edge precisely against the chosen guide line (and having decided on it, stick to it like a limpet). This will help you to achieve a really straight stitch line an equal distance from the edge along its length.

Lower the presser foot into the material (by lowering the presser foot lever). With the hand wheel you can now lower the needle into the material just at the right point to begin sewing.

Switch on. Fingers back from the needle always. The speed at which the sewing machine needle moves can be deceptive, and needles have

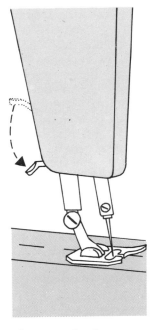

The presser foot lever at the back of the sewing machine is raised to lift the presser foot, and lowered to place it on the material.

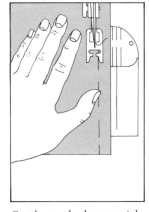

Gently steady the material with your left hand while the machine is stitching. The presser foot edges and throat plate guidelines help to make a straight seam.

been known to go through fingers!

With the threads drawn back to the left between the presser foot to avoid tangling them with the stitches, set the stitch lever in reverse, (except for zig-zag or embroidery stitching), press your foot on the foot control gently and the needle will burr into action. Change after two or three stitches to forward stitching. Guide the material with both hands, steadying it with your left hand and keeping it neatly arranged with the right, always keeping the area being sewn clear and the stitchline plainly visible. Don't push the material through under the needle, or pull it to hurry it, from the back, or a bent or broken needle might be the result. Rather let the fabric travel with the pace of the stitching.

Too thick humps at the junction of two seams in heavy weight material will, hopefully, have been trimmed away from inside the seam to reduce their bulk, during the preparation of the garment. If you do unavoidably have to take the needle over a hump, slow down to snail's pace, and if necessary, give the machine some help manually. It may even be preferable to end the machine stitchline just before the hump, and begin again after it, and join the seam with neat hand-sewn back stitches. Otherwise the machine needle could break in the material.

TO FINISH OFF: When you come to the end of sewing, slow down in sight of the last few stitches. Finish off straight stitching with a few reverse stitches, by operating the *reverse stitch lever*, except for zig-zag or embroidery. It also gives a strong finish to a machined seam to pull up the loop of the end stitch underneath. The top and under threads can then be trimmed at the ends, and hand-stitched off, or they can be tied together close to the fabric and trimmed short.

PIN BASTED SEAM: Using a hinged presser foot, it is possible to lightly pin-baste for machining, though in general, all pins should be removed from sewing before machining, except possibly marker pins at the end of darts etc.

MISTAKES: Very few people sew for long without making a mistake. Perhaps discovering a dart is slightly out of line, or the fit of the garment isn't as perfect as intended. Unpick, press and start again is a good rule to follow and will be less disappointing finally.

Operating different sewing machine types

1 HAND SEWING MACHINE: A hand-operated machine gives a straight lock stitch, but the needle moves much more slowly than on an electric sewing machine. It is operated by winding the handle over and over away from you. The bobbin is filled on a little rubber-tyred winder wheel pushed against the hand wheel, but you may have to bring it to a halt yourself if there is no cut-out to the winding. Hand sewing machines do have some attachments (except the oldest models) and can also reverse stitch quite often.

2 TREADLE MACHINE: Pushing the treadle up and down with your feet leaves your hands free for sewing and guiding the material, but though you soon learn to synchronise your movements, you may need a little practice at first. You can get the knack of operating a treadle machine by practising on paper . . . a good way of learning to stitch a straight line too, by using lined dressmaker's paper. Manuals for using the older types of sewing machine are still published by Singer, and you can also generally pick up information in old-fashioned sewing books from second-hand shops.

3 ELECTRIC SEWING MACHINES: Use the foot control at maximum speed for simple, long seams, and minimum speed for going round curves and detailed machining. Remember always to switch off between sewing, and take the plug out of the socket after a sewing session.

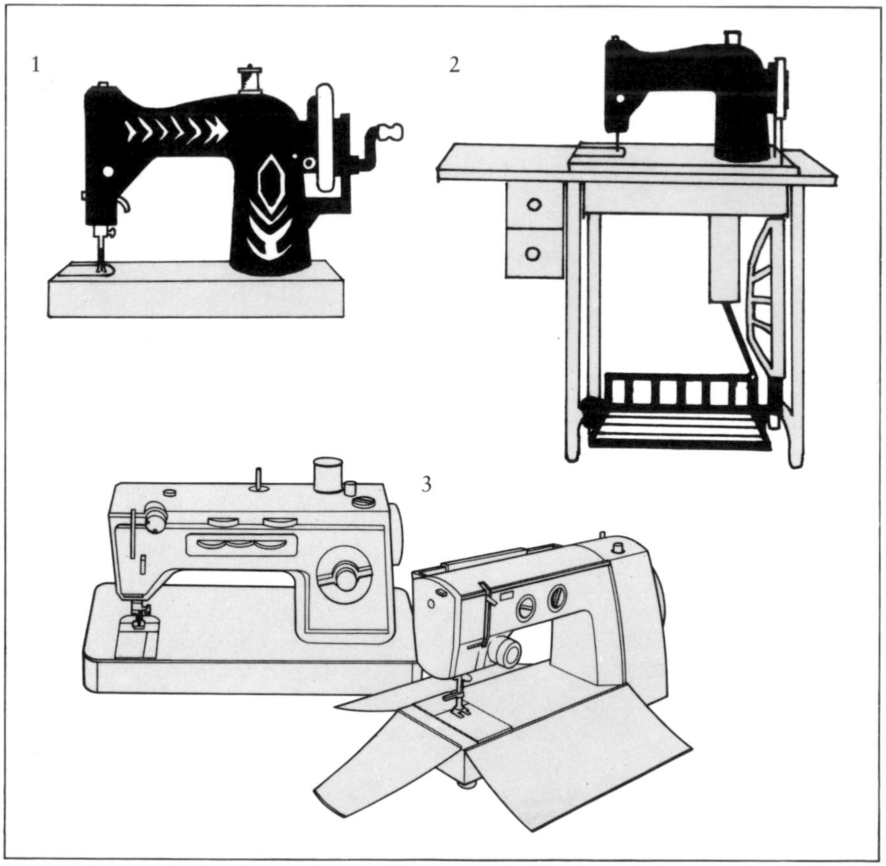

Problems

1 TENSION OF NEEDLE THREAD: A sewing machine *tension regulating dial* is shown here, very much reduced. Yours may be a horizontal type, with the numbers round the rim, and separate tension discs.

To obtain equal-sized stitches on both sides of the material, the tension of the needle thread and bobbin thread has to be exactly the same.

The upper thread pulling too tightly would cause loops to form underneath, or the under thread pulling would cause loose untidy stitches on the surface.

Normally the lowest and loosest thread tension is zero, and the highest at nine. To tighten the thread, turn the dial to a higher number, and loosen it, turn it to a lower number.

The side view shows the tension-regulating discs and the tension take-up spring.

2 BOBBIN THREAD TENSION: The bobbin thread tension is regulated by a little screw in the side of the bobbin case. It rarely needs very much adjustment, and even when it does, is moved by the smallest amount, a fractional eighth to a quarter turn of the screw to the right to tighten the thread, and to the left to loosen it. Try to avoid altering the bobbin thread tension and see if you can adjust things with the needle thread first. Test the stitches after each turn.

3 PRESSURE: A sewing machine will have a *pressure-regulating screw* at the top, or a *pressure-regulating dial* for controlling the pressure of the presser foot on the material. Refer to your instruction book for making pressure adjustments.

Too heavy pressure may drag on the material and make it heavy to sew. Too light pressure would cause material to be rather difficult to feed under the needle evenly.

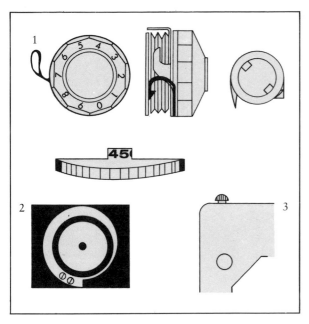

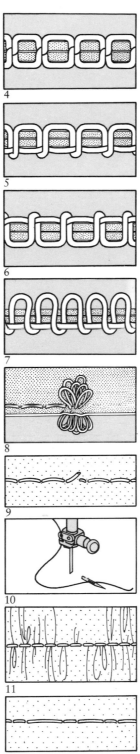

OILING THE SEWING MACHINE: It is essential to oil your sewing machine and to have it serviced regularly. Certain parts will need a drop of oil weekly. Only use fine-grade sewing-machine oil.

If the machine is moving sluggishly, after consulting your instruction book and checking for any possible faults, and removing any fluff (called 'lint') and small threads clogging the bobbin mechanism, a little oil works wonders.

After oiling, run a few stitches through a spare scrap of material to soak up any stray oil.

4 PERFECTION: A stitch line with the stitch balance just right, the upper and lower loops the same size, locked together in the material.

5 BIGWIG: Long and loose stitches on the right side of the material, and the under thread pulled in a straight line. The upper needle thread tension is too slack for the bobbin thread, and needs increasing. Test the stitches between dial turns.

6 DROOPING: The opposite problem here. The needle thread is pulled in a tight line on top of the material, and the bobbin thread is producing long irregular, looped stitches on the underside. Slacken the thread tension. If the remedies for tension difficulties by adjusting the needle thread do not work, then you may have to adjust the bobbin tension as a last resort.

7 LOOPED STITCHES: Things really have gone wrong here. The tension of the needle thread may be very loose, so try adjusting it. Look around for something holding the bobbin thread back. Has the thread been wound on the spool properly? Is the bobbin rattling in its case? Does it need resetting? Is the needle threading correct? Check back along the threading sequence.

8 BIRD'S NEST: The stitches have piled up on each other through the hole in the throat plate and are making a great knot in the material, jamming everything up. Stop everything at once and switch off, with the needle still down in the fabric if need be. Extra cautiously and carefully snip through the offending threads under and on top of the material, *avoiding cutting the fabric*. When every thread has been snipped, raise the needle and draw the material gently out, removing any threads from it with tweezers.

Now make sure that the needle thread or bobbin thread are not caught in the bobbin mechanism; remove any broken, tangled threads from here. Also check that the thread tension in both needle and bobbin is correct. Check that you are using the correct throat plate. If you are machining thin material it could be being pulled down through the centre hole. Test the stitches before you begin again, and the bobbin threading.

9 THREAD BROKEN AGAIN? Are you using the right size or a sharp enough needle? And the correct thickness thread? Is the thread tension too tight, or is the thread caught anywhere? Spiralled round the spool pin or tangled in the bobbin? Is the needle loose or not properly aligned? Is stitch length right for fabric?

10 NEEDLE BREAKS? Perhaps the needle has been bent or even broken by too tight tension or the thread being caught up, or by pulling the material out from under the needle at the end of sewing too sharply. The needle may be too fine for the fabric. Is the needle loose or not fixed in correctly so it strikes the throat plate when stitching?

11 SEAM PUCKERS? This is probably due to too tight tension in the upper or lower thread, or using the wrong size stitch for the material.

12 MISSED STITCHES: Check the needle. It may be too small for the thread. Blunt or bent.

If the fault cannot be cured by careful detailed checking and adjustment, with reference to your machine instruction book and constant stitch testing, you are probably going to need some help from the service engineer to mend it.

Measuring 5

Why measuring is vital

When sewing for yourself, whether making yourself a dress or a beach robe, you are going to have to fit them to very definite and precise dimensions: your own. The same goes for things for your home, curtains for the balcony windows, or cushion covers. Curtains of the wrong length will always look untidy. Disappointing. So will a shapeless loose cover, that fails to overlap at the fastening properly, like a person wearing too small clothes. Careful preparatory measuring, and constant checking as you go will have a lot to do with your ultimate sewing success.

When measuring for sewing, you need to make not only accurate, often three-dimensional measurements, but also to take account of various extra amounts which will need to be added to the material outside the stitch lines, called 'seam allowances', which are designed to take care of fraying. Darts, gathers, flounces, pleats, zipper turnings, design details, hems, will all require extra material, and not in standardised amounts unfortunately. Sewing is inevitably a tailored, custom-built, made-to-measure affair. So there are endless good reasons for measuring.

Household sewing, though it may look more formidable, is actually much simpler than dressmaking as far as the sewing techniques you will need to know and fitting are concerned. The biggest problem is with handling bulky, large amounts of material such as for bed counterpanes, and heavy fabric-lined curtains. After allowing for hems and gathers where necessary, an accurate, exact fit is the aim. Even more complicated armchair loose covers are going to be fitted closely over an object which will stay still and not squeak as you stick pins into it when fitting the fabric pieces!

Not so straightforward is making clothes, though they can be constructed very, very simply. A garment is going to have to be a comfortable fit, to have sufficient 'ease' built into it to enable you to move about freely in it yet still look tidy and the right size. A loose, voluminous kaftan has after all got to be the correct length not to trip you up, or have sleeves which do not fall long over your hands.

You will need to be able to bend to pick up the morning post without fear of your new trousers splitting apart at the seams, because of being too tight; to reach up and pick an apple from

MEASURING FOR A SIMPLE CUSHION COVER

1 Take a basic stuffed cushion bought ready-made. Pull the cushion side out to its true length and measure. Make a little sketch plan and note the measurements on it.

2 Using a ruler and felt tip pen or pencil, draw the cushion shape's exact full size dimensions on dressmaker's squared paper (obtainable in paper pattern departments) or on brown paper.

3 Add extra at each side for the seam allowances, about 2cm. or ¾in. This is going to be a simple cushion cover with no corded edges or zipper insertion. If you would like to go ahead and make the cover, cut out the pattern round the outside edges.

TO MAKE THE CUSHION COVER: Pin the pattern to an oddment of material, gingham, chintz, satin, even wool. Cut out. Remove the pattern and cut a second shape, not necessarily in the same material.

Place the two shapes together, right sides facing. Pin, tack, remove the pins, and machine them together (with straight stitching) on

three sides, leaving the fourth side open. Or backstitch.

Remove the tacking. Turn the cover right side out and press it. Slip it over the cushion. Turn in the raw edges of the sides of the opening and oversew them together by hand. When you want to launder the cushion cover, you merely have carefully to unpick the oversewing stitches.

OTHER MATERIALS WHICH NEED EXTRA ALLOWANCES: Any woven or knitted material with a one-way surface.

PLAID: Plaid checks have to be exactly matched at the joins. Allow for several extra repeat patterns when buying the material. Remember plaid will also have to be matched in several directions, at the shoulder seams as much as at the sides simultaneously.

STRIPES, CHECKS: Allow extra for bold stripes and checks too.

PILE FABRIC: When making a garment out of velvet or fake fur, or some knits, the pile must lie in the same direction for every part of the garment. If not it will reflect the light in a varied way, which would alter the look of the colour, even with short pile. Use a pattern layout when cutting out 'with nap'. As with plaid extra material may have to be allowed for cutting out shapes side by side instead of being placed in opposite directions to each other more economically.

LACE: Lace or material with large woven or printed patterns may need extra amounts for matching at joins.

the tree without the raw edge of synthetic material, which can be very tough, cutting into your armpits and round your neck. When you sprawl comfortably reading or fold your arms listening, you will want to feel equally comfortable and happy in good-looking, roomy clothes. And you won't want to spend weeks and use up expensive material, to make what is intended to be a slip of a dress and ends up like the proverbial sweater, an indeterminate outsize garment with no obvious purpose in life.

This is why it is wise to have your tape measure beside you as constantly as scissors, needle and thread, when sewing.

Measuring yourself

You will always be recommended by dressmakers and pattern manufacturers to make a certain series of body measurements. By the one, for use during dressmaking, and the other, for choosing a pattern to your nearest standard pattern size.

For taking your own measurements, you will need to ask the help of another person to hold the tape, and have to hand a tape measure, pencil or felt tip pen, and a notebook or piece of paper.

It is quite a good idea to have an envelope file for storing items like this, which you can keep for future reference in your sewing machine cabinet drawer, or on the bookshelf in the sewing area.

Take the majority of measurements standing up, over your under-slip and wearing shoes.

Hold the tape round the body, pinch the metal tag end over it, and read the measurement where they meet.

Check list

BUST: Hold the tape round the bust at its widest point.
WAIST: The tape should fit snugly round the waist.
HIPS: Measure round the widest point, angled up in front slightly.
BACK WAIST LENGTH: From nape of neck to waist.
NECK: Round base of neck.
SHOULDER: From base of neck to shoulder joint.
ARM: Outside arm with elbow bent, from shoulder to wrist.
ARM CIRCUMFERENCE: Round upper arm.
WRIST: Round wrist.
CHEST: Across chest below shoulders.

BETWEEN WAIST AND HIPS: An extra fitting check.
UNDER-ARM SIDE SEAM TO WAIST: For bodice length.
WAIST TO HEM: For skirt length.
NECK TO HEM: Centre neck to hem, nape of neck to hem, shoulder to hem and under arm to hem. For dress length.
ARMHOLE SEAM: To check armhole curve. From shoulder to arm sinew, then angle to under-arm (not an accurate fitting measurement, but a rough guide as an extra check).

Measuring for women's trousers

OUTSIDE LEG: Outside leg length from waist to ankle
WAIST: As for a dress or skirt.
HIPS: As before.
LEG CIRCUMFERENCE: Round the thigh, knee, calf and ankle.
TROUSERS' WIDTH: Across leg ends.

CROTCH LENGTH: Sit and take your measurement from the waist to where your seat touches the chair. Check against favourite trousers' measurements.

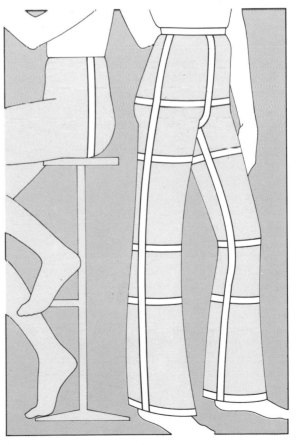

Making clothes 6

Choosing a pattern

These days most people prefer to use commercially produced paper patterns, which have been developed to a marvellously high standard, and today are easy to use.

The three people shown here are all fond of making their own clothes, but have specific ideas on what suits them, the standard of dressmaking they can cope with, and what suits their budget, and timetable.

ELIZABETH is eighteen. She has a monthly allowance to cover all expenses, including clothes. She is able to use an automatic sewing machine at home and has now been given her own portable sewing machine.

With a limited budget Elizabeth needs to use inexpensive materials such as gingham or brushed rayon, which are also easy to handle when cutting out and sewing. She can make a simple garment and is used to altering and repairing her clothes.

'Because I'm short I like to wear high-heeled shoes and straight jeans, which makes me look taller. I like to collect clothes which go together, and I go for a complete image, with top, skirt, scarf, hairstyle, make-up, shoes all of a piece.

'I don't want the bother of a lot of hand sewing and like to use the sewing machine for everything. I'll admit that I'm sometimes given help with finishing off tedious parts of sewing, such as sewing on waistbands. But I do like a well-cut-out garment that isn't going to fall apart, and that is reasonably properly made.'

Elizabeth obviously needs to buy only the simplest pattern for a basic garment, a flared skirt, or vest top, and can make it up over and over again in different materials. It is an advantage to her to be able to use every part and attachment of the sewing machine.

HELEN is a busy young schoolteacher working in a comprehensive school. She likes romantic-looking clothes such as Victorian-style cotton print dresses with long skirts or peasant cottons, and denims. Helen looks beautifully slender in all of her clothes, and tends to choose a pattern which balances the proportion of her figure taking account of her slightly wider hips in proportion to her bust.

Helen owns a fairly advanced model of a portable sewing machine which will sew some embroidery stitch patterns, though she loves hand embroidery too. Again, like Elizabeth, she finds skirts, especially long skirts, are the most useful items she makes, along with renovating the period second-hand clothes she is fond of buying.

JANET has always made her own clothes, and enjoys sewing for pleasure and economy. Indeed, she finds it labour-saving to do her own dressmaking, rather than spend fruitless hours searching the shops for a garment in the right style and size at the right price. The right patterns and materials are so much easier to buy, she finds.

She has an advanced automatic sewing machine and plenty of sewing equipment. As she finds fairly simple classical styles suit her, the patterns she buys – such as for shirt waisters, skirts and blouses, or soft dresses – don't date over years except for varying the skirt length with fashion. These include extra simple patterns or advanced couturier designs.

Three different people, with clear ideas about what styles suit them best, and different sewing requirements.

When choosing your own pattern, apart from choosing a style you feel is practical and flattering for you, you won't go far wrong if you keep to a beginner's/jiffy/so easy/very, very simple sewing pattern. These are patterns for which the number of pattern pieces have been kept to a minimum, and from which complicated sewing construction details have been eliminated. They are still well designed and in fact often gain by their stylish simplicity.

Your pattern size

Standard pattern sizes have been worked out by the manufacturers, on a series of body measurements for different figure types, based not only on the dimensions, but the build too, which is often influenced by age. A mature woman is more heavily built as a rule than a teenager, even though some of their measurements are similar. Your standard pattern size will have a code number which corresponds with the nearest equivalent to your body measurements in a particular group. Some adjustments may still be needed to the pattern when you come to use it, but it will be the closest to your own size available.

To choose a pattern from the range of standard pattern sizes available, we experimented in

Elizabeth: aged 18
Height: 5ft. 1½in. or 156cm.
Bust: 92cm. or 36in.
Waist: 61cm. or 24in.
Hips: 92cm. or 36in.
Back waist length: 42cm.
or 16.in.

Helen: aged 25
Height: 5ft. 6in. or 167cm.
Bust: 81cm. or 32in.
Waist: 55.5cm. or 22in.
Hips: 89cm. or 35in.
Back waist length: 43cm.
or 17in.

Janet: aged over 35
Height: 5ft. 5½in. or 166cm.
Bust: 92cm. or 36in.
Waist: 71cm. or 28in.
Hips: 99cm. or 39in.
Back waist length: 41cm.
or 16in.

choosing the right one for Elizabeth, Helen and Janet, using their measurements as a guide.

ELIZABETH: Her bust size of 92cm. (36in.) is in several of the tables. So is her hip size of 92cm. (36in.). So indeed is her waist size of 61cm. or 24in. though usually in association with smaller bust and hip measurements, and also with a different back waist length. Elizabeth's long back waist measurement would make Misses' size 12 the most suitable for her, though the bust and waist size would need some adjustment.

HELEN: Helen is photographed in a garment made from a Butterick size 10 (Misses') pattern without a single alteration being made to the pattern, and it fitted her perfectly everywhere. The flared skirt with its elasticated waist easily took care of her smaller waist measurement and took account of her slightly wider than the pattern measurement hip size. She prefers a size 10, but sometimes buys size 12 and drastically alters the bodice fitting. (It is simpler to alter the skirt as a rule.)

JANET: Experience has shown Janet that a standard pattern Misses' size 14 fits her well, with some adjustments to the hip measurement. Women's Half-Size 14½ is also suitable.

The basic body measurements needed for deciding your standard pattern size are:

Girls and women:
Bust
Waist
Hips
Back waist length

Children and girls:
Breast
Waist
Hips
Back waist length
Approximate height
Finished dress length

Babies:
(up to 6 months)
Weight
Height

Men:
Chest
Waist
Hips
Neckband
Shirt sleeve from nape of neck to wrist with arm bent.

The main measurement usually quoted for a dress pattern is the bust size, and for a skirt and trousers, the waist size.

If you haven't already worked out your standard pattern size you will find all the tables printed at the end of pattern catalogues in the pattern department in a store. Home pattern catalogues on sale at your newsagent also include the tables.

Basic fitting patterns are available in your standard pattern size. They give directions for making up a muslin version of the pattern, called a toile, and for adjusting the shape to fit you perfectly. By recording details of the adjustments made on the toile in charts provided, you can instantly transfer them to any other pattern in the same size made by the same manufacturer. This cuts out the necessity of laboriously altering each new pattern to fit you afresh each time and provides you with an invaluable fitting blueprint of your own figure.

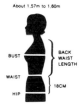

About 1.85m to 1.68m

MISSES'

Misses' patterns are designed for a well proportioned, and developed figure; about 1.65m to 1.68m without shoes.

Size.....	6	8	10	12	14	16	18	20	
Bust ...	78	80	83	87	92	97	102	107	cm
Waist..	58	61	64	67	71	76	81	87	cm
Hip.....	83	85	88	92	97	102	107	112	cm
Back Waist Length	39,5	40	40,5	41,5	42	42,5	43	44	cm

About 1,57m to 1,60m

HALF SIZE

Half Size patterns are for a fully developed figure with a short backwaist length. Waist and hip are larger in proportion to bust than other figure types; about 1,57m to 1,60m without shoes.

Size....	10½	12½	14½	16½	18½	20½	22½	24½	
Bust ...	84	89	94	99	104	109	114	119	cm
Waist..	69	74	79	84	89	96	102	108	cm
Hip.....	89	94	99	104	109	116	122	128	cm
Back Waist Length	38	39	39,5	40	40,5	40,5	41	41,5cm	

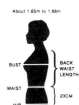

About 1,65m to 1,68m

WOMEN'S

Women's patterns are designed for the larger, more fully mature figure; about 1,65m to 1,68m without shoes.

Size	38	40	42	44	46	48	50	
Bust........	107	112	117	122	127	132	137	cm
Waist	89	94	99	105	112	118	124	cm
Hip	112	117	122	127	132	137	142	cm
Back Waist Length......	44	44	44,5	45	45	45,5	46	cm

Making your own patterns

If you would like to design your own clothes, there are a number of ways you can do so. You could go to evening classes and learn how to make your block pattern, which is a basic fabric pattern made to your own exact dimensions, as well as creating your own designs using it. You can also teach yourself the techniques of block and pattern making. There are several suitable books a beginner could use, some of which are listed at the end of this book.

Or you could begin from some of the ideas for making your own patterns shown here, which are mainly money-saving suggestions, enabling you to make the best of the alternatives to buying a commercial paper pattern: using magazine charts or making patterns from your own favourite old clothes and using your own creative design adaptations in the process.

PATTERN BARGAINS: Watch out for special pattern offers in magazines. These patterns are quite frequently made up for the magazine by a regular pattern manufacturer, and as they are usually sold at a low price, can be a real saving.

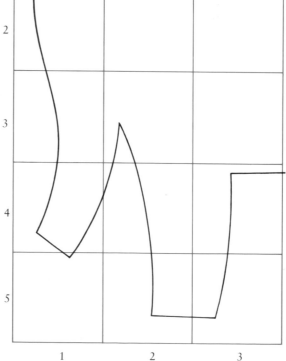

ENLARGING A CHART: This is a simple way of obtaining a free pattern, if you know how to enlarge a chart design to full size.
Method
1 Materials: paper; a ruler; a felt tip pen.
2 Number along the four sides of the chart.
3 Draw a similar number of full-size squares to the scale given. Number these to match the chart.
4 Where the lines of the pattern shapes cross a square, and at the angles and corners, draw a dot on the full-size pattern. Join the dots. Copy any figures and wording on the chart and to the enlarged pattern. Save the instructions for making up the item too.

TO MAKE A PATTERN FROM A FAVOURITE GARMENT: (Cast-off, of course!).
1 Unpick the garment, seam by seam, stitch by stitch, using a seam ripper. Save every piece, including the lining.
2 Press open all the pieces and pin to paper, or dressmakers' squared paper, if possible with the fabric grain in perfect alignment with the lines of the paper. Draw round shapes. Transfer darts, etc.
3 Cut out paper pattern shapes. Write the names of the pieces on the shapes: i.e. leg; waist; front; back. Pin to material and cut out.
4 Make up the garment the way it was sewn together in the cast-off version. Or invent your own design variations.

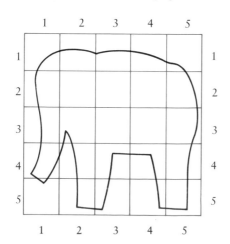

Shopping for patterns

Suppose that you want to make some clothes for your holiday. You are going to need to think about them at least a couple of months ahead, so that you can have time in which to plan which patterns would fit into your wardrobe scheme, and to shop for them and the material. Apart from having to carry out the actual dressmaking to be ready in time.

MAIL ORDER SHOPPING FOR PATTERNS: If you cannot get to the shops easily, perhaps because of having a young family or living a distance from a large town, you can choose your patterns from a home pattern catalogue, and buy them by mail order. All the leading pattern manufacturers publish their own every season, available through your newsagent.

They give the same pictures and information about the patterns as you will find in the shop catalogues, though only the latest designs are included in each issue, so you will be right up to date. Firms add new designs and discard back numbers frequently to keep well ahead with the latest fashions.

MAIL ORDER FABRICS: Fabrics are often available direct from the mill or from certain discount or factory off-cuts and ends of lines, by mail order. For these keep a watchful eye on newspaper, dressmaking or other magazine small advertisements.

AT THE SHOP: In the paper pattern department, when choosing a pattern from the big store catalogue, make a note of the pattern maker's brand name and the style number of the chosen pattern, with your standard pattern size.

THE PATTERN CATALOGUES: Looking into the big pattern books, you will find them filled with glamorous sketches and photographs of people dressed in the garments you can make out of the patterns available.

Pattern styles are classified in sections under different headings, such as Sportswear, or Young Fashions, or Bridal Fashions, or Men and Boys' Wear. *Designer Patterns* or a section with the word *Designer* on the tab is where you will find patterns created by individual designers, rather than in the design department of the pattern firms. These designers are often couturiers with world-famous names, or the most well known young fashion makers.

One of the marvellous things about being your own dressmaker is that you too can own a dress designed by Dior.

Sections for patterns for making toys, fancy dress and a wide range of accessories, and even for furnishings and furniture, are often included.

MORE ABOUT SELECTING A PATTERN: If you are a sewing beginner you will find, as a rule, a special section for very easy-to-sew patterns, and would be wise to choose from among these.

Look at the sketches of your chosen pattern closely. They will show you clearly the construction details of the garment; where there is a pleat, where gathers – whether the cuffs are buttoned or elasticated or if a zipper or buttoned fastening is used. Sometimes several versions of the same basic garment are included, and quite often patterns for several different garments, from which you can sometimes construct an entire mix-and-match wardrobe.

Back views are shown in the tiny black and white sketches beside the illustration. The price of the pattern is usually given in several different currencies and for different countries. Patterns in Britain usually come under U.K.

Double check all the printed information by the pattern sketch. If you have already bought some material in woven wool, you won't want to open your pattern at home only to discover it was intended for knit fabrics only. The hem width measurement will tell you a lot about whether the skirt will require an extravagant amount of material, especially if you are thinking of using material with nap, such as velvet, a one-way surface which requires more fabric.

THE REVERSE SIDE OF THE PACKET: The reverse side of the packet tells you the materials required to make up the pattern. To find out how much fabric you need to buy, look down the list on the left, and ring the garment you wish to make, in the chosen version, and your standard size. The ringed figures will tell you the amount of material depending on the width of the fabric. You will also have to take into account whether you are using plaid, or knit or pile fabrics which take extra material, and a 'with nap' cutting layout.

One piece of advice. It is wise to buy everything you need before you leave the shop: material, lining, interfacing, thread, zipper, skirt tape and all the list given and keep them together until you are ready to sew.

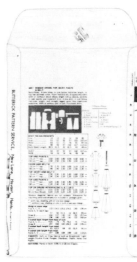

Prepare for sewing

When you are ready to start sewing, with the essential tools gathered and (if you have not your own) a sewing machine borrowed, 'clear the decks'. If you have ever watched a good dentist at work, or seen a television film of a doctor performing an operation, or the real thing, you couldn't do better than to take a tip from their tidy way of working.

Have only the sewing that you are attending to on the work-table and the rest neatly folded away in clean wrappers in a tray or basket until you are ready to deal with it. You won't actually be calling out 'Scalpel, please' or 'Amalgam, nurse' but you will want to have the scissors close at hand so that you can reach out and find them instantly when you need them, instead of having to stop everything to search for them in a heap of material.

This is an important reason why it adds greatly to the convenience and efficiency of your dressmaking if you have organised a special sewing area, with the tools hung up as in a proper workshop, and everything well-placed by the sewing machine and work-table.

Dressmaking check list:

CUTTING TABLE: completely cleared and dusted down.
CARDBOARD CUTTING BOARD: as an alternative or addition to the cutting table.
SCISSORS: on their hooks on the wall.
PINS: in the correct size for the material.
TAPE MEASURE: marked in centimetres and inches.
RULERS: various sizes.
GAUGES: for repetitive measuring.
METRE OR YARDSTICK: sometimes handier than the tape measure for longer lengths.
T-SQUARE: for aligning straight grain of fabric symbol with selvage on material, etc.
NEEDLEWORK BASKET: with tacking thread, thimble, needles, small embroidery scissors, etc.
THREAD BOX: containing assorted reels of thread.
BASKETS FOR WORK STORAGE: plastic-coated office trays or an office trolley with trays are both ideal. So is a lined and covered wicker basket.
MARKING MATERIALS AND TOOLS: for transferring the pattern marks to the material.
CLEAN PLASTIC BAGS: Large ones, small ones, carrier bags, cleaner's transparent plastic dress

covers. All fabric pieces will be safely clean if stored in them whenever they are not being sewn.
IRONING EQUIPMENT: with the board and iron set up and ready to go to work, with pressing cloths and other ironing items handy.
THE SEWING MACHINE: Oiled and ready to sew, with all the parts and attachments dusted, tidied and in perfect working order.
With all these items ready, collect for immediate action on or near the work-table:
1 Cutting tools for immediate use and any marking equipment suited to the material.
2 Your measurement chart and dress form.
3 The pattern, with any size adjustments carried out on it.
4 The material, lining and interfacing.

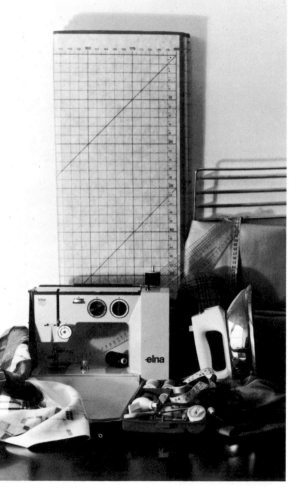

DRESSMAKING CHECK LIST
1 Prepare sewing work area and assemble sewing tools and materials.
2 Open pattern envelope and select the pattern pieces required for the garment you have chosen to make, as well as the instruction sheets and cutting layout.
3 Cut out the relevant pattern pieces roughly, fold the remainder neatly and return them to the packet. Keep the packet by you for any information printed on it you may need.
4 Fit the pattern to you and make any adjustments necessary, comparing the pattern pieces for size with your personal measurement chart, or refer to your basic fitting pattern.
5 Following the cutting layout pin the adjusted pattern shapes lightly to the material, placing all the pattern pieces you will be cutting from it along it to make sure they fit in. It certainly could be disastrous to start cutting the material until you have made this check. Remember to reverse right and left shapes, too.
6 Lift off the pattern pieces, and repin carefully following the appropriate cutting layout whenever possible.
7 Transfer all the pattern markings to the material cut out shapes, except for the wording.
8 Following the order of construction from the instruction sheets step by step, make up the garment.
9 Press at each stage and when completed unless pressing is unsuitable for the fabric used.

Sewing countdown

Here is a picture of the finished outfit of a top and trousers made from the pattern we chose, Butterick Fast and Easy, style number 4657, which also includes patterns for variations of the shirt, and trousers and a dress.

All the sewing techniques used to make and fit and finish both garments are described and illustrated in the following pages, as well as many others which weren't required for this particular pattern. The pattern has been used to show you how to find your way about the complexities of the pattern envelope contents and the printed illustrated instruction sheets that come with them.

When you are setting out to make clothes, if you work in a calm and orderly way, giving time to the various procedures, and if you take things step-by-step, preparing each stage thoroughly, without hurry, you can hope for really good results.

It is better to do a little every day than to try to make a dress in haste – in the end experience will help you speed up your sewing anyway.

For sewing procedures: always pin first, then tack. Try on for fit. Make any fitting adjustments, pinning and tacking again if necessary, and try on for fit again. When fitted perfectly, remove the pins, except for some used as markers, and sew. Press each stage neatly as you go, except when the fabric is unsuitable for ironing. Complete by finishing machine thread ends and removing unwanted tacking stitches. Leave those in still needed, such as for guidelines.

Never cut away material until sewing is complete. You may want to make last minute alterations for size, and everything would be ruined if you had cut away material already. The exception would be trimming away the bulk from inside seams on heavy-weight material, but this too would need to be only when you were absolutely satisfied of the garment fitting perfectly. Motto: Beware of being 'scissors happy' in dressmaking.

Before counting the garment as completed, turn it inside out and finish all seams and sew off loose ends of zipper tapes neatly. Add loops for hanging it in the wardrobe.

Press thoroughly and carefully.

Wear with well thought out accessories which can bring out the best in any garment.

1 Check by looking at the pattern envelope to make sure which version of the garments you are selecting from those included.

2 In the instructions sheets each garment has its own list of pattern pieces required, given under the name of the garment: 'Top and Trousers' in this case, the shapes shown either in the form of a drawing with the piece names and numbers on each shape. Or the names and numbers printed in a list. For our trousers we had to find but two pattern pieces: the trousers front, and the trousers back. With the two shapes cut out, the remaining pattern pieces were refolded and returned to the envelope.

3 The cutting-out line on the pattern is a bold, solid line, sometimes shown with scissors drawn along it. When cutting out the material with the pattern pinned to it, be sure to cut round the outside of the black notches placed at intervals along the edges of the pattern shapes. These are for accurate seam matching later.

Inside the pattern envelope

Carefully remove the pattern from its envelope. Take care of the packet. You will need the information printed on the reverse side if you decide to use the pattern again.

What have you got? What appear to be reams and reams of white tissue paper in large sheets, printed all over with a maze of pattern shapes. Plus several printed sheets of instructions.

Somewhere on the packet or instructions you will also usually find a technical description of the construction of the garments included – worth reading because it can be quite revealing about what types of seams or sleeves you will be making, etc.

UNDERSTANDING THE PATTERN: A few basic symbols are repeated on each pattern piece, and it will save you a lot of time and effort if you follow them exactly. The instruction sheets too, are invaluable – see page 39.

It all adds up to a closely-packed and printed assembly line blueprint for your home dressmaking factory, and properly followed should give you results which will compete with anything you can buy.

STORING PAPER PATTERNS: Home dressmakers tend to accumulate a number of paper patterns as time goes by and storing them for future use can become a problem. A 36cm. wide (14in.) filing cabinet with drawers about 28cm. (11½in.) deep makes an ideal place to keep them.

Selecting the pattern pieces

Before separating out the pattern pieces you will be using, take the printed instruction sheets and get them into order, like a book. In most patterns they do follow each other in sequence. Some even have sheet numbers. Pin them together at the top left-hand corner, then you will be able to leaf backwards and forwards through them conveniently.

Each pattern piece carries the style number of the pattern and maker's name; a serial number, and the name of the pattern piece, and the number of pieces of the shape to be cut out and pattern symbols to follow when cutting out. Pattern pieces for the left and right side, when not cut double, are reversed for the second shape.

The key to the pattern pieces for the garment you wish to make is given in the instruction sheets.

Helen surrounded by the contents of a pattern envelope.

Pattern illustrated instruction sheets

The instruction sheets include information you need to complement the pattern and help you to make it up successfully. Everything in them has a bearing on the best use to make of it.

They include advice on preparing and cutting out the fabrics, and any special stitches and sewing techniques needed; a key to the pattern symbols; the cutting layouts; and a fabric key to tell you whether – in the step-by-step in-structions – the material should be right or wrong side out or you are using lining material here etc.

A numbered illustrated guide to the pattern pieces is included, plus individual garment pattern piece requirements. Finally come the step-by-step instructions which you follow through to the completed garment.

It is a case of following them through from beginning to end – as simple as that!

A page from the Butterick pattern used for making the outfit described in the text.

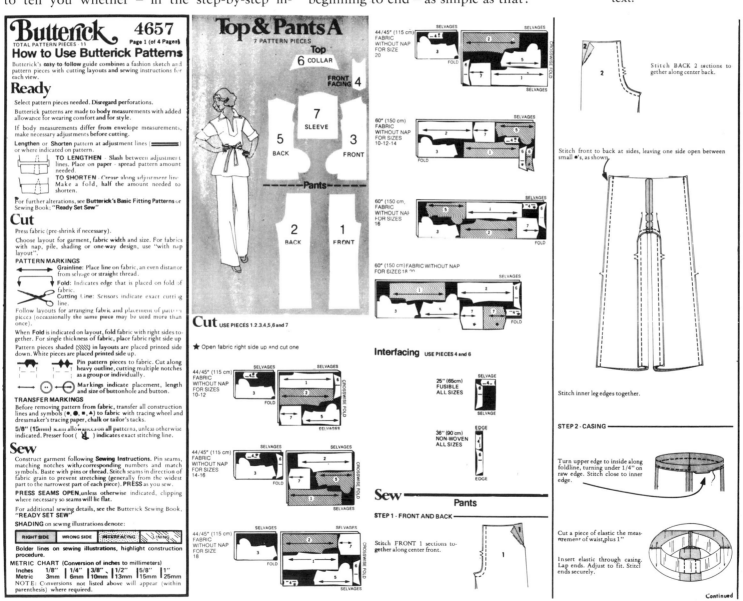

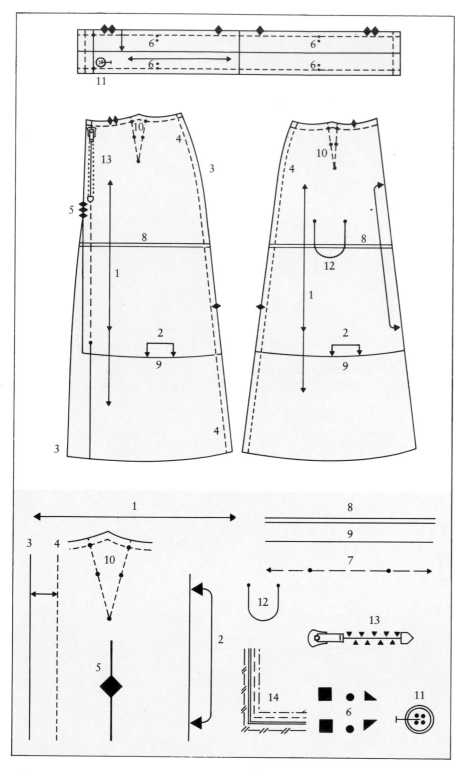

The pattern marks and symbols

A key to the marks and symbols printed on your pattern is always given in the instruction sheets. These marks and symbols are a sign language, a quick code to using the pattern; it will help the speed and accuracy of your dressmaking if you always make use of them.

1 GRAIN LINE: Also called *lengthwise grain of fabric* or *straight grain of fabric* (the grain line across the material at right angles to this line, not marked, is known as the *crosswise grain of fabric*).

The grain line symbol gives you your bearings when placing the pattern pieces, so that you cut the material with the weave lying in the right direction. It makes a big difference to the way the garment hangs when made up.

This line, with an arrow at each end, should be parallel with the woven selvages at the sides of the material, including for bias cut shapes.

2 FOLD: Indicates that this edge of the pattern should be placed against folded fabric, thus cutting the shape double. Or hem fold.

3 CUTTING LINE (sometimes with scissors drawn along it): The line to follow when cutting out the material.

4 STITCH LINE (sometimes with a presser first drawn along it): The seams of the garment etc. are stitched along this line.

5 NOTCHES: Indicate matching points on the garment. Notches come in ones, twos and threes, and are matched together on the corresponding pattern piece. Cut outside notches.

6 BLACK SPOTS, TRIANGLES, SQUARES: Indicate matching points in sewing.

Small spots are matched to small, large spots to each other, triangles together and so on. For example, if you gather a longer edge to sew it to a shorter edge, the length of the gathering line will be shown by a black spot at each end. The shorter edge will also have a black spot at each end in the same way. The gathering line is drawn up until the black spots match. Also for matching darts' sides together, folding pleats etc.

7 A SINGLE OR DOUBLE BROKEN LINE: Usually with black marker spots. A gathering line.

8 A DOUBLE SOLID LINE: Shorten or lengthen the garment here.

9 A SINGLE SOLID LINE: Across the pattern indicates a hem turning.

10 TRIANGULAR BROKEN OR SOLID LINES: Often with centre fold line and marker spots. Dart placement.

11 BUTTON AND BUTTONHOLE PLACEMENT: For placing buttons and buttonholes.

12 POCKET PLACEMENT: Position the pocket here.

13 ZIPPER PLACEMENT: Sew a zipper where the zipper drawing is shown.

14 MULTI-SIZE PATTERN: Each size is usually indicated by a different type of line. Cut the pattern shapes round your size outline.

Altering a pattern to fit

Before cutting out the material, you will need to make sure that the pattern fits you perfectly. As can be seen from Elizabeth's own measurements in relation to her pattern size, she would have to make the waist smaller and the bust larger on the pattern to make it fit her personally.

The first requirement is your measurements list. You will need to refer to the basic measurements of the pattern too, including the back waist length, adding the length of skirt and sleeves you've decided on. If your waist measurement is, say, 4cm., or 1½in. less than the pattern, this is the amount you would have to take out.

If you made the pattern fit you like a glove all over, you would remove the 'ease' – the extra room built into it for comfort so you can move in the garment easily. The amounts taken out would need to be distributed equally all round the garment too. Back to Elizabeth's waist . . . a centimetre would need to be taken out equidistant from the centre, about half-way along the waist at each side, front and back. Adding up to four centimetres or one and three-quarter inches in all.

The amounts would be taken out in tapered, pinned folds in the pattern, tapering up under the bust. For the larger bust measurement, cuts would need to be made at each side of the bodice pattern, and extra paper fitted underneath to the required amount, comparing too the width of the bodice back with Elizabeth's own back measurements.

When the alterations have been made to every part of the pattern, the shoulder seam pinned to the correct length, the bodice length right, the skirt length and circumference decided, and all seam and other allowances taken into account, the outside edges of the pattern will need to be drawn into level shapes, to align with each other as originally planned, notches matching.

Before going on to cut out, try the pattern against you critically, as well as checking it on your dressmakers' form, provided that has been made or adjusted to your own dimensions.

If you have prepared a basic fitting pattern, you can be saved the trouble of repeating this procedure of altering the pattern each time, by making use of it now.

MATERIALS: Have ready paper (tissue, greaseproof or dressmakers' paper), a ruler, tape measure, T-square, metre or yardstick, pencil, Sellotape, pins. Avoid using your best cutting-out shears. Less valued scissors are preferable for paper cutting.

Your personal measurements will be needed, and your dressmakers' form helpful.

Method: 1 To make a pattern piece narrower, pleat it vertically and pin the pleat. Or for a simple shape, turn in the edge of the pattern piece, and pin it.

2 To make a pattern piece wider, add the extra amount needed in pinned on strips of paper, tapered to fit where necessary.

Pin to the outside edge for a simple shape, or in one or two vertical cuts. Link up the outside edge of the pattern where it has become irregular as a result.

3 To make a pattern piece longer, add paper strips inserted in one or two cuts across the pattern, or at the edge of a simple shape,

and redraw the outside edge as before if necessary.

4 To make a pattern piece shorter, pleat it horizontally in one or two places, and pin the pleats. Or for a simple shape, turn in the pattern piece at the edge and pin it.

Distribute the alterations in an even, balanced way on the pattern.

Cutting out 7

Material know-how

Material is usually woven or knitted, with few exceptions, such as when the fibres have been compressed and matted together, as for felt, or bonded with latex foam, such as for non-woven interfacing or joined by stitching in the factory . . . a recent technical innovation.

PRE-SHRINK MATERIAL BEFORE CUTTING OUT: All natural materials, such as cotton and wool are liable to shrink more or less, unless they have been through a pre-shrinking process before leaving the mill. Try to discover from the label on the fabric whether it is washable, or recommended for dry-cleaning only. Or ask when buying the material. A cotton lace blouse for example, or denim jeans, could shrink one or two sizes in the wash if not pre-shrunk.

If you are in any doubt, it will be wise to pre-shrink the material yourself. Lightweight material, its edges carefully matched, and the length folded in a neat rectangular shape, can be immersed in cool water for thirty minutes or so, then hung over a clothes-horse or rail carefully, so that the straight grain of the fabric is retained without distortion.

Wool can be damp-pressed to pre-shrink it, or steamed and pressed at the dry-cleaners in the length, before cutting out. Synthetic fabrics should not shrink, though they can lose their shape if not hung up after washing, and also when being stored.

WAVY MATERIAL: You may notice that the weave, or the selvages, of your material have become rather uneven, with a wavy thread rather than a straight one, which may also distort the pattern. Before cutting out, pull the grain straight by taking hold of the material at opposite corners, and tugging it. Tug it both ways, then pull it straight, and level the selvages together.

MATERIAL STRAIGHT ACROSS: Before you begin sewing, it helps when aligning the pattern to have the material straight and level on the crosswise grain across the end. You can make it straight if the material is plain woven, by drawing a thread out carefully across, and trimming the material along the line of the thread. Where it has a horizontal guideline in the form of a woven tartan band, or gingham stripe, the material can be trimmed along this. Or a cross-grain cutting line can be made with pins, and a T-square, squared on the selvage, and a tacking guideline.

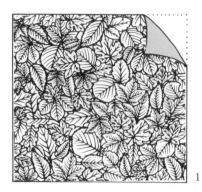

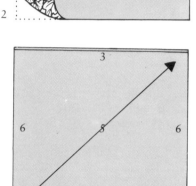

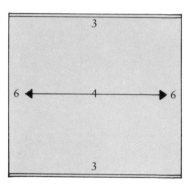

1 *Right sides facing* or *right sides together*: means that the right sides of the material are faced together for sewing at this point.
2 *Wrong sides facing* and *wrong sides together* means that the wrong sides of the material are faced together for sewing at this point.

Some material is *reversible*, for example check gingham, which looks exactly the same from both sides. In making clothes, the fact that there is a right and left side to a garment would mean that you have to place the fabric shapes in opposition when making up the garment, even where the material is reversible.
3 SELVAGE or SELVEDGE. 'Selvage' is American spelling; 'selvedge' traditional English spelling. It is the name

given to the woven edges which run down each side of the material in the piece.
4 These are the woven edges to which the straight grain of fabric symbol, the line with an arrow at each end, must be placed parallel.

In general, it is best to cut out pattern shapes inside the selvage. In some cases the woven edge can be used for a single hem turning, such as down the front of a blouse opening. The woven edge, if built into the garment, might prevent the material being sufficiently flexible for ease or movement, apart from the fact that it is often different in appearance, with the pattern irregular and even stripes along the edge. So it is better to cut it away.
5 BIAS: When deciding the bias of the fabric, take a

square on the selvages, then fold the fabric across diagonally from corner to corner. Along this diagonal fold is called the *bias* of the fabric, and apart from being used for bias binding strips, is used for bias cut garments. Tartan skirts with the plaid stitched together on the diagonal, giving it a diamond patterned look, are cut on the bias. It is a way of making softly flared skirts and sleeves, which are inclined to cling, or godets, that is, flared panels.
6 CROSS-WISE GRAIN: The grain of the weave across the material, at right angles to the selvages.
* All of this information can be found on other pages . . . but this is a convenient place to remind you of it, before you begin to cut out your material.

Folding material for cutting out

Sometimes material comes off the roll folded in half from side to side; sometimes in a single layer with the selvages at the sides. In order to place the pattern pieces on the material for cutting out, you may need to refold it, bearing in mind that when doing so it is wise to follow the appropriate folding and cutting layout given with the printed sheets of illustrated instructions that accompany every pattern.

To place every pattern piece marked 'on the fold' against the folded edge of material simply doubled over in half would be uneconomical.

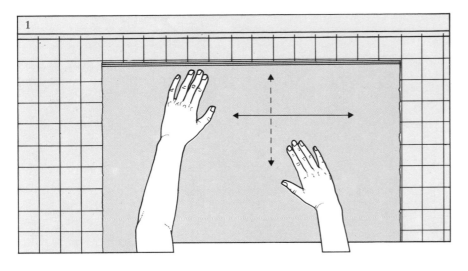

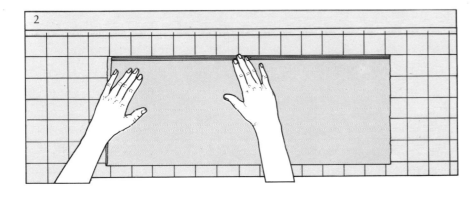

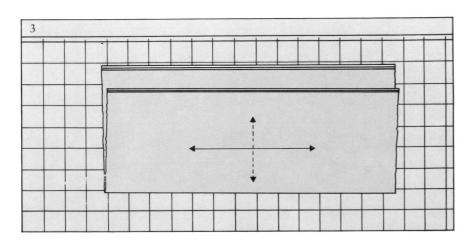

1 FOLDING MATERIAL: Clear the work table or cutting board except for scissors, T-square or dressmaker's ruler, pins and Sellotape. Spread the material out level. Pattern pieces are usually pinned to the right side of material for cutting out, including when cutting on the fold.

Straighten the selvages and level the raw edges on the crosswise grain at right angles to them, checking with your T-square or dressmaker's ruler. If you are working with the material on a cutting board, printed guidelines on the grain both ways will assist you in placing it.

Any surplus material too long for the table can be folded in a neat pile at one end. When the material has been correctly folded and arranged, anchor it in place on the table with Sellotape or to the cutting board with pins.

2 For material folded in two across the width, carefully lift one edge and take the selvage across to the other selvage. Smooth and pin the layers together along the selvages and the raw ends of the crosswise grain, matching plaid or patterns carefully.

3 ECONOMICAL FOLDING: If you have a pattern piece 30cm. or 12in. wide, to be cut out from a length of material which is 45cm. or 18in. wide when folded, or 90cm. or 36in. wide when opened out, you will be cutting out a width of 60cm. or 24in.

If you were to cut this pattern piece out of material simply folded in two across, you would be left with two pieces of material each 15cm. or 6in. wide, which would be wasteful. If you refold the material with one selvage on the fabric, true along the lengthwise grain, taking up a width of about 32cm. or 12½in. when folded (so the folded material extends just beyond the pattern piece) you will have a large piece of material left, about 28cm. or 11in. wide.

So it is wise to fold the material carefully when cutting out, with the proviso that you follow the cutting layout. It is sensible too, to place the pattern pieces close to one another without overlapping, in order to get the best value out of a length of material, again, after reference to your cutting layout.

Plaids, checks, stripes

A garment made of plaid or check material, or in stripes, can be made or marred by the way in which the woven or printed bands and patterns match together at the seams. Next time you see a plaid or striped garment, look at the seams. If these are out of true, the attractiveness of the fabric pattern and the garment's appearance will be spoilt.

Always have an eye to their position, and indeed the balance and placing of any large, repetitive pattern (including flowers or designs in lace).

When cutting out, pattern pieces have to be placed on the plaid so that when it is sewn, all the band match at the seams perfectly, as well as being equally balanced across the garment.

Sometimes the plaid or stripes are not equal both ways. These are called 'uneven' and match one way only. You can test this by folding back a corner of the fabric. You will see the bands which don't match perfectly both ways.

The plaid will not only have to match down the side seams, but across any panel seams too, front and back, to form a continuous plaid round the garment, and across the shoulders through the shoulder seams. The top of the sleeve would need to be cut so that the armhole seam front and back, though deviating at the shoulder inevitably, would nevertheless mainly match across.

Where the seams are not straight and parallel, matching the plaid bands at the seams would still make checks chevron away from each other gracefully.

All this includes perfect placing of the horizontal edges of the pattern pieces, so that when the garment is made up, with facings turned in the centre plaid check will be exactly centred on the garment, with an equal number and amount of checks at either side. This is known as 'balanced plaid'.

This information applies to checks and striped material, except for very narrow or tiny patterns.

To match plaid or stripes at the seams, first check that there is room for all the pattern, following the cutting layout, then pin the first piece, as planned, to the material. Cut out the first shape, then place it beside the next shape, matching the notches. If the bands do not match perfectly, all ways, realign the next shape till they do. Continue for all shapes. See drawing above.

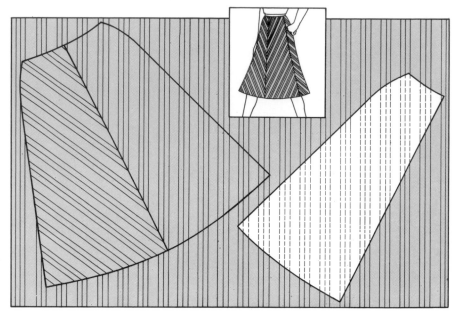

4 FOLDING PLAID OR PATTERNS: When refolding plaid, or patterned material, you will need to check that the fabric is folded so that the pattern balances on either side of the fold edge . . . or it will come out unequal when cut out, and that the design matches at the selvages. Pin the plaid selvages together exactly matching to help align the bands for cutting out.

SLIP BASTING: It will simplify the job of matching plaid or stripes perfectly at the seams, if you slip baste them together from the right side. To do this, fold under the seam allowance of one of the shapes, and place it over the edge of the adjoining shape, aligning the plaid or stripes perfectly. With the fold edge of the turned under seam allowance exactly on the stitch-line of the adjoining piece, pin them flat together. Tack through the fold edge and stitch line along the seam. Open out fabric. Now you can re-tack the seam from the wrong side as for any plain seam, knowing that your stripes and plaid matches perfectly. Machine and remove tacking.

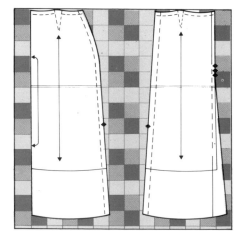

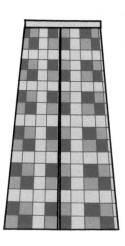

Cutting layout charts

A pattern of a top, trousers, skirt and dress ensemble may well have as many as thirty or more cutting layout charts, even for a simple pattern like ours. No wonder that people not having had a five star Cordon Bleu course in dressmaking fade away in bewilderment looking at this maze of small black and white diagrams, decide the whole idea was a mistake in the first place and give up there and then.

A cutting layout is really an easy guide, a simple drawing to show you how to place the pattern pieces on the material for cutting out, so that you don't have to work it out for yourself, and so that you are sure of being able to cut them out of your material the right way, and without too much waste.

As separate layouts are included to cater for every width of material, and additionally, for material with nap, the interfacing and sometimes for lining, the number of them tends to proliferate. To find your way among them and ring the ones you want to use is, fortunately, not as difficult as it looks.

1 From a package which includes patterns for a top, trousers, dress, skirt and belt, we are looking for the cutting layout for the top and trousers. Job number one is to find the cutting layouts under this heading and ring them round.
2 There are several alternative cutting layouts for the outfit. As our vermilion red polyester jersey is in 150cm. (60in.) wide fabric, the one we need is for placing the pattern on material of this width. It is there, among the cutting layouts, and is now ringed round. Any special pattern pieces for lining and interfacing have their own cutting layouts to be tracked down too.

From a study of the cutting layouts, you can see the difference between an ordinary cutting layout and one for a chart for 'without nap'. Here the pattern pieces can be placed facing from opposite ends of the material. For a 'with nap' pattern, such as one used for velvet or fabric with a one-way surface, the wide lower edges of the skirt or similar shapes have to be placed side by side.

Some of the shapes on the cutting layouts are plain white; others are covered with diagonal black lines. (In some pattern makes shown as shaded areas.) These give further clues to placing the pattern pieces on the material. The white

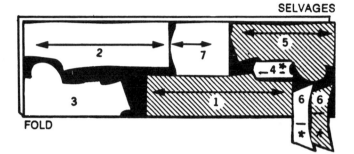

60″ (150 cm) FABRIC WITHOUT NAP FOR SIZES 10-12-14

SELVAGES

2 7 5

3 1 4*

6 6

FOLD

shapes mean that the pattern pieces shown like this should be placed on the material right, or printed side up. The pattern shape with diagonal lines, means that the pattern piece should be placed printed side down, against the material.

You can also see how the material should be folded. The word 'Fold' is placed by the fold edge of the material, which is not necessarily at the top or lower edge of the fabric as shown in the layout, but may be along the crosswise grain. Selvages on the material are placed to correspond with the word 'Selvage', usually drawn with a double edge to indicate two layers of material. The straight grain of fabrics symbol, the line with an arrow at each end, on the layout, shows the position for this symbol when the pattern is placed on the material.

The collar shape for our top pattern, as shown on the cutting layout, has a little star on it. For our Butterick pattern this symbol is to draw attention to the fact that the pattern shape should be cut out of a single layer of fabric, as directed: 'open fabric right side up and cut one'.

Other pattern makers sometimes show this as a pattern shape extended beyond the fold of the material on the layout. Whatever method they use, you will always find complete instructions for using the cutting layouts in the instruction sheets.

The pattern pieces are left pinned to the material ready for the next stage, which is marking: transferring the pattern marks on to the material.

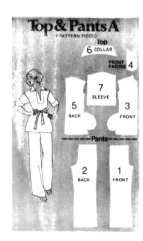

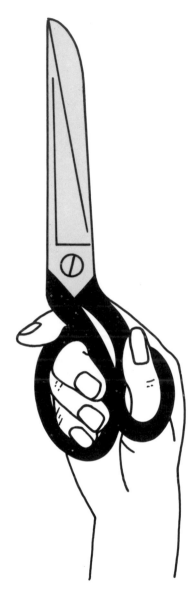

Cutting out

The moment arrives for cutting out. The cutting out tools arranged alongside the material correctly laid out and folded on the work table.

CUTTING OUT TOOLS CHECK LIST: Cutting out shears; medium-size scissors; small pointed scissors; steel pins (the right size for the material); pincushion; T-square or dressmaker's ruler; prepared pattern shapes already adjusted for size Check that the pattern cutting layout is the appropriate one for your fabric, that it is for the correct width, and 'with nap' if required.

CHECK THAT THE PATTERN PIECES WILL FIT ON THE MATERIAL FIRST: To do this, lightly pin the pieces to the material as shown in the cutting layout, with the straight grain of fabric symbols correctly aligned with the selvages.

IF YOU FIND OUT YOU HAVE NOT ENOUGH MATERIAL: If you find out that you cannot cut out the pattern from the material available, or you want to squeeze a garment from a remnant, there are one or two things you can do.

FACE THE HEMS: By facing the skirt or sleeve hems you can probably save about 5cm. to 7cm. or 1¾in. to 2½in. on the length. In this case, you would need to place the pattern with the hem turning allowance pinned up, except for the seam allowances needed, close to the raw edge of the material. For the facing, use taffeta cut to the depth of the hem plus seam allowances, or ready made bias facing. Or you could face the hem onto the right side using contrasting fabric.

REDUCE THE FLARE OR FULLNESS: Provided the basic fitting dimensions of the pattern are not reduced, you can save material by reducing the flared width of the skirt, or the gathers. By doing this you can sometimes cut out from a single width of material instead of needing two lengths, or you may be able to close up the pattern pieces more.

USE CONTRASTING MATERIAL: For almost any part of the garment: the yoke; bodice front, and/or back; sleeves; or skirt. Collars and cuffs can be made of broderie anglaise or organdie. A skirt can be lengthened with a yoke of pleats.

One precaution: use similar types and weight materials so that you do not run into trouble with cleaning and laundering, unless as for a collar the part is detachable.

YOU WOULD NEED TO KEEP: The position of the straight grain of fabric symbol in relation to the selvages, always, or you could end up with a badly hanging hemline or an off-true bodice. The size and position of the darts should also be retained, and any important details which affect the fit of the garment.

FOLD MATERIAL: and pin at edges.

PIN THE PATTERN PIECES TO THE MATERIAL FOR CUTTING OUT: Having tested the cutting out layout by pinning on the pattern pieces roughly, remove them and replace the material on the work table as before. Check the grainlines. Now pin the pattern pieces more securely and finally to the material for cutting out, following the cutting layout again.

The first time a pattern is used, it will still have its paper margins outside the cutting lines. These can be left on and cut away at the same time as you cut through the material. When a pattern is used again, there won't of course be any margin. Use ruler or T-square to check straight grain of fabric lines are parallel with selvage.

Margins can be overlapped, but not cutting lines, though these can be placed fairly close.

IN GENERAL:

* Material should be kept level and moved as little as possible during cutting out.
* Avoid stretching and creasing the fabric underneath the pattern.
* Lightly press the paper pattern if necessary before using it.
* Use steel pins, fine ones for sheer material (or special brass silk pins) and velvet, and pinned inside the seam allowance.
* Pin diagonally or at right angles round the pattern edge, about every 15cm. to 18cm. or 6in. to 7in.
* Pin at more frequent intervals for drifty or sheer fabrics, or for soft stretchy fabrics which move out of shape easily.
* These fabrics can be mounted on tissue paper and cut out as one.
* Knits stretch one or two ways, and vary considerably in their degree of stretchiness. Use the direction of the knit for the straight grain of fabric, and cut generous seam allowances.
* Be sure to cut out a right and a left shape where required, such as for sleeves.
* Cut out the correct number of each shape required.

CUTTING: This is the job for which your sharpest cutting-out shears are reserved. Pinking shears are not used for cutting out, but are for trimming seam and other fabric shape raw edges.

Take the shears in a firm grip, your thumb through the smaller handle.

Open the blades wide, and holding the scissors level on the table, slide the lower blade under the fabric, in the direction of the cutting line. Try to move the material as little as possible as you cut. Rest your hand lightly on the pattern on the material to keep it steady as you cut.

Clip along the cutting line of the pattern piece with long, clean, incisive cuts, keeping the shears as level as possible as you go. Change your position by the table, rather than the position of the material and the pattern, as you cut along the other side. If you take your time, and cut with care, you will be delighted with the results. Reminder: cut round *outside* the notches, and trim them later.

Later you may want to finish some details with the medium-size scissors or even the small sharp-pointed scissors.

ONLY UNPIN THOSE PIECES you have to remove for cutting a reverse shape through a single thickness of material elsewhere along the length.

LEAVE PATTERN PIECES pinned to the material otherwise, ready for transferring the pattern marks. As each piece is cut out, fold it lightly and place it to one side in the tray prepared for it.

INTERFACING AND UNDERLINING: After the main material shapes have been cut out, if you intend to underline the garment, you will need to use the same pattern pieces to repeat the shapes in lining material. For lining or interfacing you will also need to use any special pattern pieces included in the pattern for the purpose, with their own separate cutting layouts. Non-woven interfacing does not have a direction of fabric, or lengthwise, bias and crosswise grainlines, so you can place your pattern shapes on this material in any direction, economically.

TIDYING UP: Carefully fold up any scraps and odd pieces of material, each type in a separate bundle. Keep out a few odd scraps of each kind for testing stitches on the sewing machine etc. Put the rest away in a plastic bag, ready for use during dressmaking, such as for cutting out bias strips, or for belt carriers.

Later on, the larger pieces can be put to use for some other purpose, such as patchwork, or making accessories or small toys.

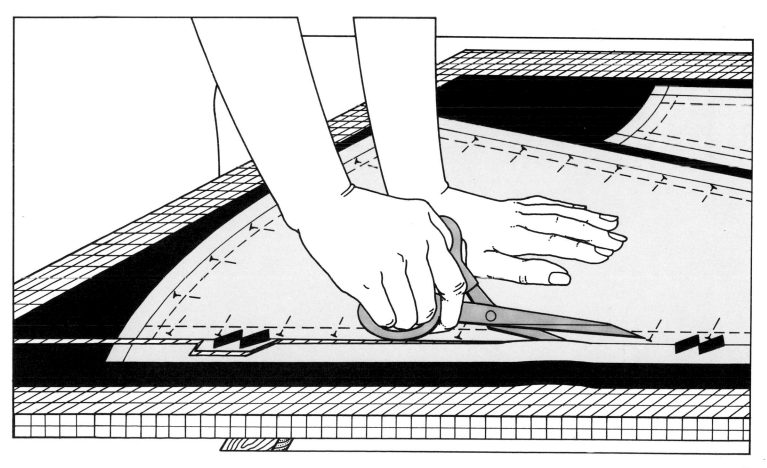

Transferring pattern marks to the material

It will save you hours of time, and help the accuracy of your dressmaking, if you transfer all the pattern markings . . . apart from the printed words and numbers . . . from the paper pattern onto the material. Marks such as seam lines, darts, pocket placement, button and button-hole placement, taking into account any pattern alterations.

There are several methods of transferring marks, each one particularly suited to marking a certain type of material. For example, you would not find that a printed line of dots, made by running a serrated tracing wheel over dress-makers' carbon paper, would show up well on rough-surfaced woollen material. This would, however, be an ideal way of marking on plain, light-coloured smooth cotton fabric. For woollen material, marking with stitches such as by tailor's tacking would be more effective.

It is wise, as you can see, to be familiar with the small number of different ways used for trans-ferring marks, as you will be sure to need to use one or other of them at some time in dressmaking. (Prepare a special board, padded with foam plastic on one side, for use when marking material. Leave one side unpadded, as a flat surface for the tracing wheel and carbon paper method.)

TRACING WHEEL USED WITH DRESSMAKER'S CAR-BON PAPER: This method, used in conjunction with a ruler or a curved guide, is suitable for relatively smooth, firm-surfaced materials such as cotton, rayon, or medium-weight fine-woven fabrics. The tracing wheel with its fine cog wheel edge is fixed between prongs at the end of a handle. Dressmakers' carbon paper is sold in packs of several sheets each, various colours included. A coloured sheet is chosen for the material so that the dots will show up well, though some packages carry the recommenda-tion that not too strongly contrasting a colour is preferable. These sheets are quite small, usually about 38cm. × 20cm. or 15in. × 8in. each, and have to be moved along between the pattern and the material in stages.

METHOD: Test the carbon first on a fabric scrap for suitability. Rest the material shape flat over a piece of card or thin board, the pattern shape facing onto the wrong side and pinned in position so that the darts and seam lines and

other marks are placed correctly. Except for reverse shapes, the printed side of the pattern will be face up. For single thickness fabric slip the carbon paper sheet, coloured side down, between the pattern and the material. Place the ruler over the pattern beside the line being transferred, say, down one side of a dart, and carefully and firmly run the wheel over the line. Wherever there is a black marker spot, make a little cross, or short horizontal line across the dart line. Repeat this process for all the printed lines on all the pattern pieces being used. For double thickness fabric (right sides facing) or the reverse pattern, the carbon can be slipped over the board face upwards, under the material and pattern, at the same time. Pin in place. Tack marks to right side if necessary.

A PLAIN, SMOOTH-EDGED TRACING WHEEL is used without carbon paper, though still over the pattern pinned on the wrong side of the material, with cardboard underneath (to protect the table top). In material soft enough to hold a groove, such as silk chiffon, or certain wool fabrics, the smooth edge of the wheel indents a solid line.

This type of wheel could of course be used instead of the serrated wheel with carbon if wished.

TAILOR'S CHALK OR CHALK PENCIL (or powder used with a tracing wheel): Tailor's chalk is

TRACING WHEEL AND DRESSMAKERS' CARBON
1 Place the fabric wrong side up over a board.
2 Slip a sheet of carbon in a contrasting colour face down on the fabric, then the pattern on top.
3 Roll the tracing wheel firmly over the pattern markings, using curved and straight rulers. Make a line across for any special marks such as black spots down dart sides.

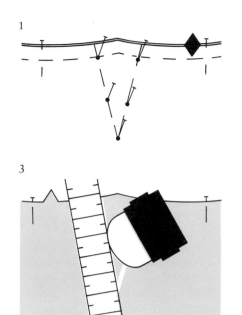

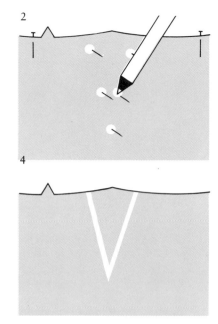

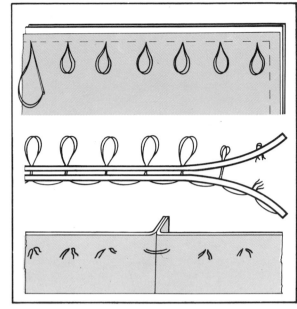

TAILOR'S CHALK

1 With the pattern pinned to the right side of the material, push pins through onto the wrong side through the pattern markings.

2 Turn the fabric over so the wrong side is uppermost with the pin points sticking through, still in position. Mark the fabric by the pins with tailor's chalk.

3 Remove the pins and complete the chalk line along the chalk dots, using tailor's chalk and a ruler.

4 Reverse the pattern for the other half of the garment and repeat the procedure.

TAILOR'S TACKING

Use a long needle with long tacking thread, double and knotted at the end.

useful for many different marking requirements. This dry, firm chalk, which usually comes in white, but is also available in pale blue-grey or pink-beige is fine textured, and can be employed for drawing on material, with the great advantage that the powdery line it makes brushes off without a trace.

It is used, as well as for marking, for temporary alteration marks during fitting operations, such as for noting a changed shoulder seam line, or depth of armhole. It is normally best for smooth-surfaced woollen or similar weight synthetic fabrics.

TAILOR'S TACKING: Tailor's tacking consists of looped tacking stitches which are taken right through the pattern and two layers of fabric. When all the stitching is completed, the materials layers are pulled apart, and the stitches snipped through.

When the pattern is removed, a line of cut threads marks darts, seam lines, etc. This is the main method for marking on wool cloth.

Have material right side out and the pattern pinned on. Push the needle through the pattern outlines and both layers of material onto the underside. Pull the thread through underneath. Bring the needle out a tacking stitch further along the marking line, repeat, being careful not to pull the loop through. Push the needle in again on the

same spot, making a loop on the surface.

When the tailor's tacking is complete pull the material layers apart, so the loops are stretched, and carefully snip through the centre of each stitch, between the fabric layers. Short cut threads will remain in the material as sewing guidelines.

Loops can be made on one layer of material but would need to be snipped through the centre above. After marking lift the pattern off.

There are several tailor's tacking tools on the market which enable you to carry out this method of marking with stitch lines quickly and easily. As with the tracing wheel, a board would need to be slipped underneath the material when the tailor's tacking tool is being used.

For using a tailor's tacking tool, refer to the instructions which come with it.

TACKING STITCH GUIDELINES: Tacking stitch is useful for marking guidelines in dressmaking. For instance for placing the centre line of the bodice front and skirt, a line of tacking stitches sewn along pin markers on the centre fold will be an invaluable guide, when the pins are removed, to balancing darts or pleats at each side.

PINS: Pins are excellent for marking purposes. They can be used to set the position for tacking lines, or to fix the exact position of the length of darts, to balance them equally, to pinpoint them in fact.

Clothes fit for a palace

'I should love to make my own clothes,' says a smart woman, 'but whenever I've tried, they never look right. There is always something clumsy and unprofessional looking about them.' It isn't necessary to feel this dissatisfaction with clothes one has made for oneself however.

Observe models in a fashion show wearing quite inexpensive clothes from chain stores. Their outfits always look a million dollars. What is the secret?

Notably the trim, neat fit. A garment which hangs well from the shoulder, with an easy, though elegant line, of the right length and immaculately brushed and pressed. Worn too with well-thought-out, usually rather simple but good and complete accessories. Shoes, stockings or tights, hats, gloves, bag, scarf, flower or jewellery, hair colour and make-up all contributing to the image.

Even where outfits are ornate they are often founded on a plain basic design, with well co-ordinated ornamentation. For colour schemes, a mixture of tones and dyes with one or two dominant colours setting the theme, work well together, enhancing and contrasting with one another, rather than going for a solid chunk of matching bright pink or green for a whole outfit.

Knowing when to stop is one thing. Using one's imagination is equally vital. It takes imagination to judge a good shape, so essential in dressmaking, and to think out a beautiful, lively colour scheme. To know how to cover a garment with elaborate embroidery which is still in keeping with the design, or to sew braid over every seam with all the style and panache of a soldier's coat, without vulgarity.

Training one's visual perception can help. Going to every fashion show possible. Fashion firms or magazines or pattern manufacturers often have store or trade fair promotions. So do local shops. Associations often run fashion shows for fun.

Looking at the leading fashion magazines helps. So does looking at paintings, old prints. Visiting costume exhibitions in museums. All these things help to extend one's knowledge of the subject and give ideas.

With a well-chosen pattern, made with care, you will have clothes fit for a palace.

POINTS FOR A FINE FINISH

* Aim at keeping darts aligned perfectly and gracefully tapered.
* Avoid bulky, large, clumsy darts.
* Aim at straight, well pressed seams which hang in a good line down the sides and centre front and back.
* Avoid seams in the wrong places. A waistline seam slightly off the waist and unintentionally ill-fitting.
* Aim at a neat, comfortable fit.
* Avoid tight armholes. Too tight a fit across the hips or in the bodice, which drag the garment out of shape apart from being uncomfortable to wear.
* Aim at a perfect hem, with not too deep a turning and concealed stitching from the right side, level and pressed perfectly.
* Avoid botched turn-ups.
* Aim at well-finished details. Cuffs of the right depth. Buttonholes, so tidy they are a joy. Belt kept in place by belt carriers.
* Avoid killing a good garment with the wrong or incomplete accessories.

Unit construction is a method of assembling a garment which is rather similar to pre-fabricating a piece of furniture from a kit of semi-completed parts. The garment is made up with the bodice, skirt, sleeve etc. completed as units and then joined together.

This form of construction is suited to modern mass produced garments, based on a certain standard range of measurements and it needs to be based on a very carefully fitted pattern.

If the personal fitting element has been taken care of perfectly beforehand, then there is no reason why the method of unit construction should not be a successful, quick and labour-saving way of putting a garment together. *More traditionally* the entire garment would be pinned and tacked together, and fitting adjustments made all over, before any final stitching would be carried out. Indeed, a couturier-made garment would be made up in muslin first, and any adjustments made to the 'toile' as it is called, which would then be the pattern for the garment.

Balance, line, elegance of fit would be carefully considered in a skilled and artistic way for this sort of dressmaking. Making your own basic fitting pattern would probably be the best com-

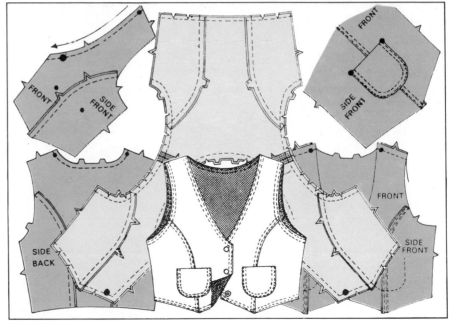

promise . . . a muslin or gingham basic garment to which basic pattern alterations are made, and recorded for immediate transfer to other patterns of the same standard size from the same maker. Most pattern firms include them in their catalogues, and they are a simple way of achieving a fine fit.

51

Sewing knitted fabrics

The stretch quality of knitted fabrics affects cutting out, pinning on the pattern, the stitches and seams used.

The stretch may go one way only, from side to side, as with cotton jersey. This is important to bear in mind when cutting out. Two-way stretch jersey stretches lengthwise as well as across.

You can check the stretchiness of your fabric by pulling a piece between your hands, and against a knit gauge if printed on your pattern.

1 Pattern normally state when they are suitable for knits. It is best to choose one of these.

2 Knit usually lies in a certain direction which affects the appearance, similar to pile fabric. Choose a 'with nap' cutting layout accordingly.

3 For aligning the straight grain of fabric symbol on the pattern it is necessary to pick out a row of knitting loops running up and down the length and to mark the row with a tacking guideline, as well as from side to side, to establish the horizontal or 'crosswise grain' of the fabric.

4 For pinning and sewing knitted fabrics, use ball-point pins and needles and machine needles.

To take the weight of stretching, a strong flexible thread is needed, such as polyester or cotton and polyester thread. For wool jersey use mercerised thread.

5 It may be necessary to open out tubular knit fabric by cutting up one folded side.

6 Pin on the pattern generously, about every 5cm. to 6cm. (2in. or more).

In the case of light or slippery knits, it may be advisable to pin or tack them on to tissue paper for cutting out and sewing.

7 Knitted material has a way of curling up when cut out, so cut extra wide seam allowances about 2.5cm. (1in.).

8 For transferring the pattern marks to the fabric, for firm-surfaced plain summer weight jersey, it should be possible to use dressmaker's carbon and the tracing wheel. Tailor's chalk would suit dark surface double knit jersey. Otherwise for soft jerseys use tailor's tacking.

9 Machine stitched seams will need to have built-in flexibility to prevent the stitches from breaking under the weight and pull of stretching material. Your instruction book will tell you which are the stretch stitches available to use on your machine, otherwise use fine zig-zag or

double parallel rows of tiny straight stitches.

Use an Even-Feed or similar presser foot to hold lightweight knits stable during machining.

10 To hold the shape of stretchable seams, especially at the waistline, stay stitch or sew tape or bias binding in with the stitch line. Only tape round armholes where it will not interfere with the comfort of the garment.

11 Hems can be turned up and machined with a double row of small straight stitches, fine zig-zag or stretch stitches. Or they can be blind stitched or overedge machine stitched and sliphemmed.

12 Press fasteners, including those clipped on by pliers, are ideal for fastening knits. So are zippers, toggles, ties.

Sewing velvet

* Velvet is a pile fabric. Use a 'with nap' cutting layout, allowing extra length for the fabric as suggested for your pattern.

* Test the velvet pile by rubbing your hand over it. If you feel the pile bristling against your hand, the pile is lying upwards; if it strokes away smoothly, the pile is lying downwards. The pile should lie the same way over the entire garment, or variations in the way it reflects the light may alter its appearance. Sewing with the pile upwards on the garment gives a richer effect.

* Use fine steel pins outside the cutting line or brass silk pins. To transfer pattern marks to velvet use tailor's tacking, sewn with a fine needle and silk thread, or tailor's chalk on the wrong side of the material.

* Mount fine silk velvet on tissue to sew.

* Test the machine stitch line not only for the length of stitches, but for the pressure of the presser foot on the material, and lighten the pressure if necessary.

* Use a fine needle both on the machine and for hand sewing, and silk thread for both.

* Velvet may be lined or underlined with silk or satin; velvet coats can be brocade or satin lined. Interline with taffeta or Vilene.

* Press velvet *very lightly* on the wrong side, over a velvet pressing mat, or rough Turkish towelling, or another piece of velvet or a stiff clothes brush. Or hold up the material over the pressing mitt worn on your hand, and then steam press the velvet very lightly on the wrong side.

* Turn up taped hems and slip hem lightly to the wrong side of the velvet, or to the silk underlining.

Fitting and equipment needed

A dressmaker's form adjusted to your measurements to work with. Remember the caution about not fitting the garment too closely on this, and to allow ease for comfort in wear.

For making the alterations you need tailor's chalk, pins, tacking thread and needle; embroidery scissors and medium scissors, and a tape measure. A well-lit full length mirror is essential, and if possible a second mirror fixed so you can see your back and side view.

In general: Fit the garment over your underclothes, or if a coat or jacket, over the dress or skirt and blouse you would normally wear under it. Wear your shoes too. Stand up straight to fit the garment, but check for comfort and ease by sitting down and moving your arms forward and to the sides freely. As a person's left and right side may differ, it is necessary to fit the garment right side out, even though this is more inconvenient for making the alterations finally considered necessary.

As a help to fitting, before a garment is even made up, tack guidelines on the fabric shapes to mark the centre front vertically, and the centre back, as well as horizontal guidelines for the bust and hips, front and back.

To begin with, tack the carefully measured and spaced darts in place on the garment front and back. Place the front and back of the garment together right sides facing and pin and tack them along the shoulders and down the side seams, as well as at any other seams where necessary. For fitting over a rigid dress form, leave one seam open for taking the garment on and off. In any case, the final fitting should always be made on you before any sewing takes place. Here the help of another person makes a lot of difference.

To fit a garment

1 Hang the dress over the dress form or wear it. Overlap and pin zipper and button openings as they will eventually be when closed. Make sure that horizontal guidelines are parallel with the floor, and that the centre guidelines and side seams hang straight vertically.

2 Begin by adjusting the fit of the shoulder and side seams. The aim should be a good fit everywhere, which sits neatly but comfortably on the body, including in movement, giving a garment which hangs well and easily from the shoulders, or if a skirt, from the waist.

3 Dragging wrinkles, gaping zipper openings, too tight armholes, botched bodice fitting, are tell-tale signs that somewhere the fitting is too tight, and perhaps the seam or darts need letting out. If there are ugly folds, or unintentionally drooping waist or armhole seams, then the garment or darts probably need taking in carefully, or some seams may need lifting or realigning.

4 When fitting sleeves, check to begin with that the right sleeve is in the right armhole, and the left sleeve in the left armhole. Darts are centred on the elbow joint at the back. Allow ease in the circumference and length.

5 To make fitting adjustments, use pins first. Either make a pleat or tapered tuck in the seam or dart, to take it in where too loose, or if too tight, undo the tacked seam or dart and repin to let the garment out. When the fit looks satisfactory, supplement the pins by chalk lines, or tacked guidelines. Or use pins as markers.

6 Now remove the garment and place it level on the worktable. Complete the chalk lines or tacking or pin guidelines. Remove those pins which were used for alterations (not the pin guidelines). Turn the garment wrong side out, and undoing former tacking if need be, repin through the chalk, tacking or pin guidelines.

Share any alterations evenly between darts and seams to retain a graceful shape.

7 With the garment repinned along the fitting lines, tack the alterations and remove all pins, including pinned guidelines, on any seams or darts about to be machined. Now try on the garment again, on yourself this time. Consider it carefully. Are any more adjustments needed? Now is the time to make them. All is well? Then you can go ahead. Remove the garment. It may be necessary to untack the waist or armhole temporarily while making up the main parts of the garment, but retain the guidelines, for sewing them later. Machine, then press.

This procedure is repeated at each stage until the garment is completed. Remove all marks and guidelines, and give the garment a final perfect pressing.

* Never cut away any material until you are quite certain that your fitting adjustments are correct for the whole garment.

Time spent on fitting is never wasted.

A good fit and finish is often the outstanding difference between a professional and a home-made garment.
Fitting begins with the pattern alterations you make based on your measurements. You may have carried these out on a basic proportion pattern first, or direct from your measurements to the pattern. It is helpful to keep your measurement list beside you when fitting too, as a check.

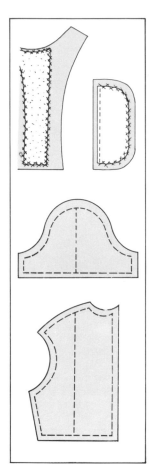

Underlining

Underlining is a method of lining a garment by facing the lining material onto the wrong side of the fabric shapes before making them up, then working with them as one.

When cutting out a pattern shape in the main fabric, cut out a repeat shape in appropriate lining material.

Underlining is an excellent way of backing stable fabrics such as lining firm linen, though it is not suitable for lining soft, flowing, draped materials. Underlining helps to hold the shape of the garment, and also enables hems and facings to be stitched down so that not a thread shows on the right side, which gives a very smooth appearance. See Lining Guide on page 135.

The pattern markings should be transferred to the underlining shapes before they are backed onto the fabric. After marking, place the underlining shapes against the reverse side of the garment shapes, wrong sides together.

As you pin the two layers together all round the edges, keep the fabric level and smooth with the lining. Tack the underlining to the fabric shape all round the edges and in addition several times down each shape. Stay stitch by machine round the edges, but not across the garment. Now work with each shape as one. A zipper is sewn on top of the folded-back underlined seam, and not between underlining and fabric.

Stay stitching

Whenever you see this term in dressmaking, it means running a line of straight machine stitching round the edge of the material where instructed, even if only through a single layer of fabric, to hold the edge firm. The stay stitch line is usually placed just in the seam allowance outside the stitch line, but can be across the top of the pleat to hold it in place before a waistband is attached.

A 'Stay' has somewhat the same function, to hold a shape, such as that of a skirt underneath pleats, but is a panel of material.

Interfacing

Interfacing is a layer of firm material stitched flat between two layers of fabric in those areas of a garment which need some reinforcing to help them hold their shape, such as front facings. Imagine how limp and shapeless a collar would be without interfacing to stiffen them.

The type and weight of interfacing material used would depend on the garment fabric. From non-woven material as light as rice paper for delicate cobwebby fabric, through to strong hair canvas interfacing for tweed.

Interfacing shapes are either cut to the main pattern shape, or have their own separate pattern and cutting layouts. The aim is to keep the interfacing smooth and flat and neat inside the garment.

It may be sewn in with the stitch line, as for a collar, then trimmed away outside the stitching to avoid creating ugly bulk along the finished edge. Or if machining will not show on the right side of the garment, it may be straight or zig-zag stitched in place. Often it has to be cut to fit inside the stitch line or fold edge exactly, and the raw edges stitched down all round with concealed hand stitches. Herringbone and catch stitch are two stitches used for this.

Interfacing materials guide

INTERFACING:	USED FOR:
Vilene Transparent iron-on (non-woven interfacing)	Transparent fabrics such as voile, chiffon, lawn
Net	Lace; sheers
Organdie	Chiffon; georgette; silk; organza; monograms; backing for motifs
Vilene Light Sew-in (non-woven interfacing)	Georgettes, polyester-cotton; lightweight Terylene and other light fabrics. Also in an iron-on version, used for small areas
Vilene Medium Sew-in (non-woven interfacing)	For medium to heavyweight fabrics
Vilene Heavy Sew-in (non-woven interfacing)	For shape and support in heavier fabrics. Also a Vilene Firm Iron-on version for crisp interfacing of small areas
Vilene Soft Sew-in or Soft Iron-on (non-woven interfacing)	For light to medium fabrics. Use iron-on version for small areas
Vilene Super-drape Iron-on (non-woven interfacing)	Stretch interfacing for knits.
Taffeta	Choose a heavy version for interfacing light to medium fabrics.
Canvas	For tailoring and also for soft furnishing
Hair canvas	Horse hair and canvas blend for tailoring
Taped seams	Twill tape or seam binding can be used to reinforce stitch lines of some seams or stretch fabrics

* Test iron-on interfacings on a piece of fabric first.

When making up the underlined garment, darts and pleats are folded and stitched in the lined fabric. Where necessary slash darts open and press them apart. Balance equally See diagram opposite.

a. Stitch line of darts from the side seams.
b. The space at each side between the end of dart and centre seam.
c. Stitch line of darts from centre of garment at top.
d. Seamline length of darts.

Darts

Darts are small tapered and stitched tucks in a garment to make it fit the body. Depending on the design, they are likely to be needed on the front and back of the skirt and bodice for fitting the waist, as well as in the bodice front in the underarm side seams, for the bust. Small darts may be placed on each shoulder at the back, as well as tiny ones on either side of the back of the neck. Fitted long sleeves often have a little row of three darts at the back for the elbow. Darts are used in furnishing too, for making soft covers fit.

Shaped panels joined by curved seams, or gathers, or pleats, are other ways of fitting a garment, sometimes used instead of, or combined with, darts.

Darts usually come in pairs, balancing the fit of the left and right side of the garment. Consequently the way they are made and positioned can make a subtle difference to its appearance. If they are crude, clumsy and unequal, they will look amateurish. They need to be perfectly placed, and follow a light graceful curve, sloping outwards slightly from the centre, left-hand darts towards the left, right-hand darts towards the right, bust side darts raised a little as they taper off.

Those at the front are usually smaller than those at the back, at the waist. They can be made in twos or threes too, for a more graduated shape.

Careful measuring is the clue to placing darts perfectly. Use the centre lines as a guide, and make sure that the spaces between each pair of darts, and between the dart stitch lines and the seams are balanced and equal at each side. Their length should match too. The easiest way of fixing this finishing point for machining is to measure the dart's length and place a marker pin where the stitch line finishes, and do the same with the other dart of the pair. Then when the darts are machined, the stitching can be tapered off onto the fold edge and be stopped at exactly the right point on each one.

MAKING A DART:

The triangular mark on the pattern for a dart has a line down the centre for the dart fold edge, and black marker spots down the sides. Having transferred this pattern mark to the material, pinch the sides of the dart together, matching the marker spots over each other, making the pleat on the wrong side.

Pin the sides of the pleat together, then tack down through the marker spots. Remove the pins. Measure the length of the dart on the fold line, and place a marker pin across the finishing point. Machine from the widest part tapering off on the fold and ending at the marker pin. Repeat for the twin of the dart.

Do not reverse machine stitch but self-sew or tie-off thread ends. Remember to use an appropriate stretch stitch for knitted fabric.

MAKING A DART

1 Transfer pattern marking of dart to fabric.
2 Pleat and pin.
3 Tack the dart sides together. Machine, tapering off on fold and ending at marker pin.
4 Press. For thick material slash the dart down the centre fold and press open. Pink edges.

TWO POINTED DART: 5a For a garment with no waist seam. The dart pleat is tapered at each end, the curve following the body line. 5b Snip dart in fold line *outside* stitch line, so the dart will lie flat when the garment is turned right side out.

6 SLASHED DART: Cut the dart as directed. Stay-stitch, tapering the stitch line at the end of the slash. Right sides facing, pin and tack the slash sides together, then machine them with a tapering stitch line.

* Dart-tucks are shown on page 59.

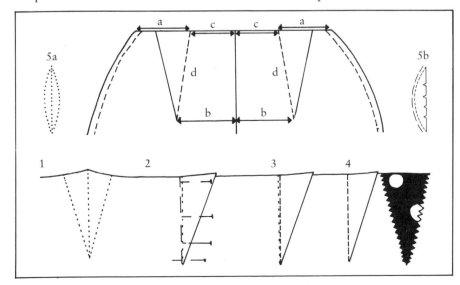

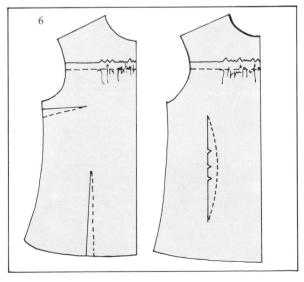

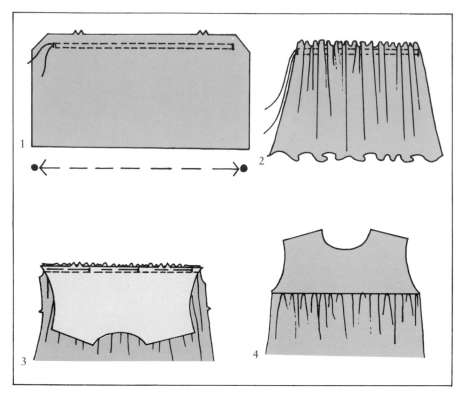

Gathers

EXTRA MATERIAL: The amount of extra material needed for gathering varies with the weight and type of fabric and the amount of bunchiness desired. Lightweight material would need three times the width of the fitted garment. Cotton or rayon material would require two to two and a half times the width, and thicker material, one to one and a half times.

Running stitch is used and the depth of the gather would depend on the size of the stitches and spaces.

MACHINE GATHERING: Use a gathering foot or long straight stitches and loosened needle thread tension. The bobbin thread can then be drawn up to form the gathers.

1 Sew a double row of gathering stitches between the marker spots.
2 Gather these threads and anchor the thread ends round a pin.
3 Right sides facing match the plain and gathered raw edges together, matching notches and marker spots and gather the threads, so that the two edges correspond in length. Pin, then adjust the gathers evenly. Machine together along the stitch line. Remove the tacking and gathering threads.
4 Turn up and press.

Ease

'Ease' is a term used when a shorter seam edge is joined to a fractionally longer seam edge, and, importantly, with a smooth seam and no little puckers, creases, or gathers showing on the right side.

It is a term used for fitting the top of a plain, fitted sleeve into an armhole, or for sewing curved seams together on a panelled bodice.

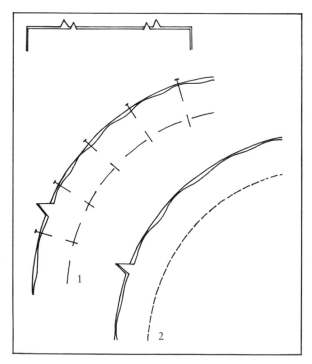

Method: 1 Run a gathering thread through between the balance notches on the longer curved edge. On top of the sleeve, these will be about two-thirds of the way down the front edge, and similarly at the back. Add a second row of gathering stitches beside the first if desired.
Match the notches on the seam edges being joined to one another and pin the two layers of fabric together at these points. Find the centre between these balance marks, and mark it with a pin. This will give you your bearings. Now work your way along the seam between centre and balance points each way, pinning, with the pins at right angles to the raw edges. 'Ease' or slightly stretch the bias of the shorter raw edge, and avoid stretching the longer raw edge. If anything, cramp it along its length slightly so the edges match.

Tack the two raw edges together just inside the stitch line, and continue the process of stretching one, and holding in the other as you do so.
2 Machine carefully along the stitch line, avoiding any creases forming, by working slowly, and stretching the tacked fabric gently as you go. Press. Cut notches outside the stitch line as appropriate.

Seams

A seam is made where two pieces of fabric are joined together along the raw edges, usually right sides facing. It consists of the 'stitch line', marked by a broken line on the pattern, and the 'seam allowance', the distance between the stitch line and the raw edge.

The seam allowance is intended to protect the stitch line from the fabric fraying, or in knits, unravelling. Today, some home sewing machines have overlocking stitch, when the garment is cut out along the stitch line and the seam sewn and finished in one operation.

Seams are aligned at the notches, the edges matched together, pinned and tacked. Remove pins, except markers, before machining.

A well-made seam helps the hang and stylishness of the garment. It should be perfectly joined without one side pulling against the other unevenly; straight or in a clear even curve. It is important to choose the correct thread, needle size, stitch length and thread tension for a seam, by testing first on two layers of the fabric.

When the seam has been stitched, it will need to be finished along the raw edges, using one of the methods shown opposite, or any flat decorative edge stitch recommended in your machine instruction book.

Finally, pressing the seam perfectly, with a steam iron or pressing cloth used dampened if needed, for woollen cloth, will have an important effect on the appearance of the seam.

PLAIN SEAM: A plain seam is the simplest seam. To make it, the raw edges of two fabrics are matched, notches aligned, and pinned and tacked along the stitch line, fractionally inside. Machine straight stitching is used, following the stitch line, and a suitable stitch length for the material thickness. For knitted or stretch material, small straight stitches are used, about 8 to the centimetre, or 15 to the inch, or preferably, the stretch stitch recommended for your machine.

A knitted or stretch seam is often taped along the shoulder and down the side seams, to help keep the length and shape of the seams stable. Seam or skirt tape, or ordinary tape, is tacked over the stitch line of these seams, and then included in the machine stitching. Seams where stretch is needed, such as armhole or crotch seams, should not be taped. (Twill tape is used for reinforcing seams in bulky tailored garments).

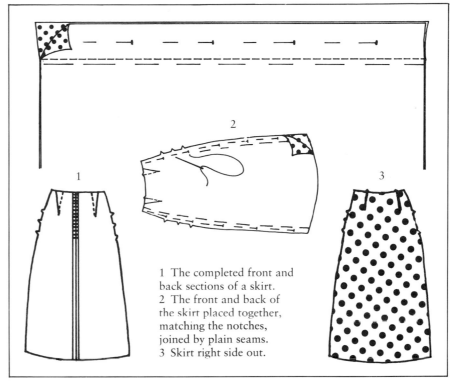

1 The completed front and back sections of a skirt.
2 The front and back of the skirt placed together, matching the notches, joined by plain seams.
3 Skirt right side out.

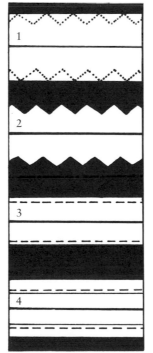
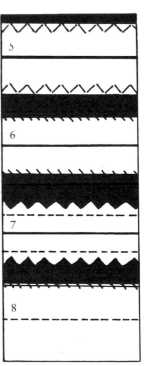

Dictionary of seam finishes

1 MULTI-STITCH MACHINE ZIG-ZAG: Used for stretch materials.

2 TRIMMED, PINKED EDGES: For non-fray materials and velvet.

3 HEMMED EDGES: For lightweight material.

4 NARROW BOUND EDGES: For thicker fabrics, especially armholes and in unlined garments.

5 ZIG ZAG MACHINE STITCHES: Inside raw edge. Stay stitches too. For fairly non-fray material.

6 OVERCAST EDGES: Easy to apply by hand. For wool and similar materials. Also velvet.

7 STRAIGHT MACHINE STITCH LINE IN PINKED EDGES: Simple, neat.

8 WHIPPED SEAM FINISH: For fine fabrics.

More seams

FRENCH SEAMS are used for sheer fabrics, because although a strong seam, being twice stitched, it can also be made neat and narrow, only visible as a fine band showing through the material at the seams.

This is an ideal seam for baby garments, and made slightly wider, (about 0.50cm. or ¼in.) is well suited to children's cotton clothes.

Make narrow French seams for curved seams or armholes. *A simulated French seam* is an ordinary plain seam, the raw edges folded and tacked together along the folded edge, and machined.

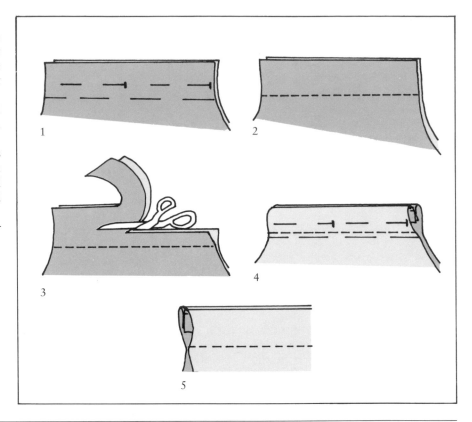

Method

1 Right side showing, *wrong sides together* match raw edges, and pin them as for a plain seam. Tack and remove pins.
2 Machine along the stitch line.
3 Trim the seam allowance to about a third of a centimetre or an eighth of an inch. Do not cut through the stitch line.

Trim any frayed threads.
4 Turn the seam over so that the right sides of the material are facing, and the seam line lies along the outside edge. Pin and tack close beside the trimmed raw edges, now tucked inside the seam. Machine. Press. Frayed threads should not show.
5 The finished French seam.

FLAT FELL SEAM is the folded over and topstitched seam used for jeans and men's shirts. It might give the impression of being slightly tricky to make successfully, but it is a straightforward seam once you have acquired the knack of folding it under neatly and topstitching it with a professional looking straight stitch line.

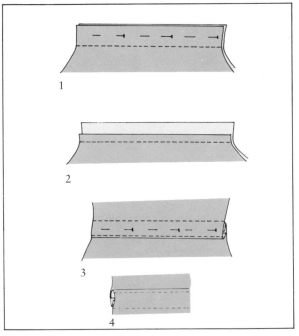

1 Make a plain seam *wrong sides* facing.
2 Trim away the front of the seam, close above the stitch line.
3 Spread the work out flat, wrong side of fabric against the table. Turn over the wider seam allowance to cover the trimmed side.

Turn under the raw edge, and pin it flat to the material, with the narrow trimmed edge inside. Tack down the folded under edge. Press. Topstitch close to the folded edge.
4 The finished Flat Fell seam.

CURVED PLAIN SEAMS
To enable a curved plain seam to lie flat when turned right side out, clip notches in the seam allowance *outside* the stitch line. This method can also be used to reduce the bulk of a concave curved seam a little, to close it up slightly, when turned.

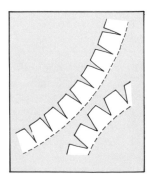

Tucks

Tucks are decorative straight parallel pleats stitched along their length, sometimes shell-edged. They can be made pin narrow or pleat wide; be spaced equally apart, or sewn in twos and threes, or groups of tucks, diagonal or fanned out. They are widely used for ornamenting thin material, such as white cotton lawn, often in conjunction with lace. Men's dress shirts are often tucked and ruffled, and they are a design feature frequently added to Victorian style print dresses, or silk or shantung blouses.

Extra material twice the width of each tuck has to be added to the basic width of the material required for the garment. Tucks should be completed before the garment is made up, and if possible, where they cover a garment, such as a bodice front, completely, before the shape is cut out of the material. Great care must be taken to be sure that the tucks lie accurately along the grain of the fabric, across or down the length. (Unless sewn at an angle for design reasons.)

As a quick check to the equal spacing of the tucks, and that they are equal in width down their length, a cardboard tuck gauge is a great help, marked with lines for each completed tuck, following the basic plan. A notch is cut out of the tuck lines. When the gauge is placed against the tacked tucks, they will show in the notches. As a further check, the gauge can be moved down the tucks.

Where tucks are a feature of the garment design they will be marked on the pattern and should be transferred to the material by the most appropriate method. A sewing machine tucking attachment helps make perfect tucks easily.

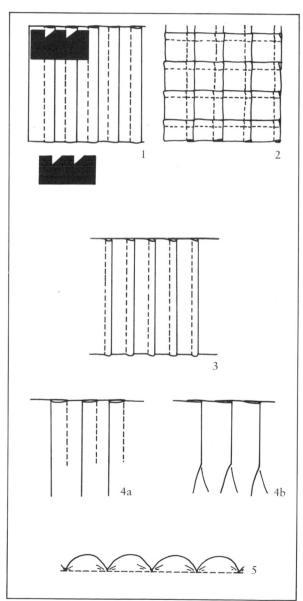

1 TO MAKE A TUCK: Follow the marking lines for the tucks transferred from the pattern, or mark your own on the reverse side of the material. Plan their placement from the centre. Pleat the tuck from its centrefold line, and pin and tack it down its length, checking with the gauge. When all the tucks have been tacked, remove the pins.
TO MACHINE: Machine down the tuck with straight stitching, following the presser foot or throat plate guidelines.
Repeat for all the tucks. Remove the tacking, and press the tucks to one side, or for tucks on either side of a centre line, to the left and right respectively, to balance them.

2 CROSSED TUCKS: A second row of tucks made horizontally across the vertical rows. Allow extra material to length as well as width of fabric.
3 PINTUCKS: Pintucks are fine tucks stitched close to the folded edge. Less extra material is needed for pintucks. Corded tucks: insert piping cord in tuck pleat and machine with zipper foot.
PLEAT OR DART TUCKS:
4a Short pleats, stitched along their length as for tucks, but with the stitch line stopped on the fabric.
4b They can also be made this way on the reverse side of the material. These are called 'inverted pleat tucks' or 'dart tucks'.

5 SHELL EDGING: Shell edging is a stitch which can also be used for a pretty, narrow hem edge. For tucks hand-stitch the tuck with small running stitches, and every few stitches (an equal number each time) carry the needle over the tuck fold and draw the stitch tight.
SHELL HEMMING OR SHELL EDGING: Prepare a narrow hem. Every few hemming stitches, the thread is taken over the hem edge, and brought back through, forming a small scallop at the edge. Repeat.
Shell edging can be stitched on some sewing machines. Your instruction book will tell you if yours will, and which stitch patterns to use.

Topstitching

Topstitching is a row of machine stitches sewn on the right side of a garment or other items, as a seam finish or decoration. To be successful it should be a perfectly level line of stitches, even when stitched round curves, evenly spaced from the edge of the material and other topstitch rows along its length. This can be achieved by accurately following the machine guidelines, or using whichever method you choose for the sewing job in hand – such as a seam guide or tacking guidelines – and a little practice.

Thicker contrasting thread may be used, such as white machine embroidery thread on navy fabric, or matching thread.

Saddle stitch is another form of topstitching: long-running stitches usually hand-sewn round pockets, collars, sleeves etc. on wool, linen or similar garments. Using contrasting colour cotton yarn or buttonhole twist, make the stitches about 0.50cm. ($\frac{1}{4}$in.) long.

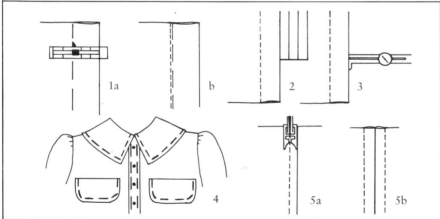

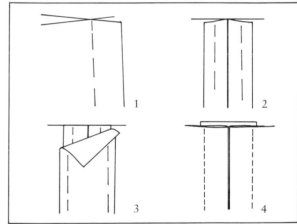

Methods

1a FOLLOWING A TACKING GUIDELINE: Measure the distance of the top stitch line from the edge, or next stitch row, and mark with pins. Tack along the line, checking with a movable gauge that the distance is kept equal along the length.
1b Stitch close by the tacking guide line.
2 THROAT PLATE GUIDE-LINES: The throat plate on most modern sewing machines is marked with guidelines. Use them to help you achieve accurate topstitching, by following the chosen guideline unswervingly with the outer edge of the material, as you stitch.
3 SEAM GUIDE: A seam guide is adjusted to the material outer edge. You can thus set the distance of stitch line from the edge.
4 SADDLE STITCH: 0.5cm. ($\frac{1}{4}$in.) running stitches in white or colour thick thread for decoration.
5a The outer or inner edges of the presser foot can all be used as guidelines for top stitching. Some are marked for this.
5b An opened, pressed plain seam can be topstitched down each side of the seam line, using the presser foot as a guide.
Or the seam, one side trimmed away, can be topstitched on one side.

SLOT SEAM
A fancy attractive seam for trouser side seams or other decorative seams, which looks like a double tuck.
1 Make a plain seam *tacked together only* along the stitch line.
2 Open out this seam and press the seam allowances. Tack the seam allowances flat down each side.
3 Make an underlay from a strip of matching or contrasting material to the width and length of the seam, covering the tacked seam allowances. Tack this underlay over the seam on the wrong side, right sides facing.
4 From the right side, top stitch at each side of the seam taking the stitch lines through the seam allowances and underlay. Pull the tacking stitches out, and press the seam.

Pleats

Pleats are not only for decoration. They have a practical purpose of allowing extra room for movement in the garment, an important feature these days when everyone walks, bicycles and in general leads an active outgoing life. We all know the swinging look of the kilt's closely pleated tartan; the charm of a silk dress with a softly pleated skirt; the small inverted pleat of a tweed skirt. They add vitally to the attractiveness of a garment.

Pleats can be made in almost any material which has a firm texture, preferably fine, and will take a crease when pressed.

Making pleats

Transfer the pleat marking from the pattern onto the wrong side of the material. These usually consist of bold and narrow solid lines with marker spots and arrows, supplemented by words, which clearly show the way the pleating goes.

You can instead work out your own pleating plan, allowing twice the width extra material for every pleat, in addition to the basic width required for the garment, and writing out a measurement chart for checking references. Though for most of us it is easier to stick to a pattern.

BEFORE BEGINNING TO MAKE THE PLEATS: Join the seam and make up basic garment, including sewing in the zipper and completing the hem.

When preparing pleats, check constantly with your dressmaker's ruler and tape measure that they are accurately spaced down their length and in relation to each other.

Commercial pleating

For a moderate charge you can have a garment commercially pleated, and with every permutation of pleats too, from knife or box pleats to accordion, or concertina, pleats, to sunray pleats on a circular skirt. All kinds of fabric too can be pleated although greater permanency is achieved with pleats heat set into synthetic fibre fabrics.

Usually the skirt or other garment is made up first with seams only and a single turning hem. For bias skirts usually the hem has to hang after pleating and before levelling. Professional pleating firms will also finish the hem edge on a sheer pleated skirt where necessary, for an extra charge.

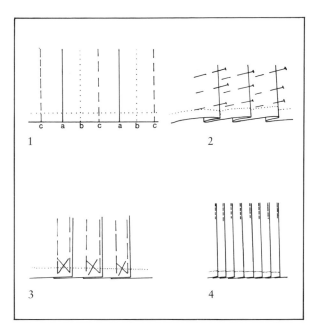

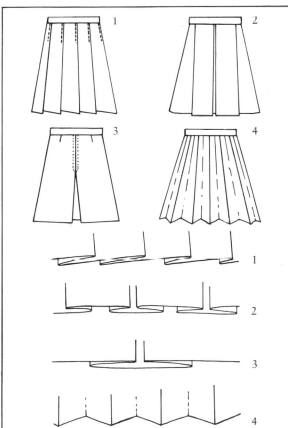

1 Crease the pleat, and carry it across to the fold placement line.
2 Pin the pleats down their length.
3 Tack the pleats down each side through all layers. Cross baste top and bottom.
Press.
4 Top-stitch the pleats where desired. Stay-stitch across the top.

There are four main types of pleats

1 KNIFE PLEATS: These pleats overlap in one direction and are sharply creased. Knife pleats are often tapered into the waist and sometimes topstitched in place on the hips.
2 BOX PLEATS: Box pleats consist of parallel pleats creased in two directions. The two inside fold edges meet at the centre at the back of the box pleats; so do the outside edges of the pleats in front.
3 INVERTED PLEATS: An inverted pleat is a box pleat in reverse, with the box pleat on the wrong side, forming the inverted pleat on the right side, often tapering narrower to the top of the pleat. Contrast material may be used inside.
4 CONCERTINA PLEATS: Concertina pleats are pleated along their length, concertina fashion.

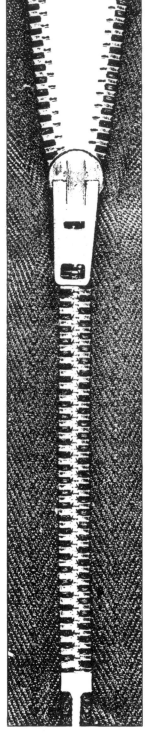

Zippers

Zippers are a boon and a blessing for making concealed fastenings. There are various kinds to suit most dressmaking applications: invisible zippers with coiled nylon spring fastenings concealed in the tapes, for extra-lightweight fabrics; dress zippers with narrow metal teeth; skirt zippers, rather stronger and heavier, and for fly fastenings in men's trousers and jeans, heavier zippers still, including a zipper with a curved end for this purpose. Separating zippers are used for anoraks and lumber jackets. They open all the way through. Then there are showy zippers with large white plastic teeth, and fancy tags, and tassels, which are not concealed when sewn in.

SEWING IN A ZIPPER: The zipper should lie flat in the seam, and the slide tag move up and down freely. It should be placed so the tag and lower end lie within the seam opening, or when sewn into a skirt, so that the ends of the tape match the raw edges of the material at the waist, before sewing on the waistband, and the zipper tag is placed just below the stitch line, with the rest of the zipper in the seam opening. The same goes for a zipper inserted in a dress opening from the back of the neck. The tape ends are turned under and hemmed to the seam allowance at each side, or concealed inside the facing or waistband.

The slot or centred method of inserting a zipper is the simplest, most basic way of sewing one in. The zipper is centred under a seam or slashed opening, with equal turnings at each side, and the zipper teeth directly under the opening. Used for dresses, pockets, bag fastenings etc. Use a zipper presser foot when machining.

Lapped zipper

A lapped zipper is inserted in a seam opening, so that one side of the closure is broader than the other, and laps right across over the zipper teeth. This method is used for skirt and dress zippers. If it is set in a side seam, the lap should go from

CENTRED OR SLOT ZIPPER
1 Make a plain seam with a zipper opening. End the machine stitch line at the opening, then tack the seam along the opening. Attach the zipper foot.
2 Press the seam open.
3 Centre the zipper right side down, over the tacked seam, tag and teeth within the opening.
Pin and tack the zipper tapes to the seam. Start from the top, first down one side then down the other.
4 Remove pins. Topstitch the zipper to the seam, first down one side, then down the other side, about 0.50cm. or $\frac{1}{4}$in. from the teeth centre, so the tag moves up and down freely. Stitch line across below. Sew off the tape ends. Press.

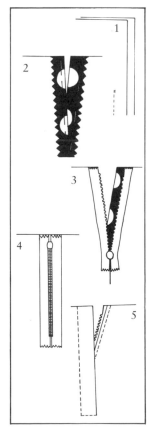

1 Straight stitch the plain seam, leaving an opening for the zipper. Change to the zipper foot on the sewing machine.
2 Turn back the left seam allowance 1.3cm. or $\frac{1}{2}$in.; on the right seam allowance: 1.6cm. or $\frac{3}{4}$in. Tack both turnings.
3 Open the zipper, with tape right side against the wrong side of the material. Working from the top pin and tack the right-hand zipper tape to the wider overlap on the right.
4 Close the zipper, and working from the top, and the wrong side, pin and tack the other zipper tape onto the narrower seam turning at the left.
5 Open the zipper and machine the underlap to the zipper tape and the other zipper tape to the overlap. Stitch across below. Hem down tape ends.
6 Lapped zipper.

front to back; if in a centre seam, the overlap should lie, for a woman, from right to left, and the reverse on a man's garment.

More zippers

1 HAND SEWN ZIPPER: Use a tiny spaced form of backstitch known as prickstitch (or use backstitch). Prepare as for other zippers. Follow the tacking line and sew down first one zipper tape from the top, then down the second tape from the top, finally across below.

2 PRICKSTITCH: Begin with small backstitches on the wrong side. Bring the needle through to the front of the material, then push it back through all the layers in a pinhead-size backstitch. Bring the needle through to the front again a long stitch forward, level with the row, and make another pinhead-size backstitch. Repeat for a row of backstitches. End with small backstitches on the wrong side.

OPEN ENDED ZIPPER: This is also called a 'separating zipper'. It unlatches at the lower end, and is inserted with the centred method. It should be machined in closed, so that the garment sides are joined evenly. If sewn in open, there could be a lop-sided effect when the zipper is closed again.

A second row of stitching, taking the outside edge of the presser foot as a guide, will prevent the tape from curling back. Afterwards hem the lining to the zipper tapes.

UNCONCEALED ZIPPERS: If you wish to sew in an unconcealed zipper, use a centred zipper insertion, and turn under the seam allowances at each side so that the folded edges lie on the tapes. Machine close to the folded edges.

ZIPPER SEWN INTO A SLASH: Snip at the corners of the slash, to form a folded-under rectangle outside the lower end of the zipper.

VELCRO: This is tape with a furry look, with hooks on one tape, and loops on the other, which grip together. It is useful for pyjama trouser fastenings or duvet covers and is an easy fastening for children or disabled people. Machine along each edge, or hand hem.

3 NARROW PLACKET: For extra sheer, soft, lightweight fabrics, such as georgette or chiffon, even a lightweight zipper may be too heavy. Make a self-bound placket opening, fastened with little press studs, and/or a tiny hook and eye.

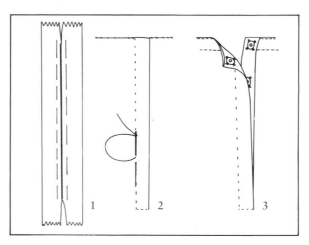

Method: Cut bias binding strips in self material, to the length of the placket plus seam allowances and turnings. Use double thickness sheer fabric, interfaced with organdie or transparent Vilene, or use seam binding or narrow corded ribbon.

On the underside of the placket, make a hem faced with ribbon, or a narrow bound edge, so that the edge extends under the other side of the placket. When the placket is complete, the seam allowance will need to be snipped, to lie flat outside it when pressed open.

Turn under and face the other seam allowance, or turn in a narrow hem. Hem across the top and bottom to keep flat. Sew on tiny press fasteners and a hook and eye at the top of the placket or half-way down on the waist seam.

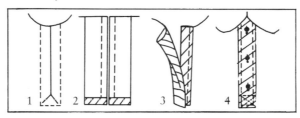

BOUND FRONT OPENING

1 Mark the slash from the neck, then stay stitch down sides and across below. Cut slash down centre and into corners.

2 *Right sides facing* on *wrong side of garment,* sew facings on each side of slash. Turn up ends to neaten.

3 Fold the facings onto the *right side,* in half as for binding. Turn in raw edges down facing sides. Machine topstitch to garment close to edge.

4 Place right over left facing (for women), and at lowest point stitch together across and down sides. Sew buttons to underlap; buttonholes to overlap.

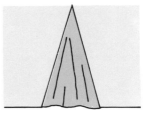

GODET: A godet is a flared panel stitched into a slash in a skirt, which gives a delightful swing and movement to a garment. It can be made in a contrasting material too. Godets are most suitable for garments made out of soft, easily draped material such as silk, crêpe de chine and other fine fabrics.

1 Carefully mark the position of the godet slash or shaped opening on the wrong side of the skirt or garment, where required. Stay stitch the sides of the marking, tapering the stitch line in the case of a simple slash towards the top. Cut out the shape, or between the slash stitch lines.

2 Right sides facing, pin the godet into the opening, working from the top down each side in turn. Be sure to keep the godet and garment opening even and smooth along the join, and avoid any puckering. Tack, remove the pins and machine.

3 Clip the seam allowance round a curved godet insertion, or reinforce the top point with ribbon, tape or a patch of non-woven interfacing or taffeta, on the wrong side. A small arrowhead tack at the point could look decorative on the right side. Press with care, and hem with the rest of the garment edge.

Waistbands

When fitting a waistband, it is important to measure carefully. It is so easy to end up with it rather too loose, or somewhat too tight, with the back a little too low, or the entire thing too high and wide. Which also leads to the boring task of unpicking an elaborate piece of sewing construction and starting again, or living with a garment which fits badly, resulting in untidiness and discomfort.

It really is worth giving attention to the size of the waistband when adjusting your pattern pieces to fit.

The waistband strip needs to be the correct length to go round your waist allowing a modest amount for a tucked-in blouse and underclothes, and adding seam allowances, and extra for the hooked or buttoned overlap, about 2.5cm. to 3cm. or 1in. to $1\frac{1}{4}$in. Although the depth may vary with the design, from a high cummerbund to a turned-in petersham ribbon facing with no band showing at all, a comfortable waistband is generally not too wide, about 2.5cm. to 4cm. (1 inch to $1\frac{1}{2}$in.); more than 5cm. or 2in. for a waistband would be coming into measurements where some shaping would be needed. Check also for comfort when sitting down as the waistline tends to expand when you are seated.

A homely tip, if you have a skirt or trousers which fit you perfectly, is to make a spot check between the waistband you are sewing and the one on the favourite garment. This will provide an instant size comparison.

A good fit for the waistband also depends on well-fitting darts on the waist, back and front, and an accurately placed waist seam.

For stiffening the waistband, sometimes heavy duty non-woven interfacing is used, particularly for lightweight fabrics. For heavier materials plain or corded petersham ribbon or thin belting usually work well.

Generally the zipper ends in the skirt or trousers' seam, and the waistband is overlapped above by about 4 or 5cm. ($1\frac{1}{2}$ to 2in.). The ends are fastened by two skirt hooks and eyes, or a flat trousers' hook; a button and buttonhole or Velcro.

A broad band of striped elastic, or strong elastic threaded through a waist edge facing can be used instead of a waistband. Not to mention a bib and shoulder straps, or braces.

Belt carriers

Belt carriers are a must for a garment with a narrow or medium width belt. The way to make these is given on page 105.

Make a carrier for each side, and possibly another two each for the back and front, unless you decide on chain stitch belt carriers which are stitched to the sides only.

Sew in with the machine stitch lines or finish the waistband first and hem and oversew to the garment in the usual way.

Hanger loops

To complete the job, make loops to act as hangers. Cut two pieces of tape or narrow ribbon, each about 15 to 20cm. (6 to 8in.) long. Double over the tapes and pin to each side, inside; sew in with the machine stitch line or hem in place.

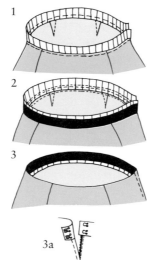

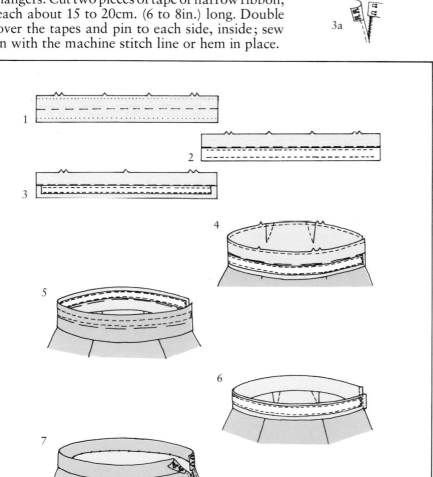

Petersham waistband

1 Pin petersham ribbon 2.5 to 3cm. (1in. to 1¼in.) wide all round inside seam allowance at the top of the skirt, on the wrong side. Tack. Remove the pins. Machine the ribbon to the skirt with two rows of straight or zig-zag stitches, including one over the petersham edge.

2 Tack seam tape or ribbon 1.5cm. to 2cm. wide, or ½in. to ¾in. wide, round the seam allowance on the right side, to cover the overlap of the raw edge on the petersham. Machine along both edges. Remove tacking. Press.

3 Turn down the petersham band inside the skirt. Turn under the ends and hem them, slightly underlapping the back under the front.

3a. Sew on two skirt hooks and eyes.

Bound waistband

1 Cut out one waistband and one interfacing. Transfer the pattern marks to the wrong side of the material and sew a tacking guideline on the centre fold.

2 Tack the interfacing strip to the lower half of the waistband on the wrong side, matching notches and other marks. Machine or herringbone stitch to the waistband all round on stitch lines.

3 Trim away the interfacing outside the stitchlines except along the centre fold line.*

4 Pin the interfaced waistband, right sides facing round the waist, matching notches and other marks, allowing an extended overlap to the right, over the zipper opening. Tack. Remove the pins. Try on for fit and adjust where necessary. When perfect, machine. Do not attach inside of waistband edge at this stage.

5 Remove tacking. Turn waistband up to fullest extent so that interfacing is above inside.

6 Fold the waistband back on itself and machine across the ends, right sides facing.

7 Turn the waistband right side out, and fold under the seam allowance of the interfaced edge. Pin and tack this edge to the waistband inside. Sew on hooks and eyes, a flat skirt or trousers hook or a button and buttonhole.

Second method: Follow the first three steps, then fold the waistband in half, right sides together and stitch across the ends. Continue with 4, leave out 5 and 6, and end with 7.

* If petersham is used, treat it as for interfacing, but do not cut away seam allowances.

Further into dressmaking 9

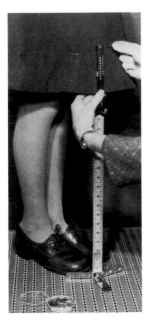

Hems

One of the prime essentials of successful dressmaking is a well hung, level hem, beautifully pressed.

Measuring for a level hem

DO-IT-YOURSELF HEM MARKER: Wearing underclothes and shoes and the garment being measured, stand level with the powder ejector fixed to the wall at the height for your hem level.

Squeeze the powder ball and a puff of chalk will form a short line on the skirt. Move round a fraction. Puff the powder again. Repeat this process for a full turn. When you remove the garment you will find an even row of chalk marks round the skirt. Before the chalk rubs off, supplement it with tacking guidelines or pins.

SKIRT MARKER: This is the familiar upright ruler on a metal stand which is placed on a level floor. You will need the help of another person to use it.

The marker arm can be adjusted to different hem levels. The edge of the skirt is clipped between the marker arm and the ruler, and marked with a pin and/or chalk powder.

Hem turnings

SHEER MATERIAL: Narrow hand-rolled, or narrow machine hemmed; faced with sheer material or transparent iron-on Vilene.
Lightweight dress hem: 3 cm. to 4cm. or $1\frac{1}{4}$in. to $1\frac{1}{2}$in. deep.
Dress hem: 4cm. to 5cm. or $1\frac{3}{4}$in. to 2in. hem.
Coat: 6cm. to 7cm. or $2\frac{1}{2}$in. to 3in.

Today machine stitching is acceptable for narrow or topstitched hems, but machine blind stitching is preferable for deeper hems. By hand, slip hemming is best. Stitches should not show on the right side.

PRESSING: Avoid pressing over the stitch line as this may create a ridge on the right side.

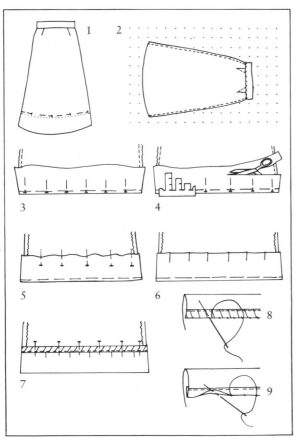

TURNING UP A BASIC HEM
1 The completed skirt is shown here with the hemline already marked with pins.
2 Wrong side out, with the plain seams pressed open down each side, place the skirt on the table, spread out level.
Collect the tools needed: pins, tailor's chalk, hem measuring gauge, needle, tacking thread, seam ribbon or tape, thimble, scissors.
3 Turn up the hem onto the wrong side of the skirt along the marked hemline. Pin and tack it all round, close to the fold of the turned-up edge. Place the pins at right angles to the edge.
4 Using tailor's chalk and pins, measure and mark the hem depth from the turned-up edge, adding extra for the seam allowance. Trim the hem depth level all round this

marked line. (Take care not to cut the skirt.)
5 Pin the hem to the skirt on the wrong side, with the pins at right angles on the hem. Tack along the fold edge and press.
6 Make small pleats or darts at regular intervals in the upper raw hem turning edge, to make the hem fit inside the skirt as smoothly as a glove, and pin.
The hem can be temporarily lowered so that the darts can be stitched in the ordinary way, then pressed. Pleats should be slip stitched down along their folds, then pressed.
For sheer material, a fine gathering thread may be run through the upper raw edge of the hem turning, and the gathered edge pressed.
7 Pin skirt tape over the hem turning raw edge. Tack and machine in place onto the hem edge, with the hem still separated

from the skirt. The tape raw end should be turned under and hemmed or machined over the other end of the tape.
Sew the hem to the skirt with concealed stitching which will not show on the right side, such as sliphemming by hand or blind stitching by machine.

STITCHES
8 HEMMING STITCH may be used for an underlined garment. See page 18.
9 SLIP HEM: Pick up one or two threads from the garment on the wrong side, then pass the needle through the hem edge, or under the tape, and pick up one of two threads in the tape.

The waistline seam

It is interesting to look through a dozen dress patterns at the different waist seams. Although the construction procedure is fairly routine through all of them, it is amazing what design variations a dressmaker can have to cope with.

One dress has an inset waistband stitched between a bloused bodice and gathered skirt, completed by a lining stitched over the inside. Another has a contour seam, dipping at the back, with topstitching. On one, the 'waistline' comes under the bust. Regency style. On the next, a bloused top is stitched to pleated skirt, with a waistline stay, a reinforcement of tape sewn along the seam allowance to prevent it from stretching.

It is important for style and comfort that the waistline seam is accurately placed, in accordance with the design, and fits perfectly. A dress should have a little more ease than a skirt or trousers' waistband, a coat or jacket even more.

Nevertheless, though these differences occur, the waistline seam is straightforward to carry out, though it is wise to follow the pattern step-by-step instructions exactly.

Waist seam stay

(a) A second line of stitching about 1cm. or $\frac{3}{8}$in. from the first on the seam allowance can act as a waistline stay. (b) Or pin and tack seam tape along the seam allowance, through all layers, on the skirt side. Remove the pins and machine through all layers. (c) Sew a belt of petersham ribbon not more than 2.5cm. or 1in. wide round the completed waist seam, after the zipper has been inserted. The ends of the ribbon, left unstitched for about 6cm. or 2½in., overlap across the zipper. Turn under hems at the end of the ribbon, and sew on two small hooks and eyes to fasten the belt, with the hooks facing *outwards*.

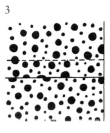

1 Usually the bodice and skirt will have been largely completed by the time you come to join them together. Previous fittings will have ensured that the centre front and back, darts and side seams align perfectly at the seam and any other details, such as matching plaid, have been taken care of. Notches should of course, match. The zipper (still not stitched in place) should extend below the waist for about 10cm. to 13cm. or 4in. to 5in. and for about the same amount above. (Most dresses have a zipper which opens from the neck to below the waist seam, usually down the centre back.)

2 Slip the bodice right sides facing inside the skirt, carefully matching darts and seams. Pin, and tack securely (for fitting) all along the seam from one side of the zipper to the other. Remove the pins.

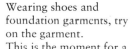

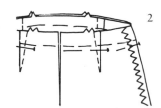

Wearing shoes and foundation garments, try on the garment. This is the moment for a critical look at the fit and line of the waist seam. Is the seam line where the pattern meant it to be? Where do you think it looks nice on you? If the seam feels a little tight, and the zipper opening is strained, then you may need to open out any darts and seams where necessary. Or if the waist looks loose, to take them in. Mark any alterations with pins and tailor's chalk. Remove the garment, and make the required adjustments. Check that the waist seam meets level and exactly across the zipper opening. It is so easy for it to be tacked a little out of line. Try on the dress again, and if all is in order, go ahead and machine the seam. Stitch slowly and carefully, usually using straight stitching (stretch for knits). A knit fitted waist can be reinforced by sewing tape in with the stitch line.

1 The seam completed on the fitted waistline.
2 A gathered bodice joined to a fitted skirt. The blouse is still slipped inside the skirt for sewing.
3 A gathered skirt and fitted bodice . . . but the way they are sewn together is still the same.

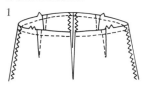

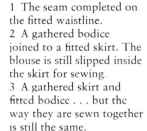

WELT SEAM

A welt seam is similar to a flat fell seam and can give a stylish finish to a waistline where there is no belt.

1 Sew a plain seam at the waist. Press the seam allowances open and trim away the bodice-seam allowance to about 1.0cm. or $\frac{3}{8}$in.

2 Press both seam allowances up, the wider over the narrower trimmed one. Tack through all layers.

3 Turn the garment onto the right side and topstitch through the wider seam allowance above the narrower one, taking your waistline from the waist seam line. Press.

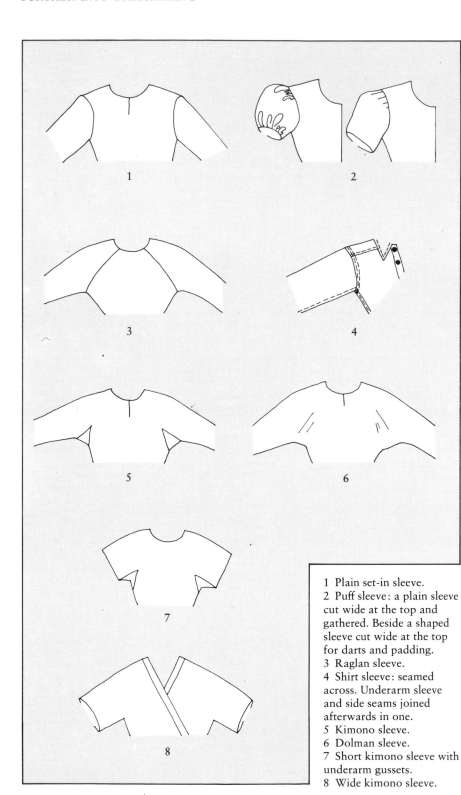

1 Plain set-in sleeve.
2 Puff sleeve: a plain sleeve cut wide at the top and gathered. Beside a shaped sleeve cut wide at the top for darts and padding.
3 Raglan sleeve.
4 Shirt sleeve: seamed across. Underarm sleeve and side seams joined afterwards in one.
5 Kimono sleeve.
6 Dolman sleeve.
7 Short kimono sleeve with underarm gussets.
8 Wide kimono sleeve.

Sleeves

Although one thinks of sleeves as coming in dozens of different styles, all are variations of three main basic types of sleeve. Tailored garments often have two-piece set-in sleeves.

SET-IN SLEEVE: Where you see a sleeve fitted into the armhole with a seam which goes all round, this is a *set-in sleeve*. The sleeve can be cut square under the arm, or mounted low on the shoulder; the top can be gathered or padded.

RAGLAN SLEEVE: The sleeve seam runs diagonally from the side seam under the arm, across and up to the neckline. There is no bodice shoulder seam, though there is usually a dart on the shoulder part of the sleeve or the sleeve comes in two parts for fitting purposes.

A raglan sleeve gives a roomy fit while looking neat, and is useful in overcoats to be worn over jackets, or baby gowns, where plenty of room for movement is needed.

KIMONO SLEEVE: This is a sleeve cut in one with the garment, whether cut wide as a Japanese kimono, or close fitted in a dress. When narrow, it usually has a gusset under the arm.

MORE ABOUT SLEEVES

On a fitted sleeve the back of the arm has a slightly longer seam, and darts or gathers to allow for fitting the elbow. The shape of the fitted sleeve head too, takes account of the shape and movements of the body, the shoulders and back. The front curve, as for the front of the armhole, is likely to be shaped in more than the back, and you may also find the wrist at the front is curved up slightly compared with the back.

These variations in the shape of the front and the back of the sleeve are why it is important to make sure you fit the correct sleeve for the left and right armholes. When fitting a sleeve care needs to be taken that it is not too tight a fit under the arm, or it will cut into the sinew where the arm joins the body at the front.

SLEEVE FINISH: The lower edge of the sleeve, whether short or long, is usually finished either by a hem, or a cuff, though it may have a ruffle or circular frill attached too. In a long closely-fitted sleeve, there is usually a buttoned or press fastened opening in the seam.

The cuff, should be neat but roomy enough for you to be able to run your fingers round inside it when fastened.

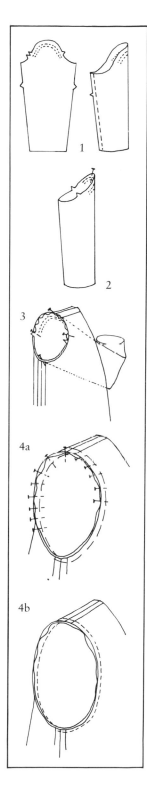

More on sleeves

SET-IN SLEEVE

1 Run two rows of gathering thread between the balance notches at the top of the sleeve. Carry out any further pattern instructions for making up the sleeve at this stage (which may include attaching a cuff). Turn the sleeve right side out. Partly make up the garment, as directed for your pattern, including sewing the side and shoulder seams.

2 Find the centre top of the sleeve and mark it with a pin.

3 Right sides facing, slip the top of the sleeve into the armhole, matching the correct sleeve to the correct armhole.
Pin the sleeve to the armhole matching the underarm side seam with the sleeve seam and the marked centre top of the sleeve with the shoulder seam. Draw up the gathering threads slightly, and match the balance notches of the sleeve with those on the armhole, front and back, and pin them together too.

4a Continue to pin the sleeve into the armhole, with pins placed at right angles to the raw edges, easing the distribution of the fullness round the head. Tack the sleeve to the armhole all round, being careful to avoid forming gathers at the seam (unless they are part of the design). More detailed information about 'ease' is given on page 56.

4b Remove the pins, and machine round the sleeve where tacked. Remove the tacking. Press.

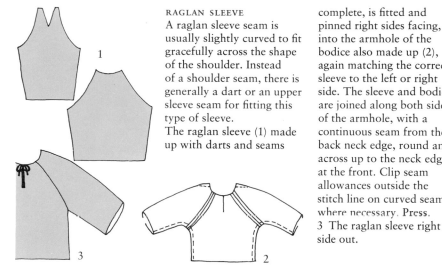

RAGLAN SLEEVE

A raglan sleeve seam is usually slightly curved to fit gracefully across the shape of the shoulder. Instead of a shoulder seam, there is generally a dart or an upper sleeve seam for fitting this type of sleeve.
The raglan sleeve (1) made up with darts and seams complete, is fitted and pinned right sides facing, into the armhole of the bodice also made up (2), again matching the correct sleeve to the left or right side. The sleeve and bodice are joined along both sides of the armhole, with a continuous seam from the back neck edge, round and across up to the neck edge at the front. Clip seam allowances outside the stitch line on curved seams, where necessary. Press.

3 The raglan sleeve right side out.

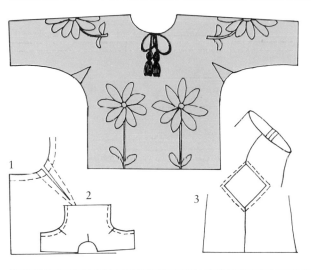

KIMONO SLEEVE

Where a kimono sleeve is wide, to prevent the sleeve tearing during wear, reinforce the underarm curve with tape, sewn into the stitch line. The seam allowance may also need to be clipped round this curve.

GUSSET· For a close fitting kimono sleeve, a gusset may be needed. This is an inset, shaped patch, sometimes interlined. It may be diamond-shaped, triangular or even come in two parts, joined across.

GUSSET

Refer to the pattern. Cut out; interface if necessary, stay stitch the edges; join any seams.
SLASH: The gusset is stitched into a slash, the length of the gusset sides matching the length of the slash.

1 TO SEW IN A GUSSET
(a) Transfer the pattern marking for the gusset slash onto the fabric on the wrong side, reinforced at this point with a strip of iron-on, non-woven interfacing, or with a patch across the proposed cut.
(b) Stay stitch the sides of the slash, marking and tapering the stitch line.
2 (c) Fold over the garment, matching front over back, right sides facing, and join the side and sleeve seams, except over the proposed slashes.
(d) Carefully cut along each slash.
(e) Right sides facing, pin the sides of the gusset to the sides of the slash.
(f) Tack, remove the pins, and machine the gusset to the sides of the slash. Remove the tacking. Press.
3 (g) Turn the garment right side out. Topstitch round the gusset seamline if wished, and press again.

Cuffs

Finishing a garment when you are dressmaking, or indeed with any other sewing, can simply be a case of turning neat hems, or binding or facing the raw edge.

By going to a little more trouble and taking extra time over it to add cuffs, a collar, a belt or other detailed finishing touches, the result will be an even more professional and attractive appearance.

You need to finish the sleeves taking the whole design of the garment into consideration, and harmonising the cuffs (or lack of) with the collar or neckline especially. A shirt collar would need shirt cuffs; a soft, faced neckline a concealed sleeve seam fastening; a stiff collar, stiff cuffs – and so on.

A cotton top might only need narrow machined and perhaps topstitched hems, or the sleeve could be gathered into the wrist with elastic or drawstrings threaded through the hem, or casing above. See page 83.

A cuff can be cut in one with the sleeve, by making a hem deep enough to turn up. For heavier or more important fabric, this would need to be interfaced, and after turning up and pressing, slip-stitched lightly about 1cm. ($\frac{1}{2}$in.) inside the folded edge to hold it in place on the sleeve.

For a fitted long sleeve, some sort of opening for the hand to pass through would be needed, and two ways of providing this are included here – by inserting a little zipper in the seam, or making a fastened placket opening.

These flat, concealed fastenings in a seam usually lie along the inside of the wrist. When a button cuff opens, it usually has the overlap on the outside of the wrist, parallel with the outside edge of the hand and little finger, with the seam positioned under the wrist about 8cm. (3in.) in. The top of the cuff overlaps the button sewn on the underside.

When fitting the sleeve or fastened cuff at the wrist, you should be able to pass two or three fingers round inside it comfortably. For a cuff without an opening, the hand, with fingers and thumb extended, should be able to pass through easily. This is something to check at the fitting stage.

On the following pages you will find information on how to make sleeve openings in the seams; and various kinds of cuffs, including turn-down band cuffs for long, gathered or short puff sleeves, ideal for children's clothes (bias binding can be used for this too; sew on in the same way). Make a detachable cuff as for a detachable collar (see page 77).

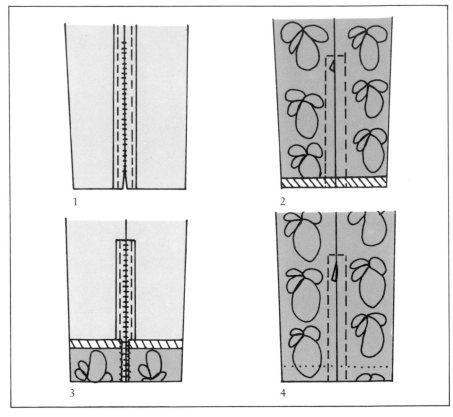

1

2

3

4

ZIPPER OPENING

1 Measure the seam opening from the sleeve raw edge to include the hem turning and length of the zipper.
Mark the top of the zipper opening, before joining the sleeve with a plain seam. Tack along the zipper opening. Press the seam allowances open.
Place the right side of the zipper against the wrong side of the sleeve, over the tacked zipper opening, with the tag, just above the wrist hem turning. Pin the zipper in position, on the seam allowances, working first up one, then up the other side. Tack the tapes where pinned, then remove the pins.

2 Turn the sleeve right side out, and topstitch the zipper in place. You may find it necessary to open the zipper to do this, or use the free arm of the machine if small enough to slip inside the sleeve. Pin, tack and machine skirt tape, or narrow ribbon over the raw edge of the hem turning.

3 Turn the sleeve wrong side out. Turn in the seam allowances at the hem sides, then turn up the taped hem. Pin and tack, checking that the slide tag moves up and down freely, and the hem lies smooth inside the sleeve. Slip hem the taped edge, and hem the hem sides to the zipper tapes. Repeat for the second sleeve.

4 Press from the right side.

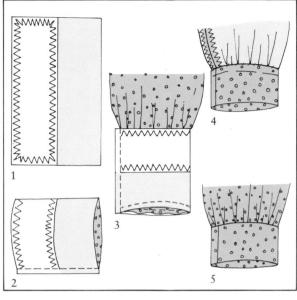

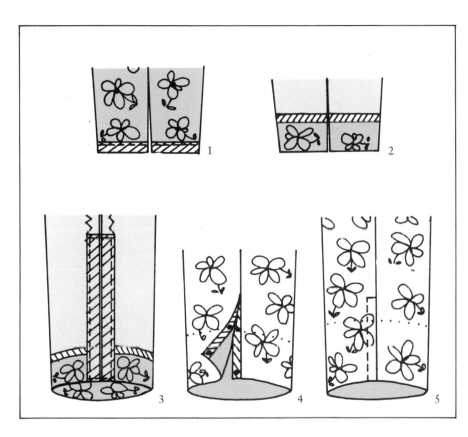

SLEEVE PLACKET:

1 Leave an opening at the lower end of the sleeve seam for the placket, plus a hem turning. With the sleeve right side out, machine skirt tape or ribbon over the raw edge all round.

2 Turn the sleeve wrong side out. Turn up the hem to the required depth and pin, tack and slip hem the taped edge to the sleeve, including along the seam allowances.

3 With the sleeve right side out, sew grosgrain ribbon over the seam raw edges beside the sleeve opening. Machine on the tape. Turn the sleeve wrong side out.

4 Clip the seam allowances above the plackets. Fold over the under ribbon edge onto the upper ribbon edge, (the upper edge would be on the front of the sleeve opening, and the under on the back). Turn in the ribbon narrow ends and hem, then oversew the under to the upper ribbon across the top. At the same time, slip hem (or machine) the upper ribbon to the sleeve.

Turn the sleeve right side out, and sew on two press fasteners inside the placket opening, or sew on small buttons and buttonholes.

5 The finished fastening. Repeat for the second sleeve, and press. Or you can bind the under edge, and face the upper edge, with bias binding or self-material.

TURNED DOWN CUFFS

This type of cuff is stitched direct to the lower edge of short or long, usually gathered, sleeves. Because it does not have a fastened opening, it needs to be at least wide enough for the hand to be slipped through, fingers pressed together. Cuffs like this look charming on children's clothes, or smock tops.

1 Mark the cuff along the centre fold on the wrong side, and interface one side with non-woven or taffeta interfacing, stitched to the cuff with straight or zig-zag machine stitching. Or use the iron-on type if suitable. This interfaced side should end up inside the finished cuff.

2 Fold the cuff in half from side to side, right sides facing, and join the sides together with a plain seam, down the narrow end.

3 With right sides facing, and the interfaced half of the cuff uppermost, and with the cuff and sleeve seams aligned, slip the cuff onto the end of the gathered sleeve, and pin them together all round the lower edge. Tack, adjusting the gathers evenly at the same time. Remove the pins and machine the cuff to the sleeve where tacked, with a plain seam. Remove the tacking.

4 Turn down the cuff, and turn the sleeve and attached cuff wrong side out. Fold the cuff along the centre line. Turn under the raw edge, and pin the cuff to the sleeve, just below the stitch line. Tack where pinned, then remove the pins. Hem the cuff to the sleeve, then remove the tacking.

5 Repeat for the second sleeve. Topstitch on the right side if wished. Press both cuffs.

The cuff can have frill insertions in the seam, or be decorated with braid or embroidery.

TURN-BACK CUFF
(VERSION 1)

Turn-back cuffs can be made in a variety of designs, and in contrasting material to the garment, though white cuffs should be made detachable for laundering, in the same way as a detachable collar (see page 77) with the sleeve edges finished separately for them. Frills, lace, embroidery, cuffs matching the collar, are all possibilities.

Some cuffs are made in two parts, interfaced and seamed together right sides facing, then attached to the sleeve end with a separate facing strip.

For a turn-back cuff open down one side, make as for version two below, but join the longest edge and narrow ends as step 1, then turn right side out. Align the cuff ends on top of the sleeve before attaching the cuff with facing.

Here the cuff is sewn direct to the sleeve, and turned back.

1 Cut out two cuff shapes and one interfacing shape for each cuff. Interface one cuff shape. Fold the interfaced shape in half from side to side, right sides facing, and join it with a plain seam. Fold and join the second non-interfaced shape in the same way.
2 Slip the interfaced shape over the sleeve end, right sides facing and seams aligned, and pin them together round the lower edge. Tack. Remove the pins, then machine where tacked. Remove the tacking.
3 Turn down the cuff and press. Slip the second non-interlined shape over this cuff, right sides facing, seams aligned and tack together round the lower edges. Machine.
4 Turn the cuff up, folding it onto the wrong side of the sleeve, so the seam is along the 'fold' edge. Turn under the raw edge, and pin it to the sleeve, just under the first stitch line. Tack. Remove the pins. Hem the cuff to the sleeve at this edge.
5 Turn the cuff up, on the right side of the sleeve, and press. Topstitch if wished.

TURN-BACK CUFF
(VERSION 2)

1 Cut out two cuff shapes and one interfacing shape. Interface one, and fold and join as for version one. Repeat for the non-interfaced shape.
2 Slip the interfaced and non-interfaced cuffs over one another right sides facing, aligning the seams. Pin together round the wider opening. Tack, remove the pins and machine. Remove the tacking.
3 Turn the cuff right side out and press so the seam lies along the fold edge. Top stitch if wished.
4 Cut a bias strip for each cuff about 5cm. (2in.) deep to the length of the sleeve circumference plus 7cm. (2¾in.).
5 Overlay the facing ends 5cm. (2in.) and cut through the overlap diagonally. Trim right sides facing with 1cm. (½in.) seams as for bias binding, and trim edges.
6 Slip the cuff onto the sleeve, right side out, and the facing right sides together, over it. Seam facing, cuff and sleeve together round lower edge.
7 Clip the facing outside the stitch line if necessary and turn onto the wrong side of the sleeve. Turn in and hem to the sleeve. Turn the sleeve right side out and the cuff up.
8 Press. Repeat for the other cuff.
9 Cut a deeper facing to the shape of the cuff and the required depth plus seam allowances.

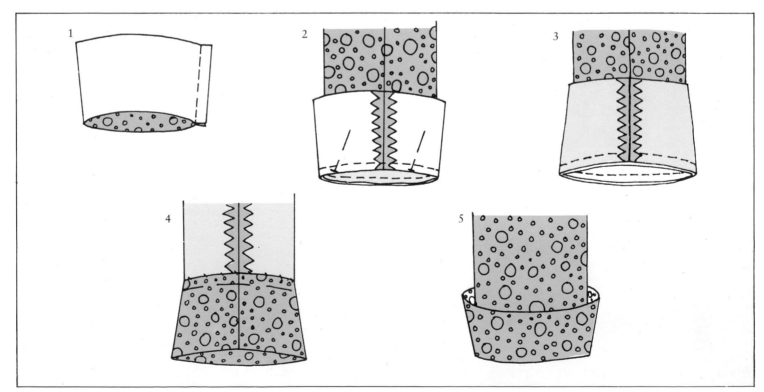

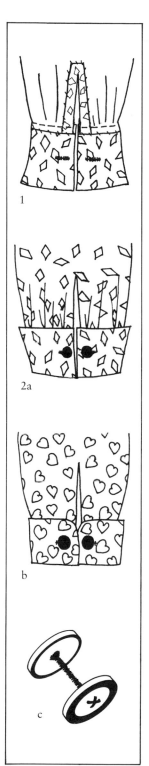

1

2a

b

c

LINKED CUFFS

1 Attach cuffs to be worn with cuff links in the same way as for button cuffs, but cut them twice as deep. The cuff is folded back and shaped as wished, plain, curved, angled or squared – even scalloped. Instead of being overlapped, the cuff is aligned with buttonholes for the links to correspond through each side, and through the turn-back too, if wished.

2 Linked buttons or cuff links are passed through the buttonholes from side to side. (a) Pointed cuff. (b) Curved cuff. (c) Linked buttons.

LINKED BUTTONS

Use two pearl or other buttons and button thread. Knot the thread and pass the needle from the back of the button to the front and back through into the next hole. Stitch the thread to the knot close behind the button. Take the thread through the second button, its back to the first, holding them apart with your finger and thumb to give the thread length in between them. Repeat until three or four thread loops between the buttons have been made, of equal length. Carefully, beginning close to the back of one button, embroider buttonhole stitches along the threads, keeping the knots close together and level on the same side in a neat corded row. Secure the thread firmly with several stitches, and trim. Small buttons can be linked with mercerised thread in the same way.

1 Finish the opening above the cuff. Right sides together centre the hemmed interfaced strip over the sleeve opening mark, and pin. Tack where pinned then remove the pins. Machine along either side of the opening, tapering the stitch line. Cut along the opening. Turn the facing onto the wrong side and press.

2 Interface half the cuff and fold in two along its length. Machine across the ends. (Or have two cuff shapes, one of them interfaced, and right sides facing seam them together down the narrow ends and along one side.) Turn right side out and press.

3 Gather or pleat the sleeve to fit the cuff, allowing for a cuff overlap at one or both ends, if wished.

4 Right sides facing, pin one side of the cuff round the sleeve adjusting the gathers. Tack where pinned, then remove the pins and machine. Remove tacking.

5 Turn the sleeve wrong side out, and turn under the cuff inside raw edge to neaten. Pin and tack and hem this edge round inside the sleeve. Topstitch round the cuff if wished.

6 Sew on a button to the underlap, and make a buttonhole in the overlap. Press. Repeat for the second sleeve.

7 A deep buttoned cuff can be made the same way. By cutting the shapes and interfacing for each cuff to allow for a double cuff, button cuffs can be made in turn-back versions.

ANOTHER WAY OF FINISHING THE SLEEVE OPENING: CONTINUOUS BOUND PLACKET: Bind the edge of the opening above the cuff, with a strip of binding, bias or straight cut.

(a) Make the cut in the lower edge of the sleeve.

(b) Sew the binding along it, stretching the two sides of the cut-out in a straight line to do so. Fold the bound edge in two as shown, and stitch together across the top, to hold the shape.

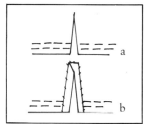

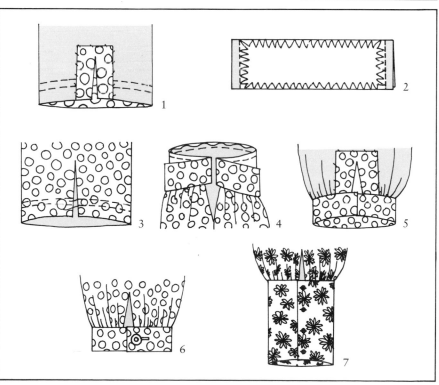

Collar close-up

A collar may be cut high, or be Byronic and floppy. It may be a white georgette pie frill on an evening dress, or velvet and tweed revers on a tailored overcoat. It may be demure, or romantic. Plain or fancy, a collar is one of the prime parts of a garment's design, and alas, one of the trickiest when aiming at the professional look.

To achieve this, measure your neck carefully, and make sure the pattern is a good fit for your measurements. The collar and neckline not only have to fit you well, but each other too. This should be taken care of by the notches, matching marker spots and other balance marks on your pattern, but it is an important aspect to watch.

When measuring, the tape is taken round the base of the neck, but when fitting, run your fingers round inside the collar. If a tailored fit, it will rest lightly, not press on your fingers,

which should move round inside it easily.

Make a point of trimming away surplus bulk from the seam allowances outside the stitch lines, especially across corners and seam junctions, not only inside the collar, but inside the neck facings and neck end of the shoulder seams. Press carefully at every stage.

The collar should be equal-sided too. Mark the centre with care, and when attaching it, match it accurately with the neck edge centre back guideline, and work from there round each side in turn to the front (when making the collar, check that the sides are equal by folding it in two and matching them). The button overlap should be square at the centre front of the neck, and the collar should meet at the centre above it, and both be aligned to the centre front guidelines of the garment.

1a
1b
2
3
4
5
6a
6
7

1 (a) The upper collar is usually cut in one piece, and the centre marked with a tacking guideline.
Align this centre guideline with the centre back of the garment, and the centre front of the collar, or its fastening over the centre front guideline of the garment. Your marked dress form can be helpful here.
(b) The under collar often has a centre seam, and is interfaced with suitable, non-woven or taffeta interfacing, sewn on by hand herringbone or machine straight or zig-zag stitching. A lightweight material collar can have the taffeta or other interfacing stitched or ironed onto the wrong side of one shape, and sewn in with the seam.
2 The upper and under collars, notches and other marks matching, right sides facing, are placed together and pinned, tacked and joined by a plain seam, down the short ends and lower edge. When

machining, equal width seams and identical corners or curves at each side in the stitch line help to make an equal sided collar, which will show to advantage in the right side of the shape. Interfacing seams and corners are trimmed away evenly close outside the stitch line to reduce material bulk where necessary.
3 The under collar is centred on the centre back of the neck edge, right sides facing, matching notches and other marks. Working from the centre back, collar and neck edge are eased and pinned together along each side, tacked, and then tried on for fit before machining.
4 Other methods for attaching collars follow on the next pages. Here the extended front and back neck facings have been joined, and right sides facing matched against the neck edge of the garment, taking in the attached collar. They are pinned, tacked, and finally machined from one end to the other in a plain seam through all layers.
5 With the seam allowance outside the stitch line trimmed, the facing is turned down, and pressed, and hemmed, or sewn to the lining.
6 The button overlap, centred exactly, has a button sewn on the underside, and a button-hole, avoiding seam-thick areas, is sewn in the upper side, and a small hook and eye (or press fastener) sewn under the corner (6a).
7 The finished collar.

Inserted frills

A collar with a frilled or piped edge is especially pretty, and the method given here for doing this can be applied to cuffs and insertions in other seams, including in upholstery.

Broderie anglaise, or lace, or pleated organdie, or other trimming can be sewn in using this method. Frills are gathered at the raw edge, but otherwise for a flat insertion the corners would need to be mitred, then trimmed and finished close to the mitre seam line with whip stitch or fine zig-zag machine stitching.

Corded piping is made up beforehand, as described in caption 4 on this page. Cord can be inserted (as a raised ridge between two layers of material) in the same way, but machined close in on either side of the cord, for decoration.

Narrow braid corded along one edge is also available. Whichever is used, when trimmed right side out the cord must lie level and even along the seam, not buckled or puckered. This is achieved by close pinning and tacking before machining.

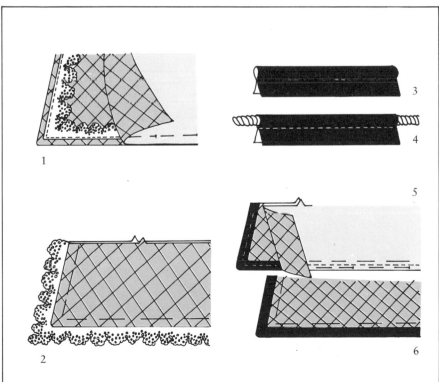

LACE FRILL INSERTION for collars, and other seams.
1 Cut lace trimming two to three times the length of the collar edge. Gather along the upper raw or woven edge. Adjust the gathers evenly, and pin this edge over the stitch line of the under collar on the right side, so the frill lies inward onto the collar. Tack, remove the pins, then machine the frill just outside the collar stitch line.
2 Pin the upper collar, right sides facing, over the under collar and lace frill. Pin, tack and machine the collar shapes together, taking in the frill in the stitch line. Turn the collar right side out, and press. If wished topstitch on right side inside lace edge.
PIPING AND CORDED PIPING for seams (and upholstery)

3 *Piping* is folded over bias strips without cord running through it. Use bias binding in cotton or thick silk etc.
4 Corded piping is folded over material strips, tightly stretched over piping cord, and machined along close to the cord, using the zipper foot on the machine.
5 Sew the piping or corded piping to the collar in the same way as for the lace frill.
6 Make sure the piping is sewn in so that it is of even width when turned right side out, and the cording is machined to the collar close in so the cord forms a smooth, even ridge along the edge of the collar.
* Piping with braid with a corded edge is sewn in the same way.

Collars

Here are some of the main methods of attaching the most popular basic collars. The instruction sheets with your pattern will of course provide step-by-step guidance. Remember to add any embroidery or other decoration such as ric-rac braid, frills or piping, before you sew the collar layers together.

For a silk or velvet-faced collar, turn in the facing edges and slip stitch onto the unattached collar round the outside edge. For fur collars see page 111, tailored collars page 113.

DETACHABLE COLLAR

1 Face the neck edge. Bind the collar edge.
2 Align the centre back of the collar and garment neck edge. Sew on press fasteners.

PETER PAN COLLAR

1 Interface the under collar on the wrong side, then right sides facing place under and upper collar together. Pin, tack and machine together. Trim away the seam allowance and clip outside the stitch line.
2 Turn the collar right side out. Press. Topstitch if wished.
3 Mark the centre of the collar and the garment back neck edge. Match collar to centre neck mark, and match notches. Pin together round neck. When made in two parts with a back zipper opening, this collar may be attached all along with a bias facing. For a one-piece Peter Pan collar the front facings can be turned back and joined to a bias facing, then sewn on as for a convertible collar – see instructions 3 and 4 except that when turned right side out and pressed, the bias facing would be hemmed to the garment inside neck edge. Or take the bias strip along the neck edge but at the opening, turn back the front facing over the collar and machine at the neck edge. When turned right side out, the collar will lie neatly inside the overlapping facings.

SHIRT COLLAR

1 Interface the under collar and one neckband. Join upper and under collar, right sides facing, as for Peter Pan collar. Turn right side out and top-stitch round edge.
2 Sandwich collar, right sides facing, between two neckbands at upper edge of neckbands. Pin, tack and machine as shown.
3 Turn neckbands right side showing. Take the under neckband only, and pin along neck edge right sides facing. (The second neckband is only attached along one edge still.) Machine the under neckband to neck edge, right sides facing.
4 Turn under raw edge of upper neckband, which lies round inside the shirt neck. Pin, tack and machine to shirt.

CONVERTIBLE COLLAR

1 Make a straight interfaced collar, following Peter Pan collar instructions 1 and 2.
2 Mark the topstitched collar edge centre and pin the collar, right sides facing, to the neck edge, matching notches. Tack,

remove pins, and machine.

3 Join ends of extended front facing to back neck facing. Right sides facing, match the over collar and neck edge, and machine together.

4 Turn right side out and press. The collar can be buttoned with a small button and buttonhole loop at the top right corner, or it can be worn open.

TURTLE NECK COLLAR

1 The collar is a strip, marked with a centre tacking thread. Interface along one side. Mark the collar and neck edge at centre front.

2 Turn in narrow ends to neaten them, then pin the interfaced collar, right sides facing, to the neck edge, matching the notches and centre front marks. Pin, tack and machine together.

3 Turn up the collar and fold it over at the centre line onto the wrong side. Turn under the second raw edge. Pin and tack round inside the neck edge, and to the zipper tapes (now inserted, and topstitched as far as the collar fold). Hem the collar round the neck edge inside, and to the inside of the zipper tapes.

4 Sew a small hook inside the under collar, and eye on the upper collar at the top edge.

Or insert the zipper as far as the garment neck edge only and join the collar opening with hooks and eyes or buttons and buttonloops.

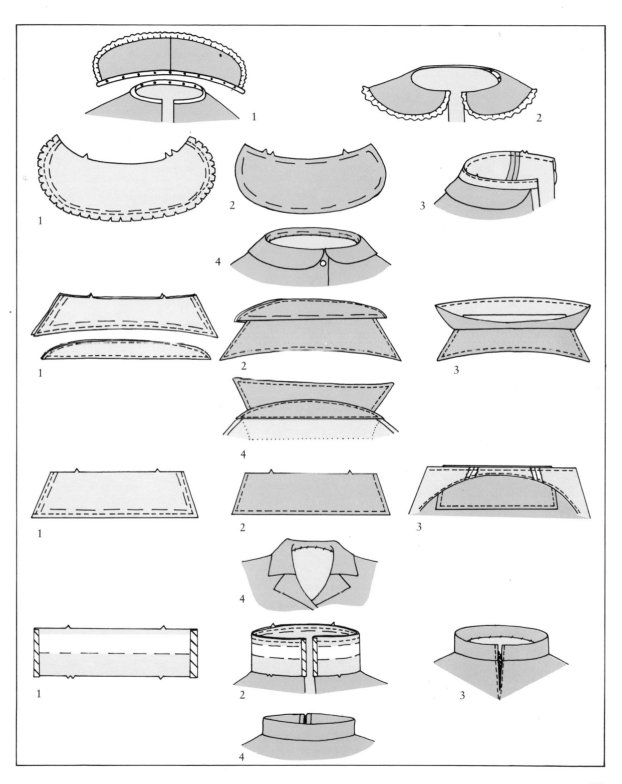

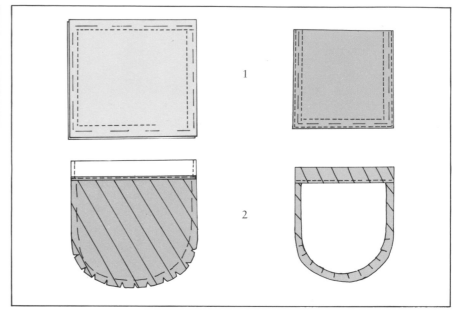

Pockets

It is usually convenient to make and attach a pocket at an early stage in dressmaking, often as one of the preliminary sewing jobs. Consult your pattern for the order of sewing on the pockets for your garment. You will find the pattern shows the pocket placement plainly. Do transfer the markings unless you have other ideas for their position. It will save you a lot of trouble when it comes to attaching the pocket.

There are various basic types of pockets; some are included in this section, such as patch pockets (the easiest to make) and the more elaborate bound 'letterbox' and 'flap' pockets usually found in tailored garments. Later in the book in the trousers section (page 92) you will find information on how to make cutaway jeans-style pockets and seam pockets.

1 SIMPLE PATCH POCKET
For this simple patch pocket, the pocket and lining are cut out to the same size and shape. Iron-on interfacing can be used too, if needed, and on suitable fabric, and should also be cut to the same shape.

Place the lining right sides facing, onto the pocket (already interfaced on the wrong side, if wished). Pin the lining to the pocket round the sides, and tack, leaving an opening in the side for turning the pocket right side out. Remove the pins, and machine where tacked, with straight stitching. Remove the tacking.

Turn the pocket right side out, and press. Slip hem the sides of the opening in the stitch line where the pocket was turned right side out, to close the gap. Pin the pocket in place on the transferred pocket mark.

Tack down the sides and across the lower edge. Remove the pins and machine the pocket where tacked. A second row of topstitching can be added inside the first if wished. Turn the stitching back at the top to strengthen the seam at this point. Remove the tacking and press. This pocket could be slipstitched to the garment to give a simple streamlined effect without topstitching. Or it could be machined on unlined, with a hem across the top and turned-in sides, if made in check gingham for example. Always aim at keeping the pocket flat with the garment, and well positioned. Two pockets should be level, and spaced equally from the centre at the same depth, if they are cast in the role of twins.

2 SECOND PATCH POCKET
(a) Cut out the pocket, and interfacing to the same size and shape. Tack or iron the interfacing to the wrong side of the pocket. (Use taffeta lining in addition, if wished.)
(b) Turn a narrow hem onto the wrong side, and machine.
(c) Turn the top edge of the pocket over onto the *right side*, right sides facing. Machine this turning to the pocket down the sides.
(d) Clip round the curved edge of the pocket outside the marked stitch line, so it will lie flat when turned in.
(e) Turn the seam allowance round the curved edge and down the sides of the pocket onto the wrong side, and at the same time turn over the turning at the top straight edge onto the wrong side.
(f) Pin the pocket in place on the garment, and slip-stitch round the edge, or topstitch to attach.

More pockets

A flap pocket is a tailored pocket, which might look rather daunting to make at first. Yet it is a pocket which often crops up in dressmaking, and adds greatly to the good looks of a coat or suit. Perhaps, next time, you would like to try your hand at making one, or if you want to pretend, just sew on the pocket flap.

Flap: false pocket

A flap, stitched to the pocket placement line, will give a false pocket appearance. (a) Make the pocket flap as for the pocket above. (b) Right sides facing, place the flap with its stitch line parallel with the placement line. Pin in place. (c) Tack the flap along this line and remove the pins. (d) Machine the flap along the stitch line with straight stitching, and along the raw edge with zig-zag stitching, or hand finish instead with herringbone stitches. (e) Turn down the flap, and top stitch inside the upper edge if wished.

LETTERBOX POCKET

1 Cut out a rectangle of self material and one in lining material. Mark self fabric opening with a tacking guideline, as on garment, for the pocket slit. Right sides facing, pin and tack to garment through the guidelines.

Accurately machine along the sides and across the ends, with straight stitching. Cut between the stitch lines through all layers, and into the corners.
2 Pull the pocket flap through onto the wrong side, smooth it and oversew the tiny pleats that form at each end. Press.
3 Stitch the lining and pocket together round the four sides, then catch stitch the top edge to the garment.
4 Remove tacking. Press letterbox pocket.

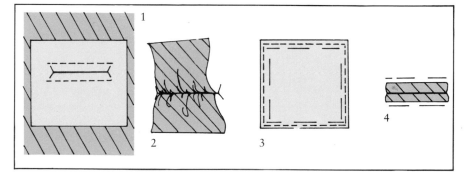

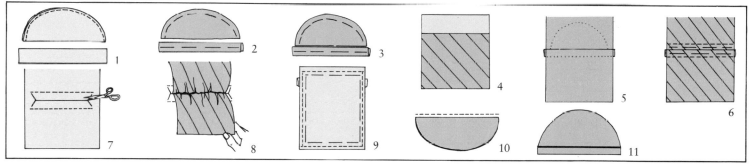

POCKET WITH A FLAP

First, transfer the mark for the pocket slit from the pattern to the material, and sew a tacking guide line along it.
1 The flap is made out of two layers of material, interfaced, or a layer of material, interfacing and lining stitched together. The binding strip for the lower edge of the pocket strip is also interfaced, and is slightly longer than the flap.
2 Turn the stitched flap right side out, tack top-stitch to keep flat, and press. Fold the binding

strip in half along its length and tack it together. Press. Use a steam iron or damp cloth.
3 Place the flap and binding *raw edges meeting* along the tacked pocket placement guideline. Tack in place along raw edges only.
4 The pocket lining shapes look like this, the same size on three sides, but one shorter than the other on the fourth side. The shorter shape is attached over the binding; the longer over the flap.
5 The pocket shapes are

separated. Right sides uppermost, wrong side against the right side of the flap and the binding, one shape, the long one, is placed over the flap, and the second short shape is placed over the binding. The lining raw edges meet over the flap and binding raw edges on the pocket placement tacked guideline. Carefully tack through the lining at this edge, through the flap onto the garment shape. Repeat for the lining over the binding.
6 Machine through all layers where tacked, on

either side of the pocket placement tacked guideline, from the right side, with straight stitching.
7 Turn over onto the wrong side of the garment, and you will see two machine stitched rows on the material where the binding and pocket flap have been stitched on, with the tacked guideline between. Snip between the stitch line along the guideline, and cut little snips into the corners at each end.
8 Pull the lining pieces through this cut onto the

wrong side.
9 Pull the pocket lining shapes flat together and match them. Pin and tack them down the sides and across the lower edge. Remove the pins and machine where tacked. Remove tacking. Press.
10 The pocket flap will look like this on the right side. Topstitch just above it if you wish.
11 When the pocket flap is lifted up, you can see the bound edge below the pocket flap, and can slip your hand into the pocket between.

Lining a skirt and dress

Lining any garment always adds to its good appearance when well carried out. Very casual gingham or cotton or denim clothes would be an exception. Sheers are treated in their own special way.

Unless special lining patterns are given repeat the pattern shapes cut out in the lining fabric. Here an ordinary attached lining is shown, stitched to the skirt and dress except at the hem. The unattached hem hangs slightly shorter inside the skirt. An attached hem is shown on the following pages.

The see-through character of sheer material or lace is a large part of its charm, and although a lining is normally needed, it would need to be harmonised with the garment, made in the right texture, colour, and even shimmer of material. The shape may be cut away to set off the design, the sleeves and often shoulders left sheer, the lining only lightly attached, or separate.

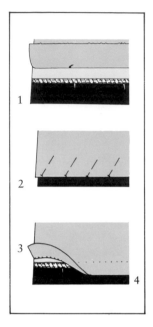

HEM – UNATTACHED METHOD
1 Turn up and hem. Finish the garment. Press.
2 Work with the garment lining side out, level, over the dress form. Turn up the lining so that the folded edge comes about 2 or 3cm. (or 1in.) above the finished skirt edge. Mark edge.
3 Trim the lining hem depth to about 5 or 6cm. (about 2in.). Turn the hem, pin, tack, remove the pins, and slip hem or machine. Press. Remove the tacking.
4 The finished lining hem over the skirt hem. The lining may be anchored to the side seams of the skirt by a buttonhole stitch chain 6 or 7cm. or 2½in. long.

SKIRT LINING
1 After cutting out the skirt pattern pieces in lining fabric, make them up in the same way as for the skirt. Leave the zipper opening unstitched. When the skirt and lining are made up, separately, press them both. Turn the skirt wrong side out, and slip the lining over it wrong sides facing. Align the seams, darts, notches, zipper opening and any other details and then pin the skirt and lining together round the waist edge. Tack. Remove pins. Look critically at the way the lining fits over the skirt inside, and hold it up to see how it hangs. Turn the skirt right side out, and try it on to make sure that the lining isn't fitting too tightly over your hips, nor dragging the skirt, nor too bulky. Make any adjustment needed, try on again, and when you are satisfied with the fit machine together round the waist edge.
2 Turn in and hem the lining to the zipper tapes, and sew on the waistband with any belt carriers and hanging loops. Turn up the lining hem following the instructions given here, or hem as for the jacket.

DRESS LINING
1 A dress lining is made up as for the skirt lining except that the neck and armhole edges of lining and dress are pinned together.
2 When fitted, the lining can be machined to the neck edge and armholes, and the facings attached afterwards. For a fitted sleeve, the lining is stitched to the armhole seam, and the sleeve lining turned in and hemmed over it later. The hem is finished as for the skirt.

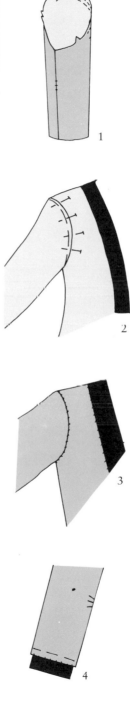

1 Using appropriate lining material and pattern lining pieces, cut out and make up the lining as directed in the pattern.

2 Slip the already seamed and softly darted lining (lining should always be on the roomy side) over the faced and interfaced jacket, wrong sides together, with the lining outside. Make a small, unstitched pleat (about 1.5cm. or ½in. deep) down the centre back from the neck, for ease. Either work with the lining and jacket together level on the work table, or preferably, use the dress form with the jacket hung over it, seams and centre marking aligned on the form marking tapes.

3 Pin the lining, raw edges turned under, round the facing and onto the seam allowance round the armholes.

Tack the lining to the jacket where pinned. Remove the pins and turn the lined jacket right side out.

Try on the jacket, over a blouse, and inspect it critically. Is the lining comfortable? Does it feel bulky inside or too tight? Is it pulling the jacket out of shape, wrinkling or dragging it in any way? Make adjustments where necessary, but do avoid making the lining too close a fit. It needs to be a little loose.

4 Starting from the back of the neck, and working down, hem the lining onto the facing taking in the centre back pleat. Repeat for the other facing edge. Try to keep the lining and facing smooth together along this sewn edge. Machine the lining round the armhole seam allowance outside the stitch line, using straight stitches. Repeat for the other armhole. Press.

HEMS

Turn up and pin the lower edge of the lining to the jacket (which has already been turned up over interfacing, and herringbone stitched in place) to the required depth. The lining hem should form a neat, loose fold on the jacket, the fold coming 2 or 3cm. or about an inch above the jacket hem edge, to allow for ease of movement in the lining. Try on the jacket when the hem is pinned to make sure it lies evenly and does not droop below the edge, or drag the jacket up. When satisfactory, hem as follows:

5 Slip hem the lining to the jacket hem under the fold.

6 Press. The finished attached lining hem. Use for any lined garment.

1 Make up the sleeve lining with darts or gathers at the elbow, and gathering threads round the sleeve top between the balance notches. To fit, slip the lining over the sleeve wrong sides facing, aligning the seams and balance marks. Make sure that the left or right lining is attached to the correct sleeve. The same goes for the right sleeve. The lining should fit inside the sleeve comfortably, with ease.

2 To sew in, pull the sleeve lining, right side out, over the jacket sleeve, wrong sides facing. Align notches, seams, darts. Turn in the lining raw edge round the top, and pin it to the armhole seam allowance, onto the jacket lining. Use plenty of pins, and adjust the ease at the top of the sleeve.

3 Tack. Remove the pins and hem in place. Repeat for the second sleeve. Remove tacks.

4 Turn under the raw edge of the lining at the wrist, and press. Pin it round to the sleeve hem turning, with gentle ease or a small fold as for the jacket lining. Tack the lining hem to the jacket, remove the pins and turn the jacket right side out. Try on. Move your arms about. If the sleeve feels good, and looks tailored and smooth, slip hem the lining under the pleat, or for the unpleated version, hem to the jacket sleeve. Press.

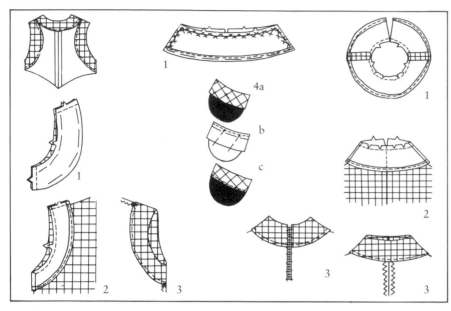

Shaped facings

A collarless neck edge, or sleeveless armholes could in certain circumstances be edged with machined narrow hems (e.g. cheesecloth tops) where there is enough stretch in the material. Handrolled and hemmed edges round sheer material and bias binding are also used.

Otherwise shaped facings would be a regular way to finish these edges, cut to the exact shape of the curved neck edge back and front, or to fit a square neckline, mitred at the corners; or for the armholes.

Facings are usually made in the garment material, unless it is too rough to wear next to the skin. In this case, suitable interfaced lining material would be used instead.

Slashed facing

A simple cut in the material, with a facing stitched over it, is called a slashed facing.

NECK AND ARMHOLE FACINGS: First alter the facing shapes to correspond with any pattern alterations, at the shoulder and side seams or elsewhere.
1 Cut out the correct number of facing shapes required, repeat in interfacing but less seam allowances.
Attach the interfacing shapes to the wrong side of the facings, within the stitch lines either by tacking or pressing. Right sides facing, pin, then tack the interlined facings together at the shoulder,

and for armhole facings, side seams as well. Remove the pins. Machine. Remove the tacking. Press.
2 Right sides facing, fit the joined facing shapes over the garment, matching the seams, notches, raw edges. Pin each facing to the garment round the edge. Tack. Remove the pins. Machine all round on the stitch line. Clip the curved edges outside the stitch line.
3 Turn the facing onto the garment, wrong sides together. For an underlined garment, the facing

raw edge can be turned under and hemmed to the underlining, but for an unlined garment, the facing should be narrow hemmed or otherwise finished, then anchored with a few hemming or oversewing stitches onto the seam allowances only.
4 SHAPED POCKET FACINGS
(a) The facing shape.
(b) Facing stitched right against wrong side along top edge.
(c) Facing turned onto right side, turned in and hemmed or topstitched.

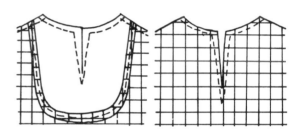

1 Cut out a panel bib to fit the shape of the neckline and shoulders, and longer than the proposed cut. Repeat the shape in interfacing, tacked or ironed to the wrong side of the facing shape.
2 Turn in a narrow hem down the sides and round the lower edge and machine, or hem.
3 Mark the proposed cut on the wrong side of the interfaced shape. Pin the facing right sides together to the front of the bodice, matching the neck edges. Tack where pinned, and remove the pins. (Check by measuring that you have done this accurately so the

proposed slash is really vertical and central on the bodice. It is so easy to go a little offside in this.)
4 Machine the facing shape round the neck edge, and along each side of the mark for the slash, tapering the stitch line at the inside end of the cut, and reversing the stitch line round the point as an extra reinforcement, forward, back, and forward again.
5 Snip carefully along the cut inside the stitch-line.
6 Turn the facing onto the wrong side of the bodice front. Press. Hem to the shoulders. Topstitch if wished.

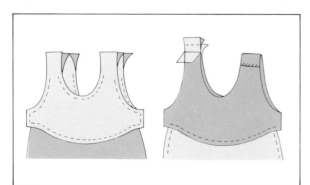

YOKE SHAPED FACING
(a) Made-up yoke stitched in place right sides facing, but both garment and yoke left unstitched at shoulders.
(b) Yoke turned onto wrong side of garment. The garment shoulder seam is joined first, then the yoke turned over and hemmed down.

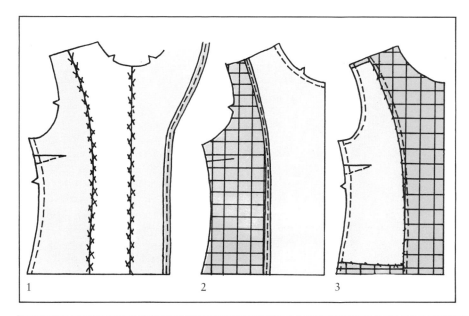

1

2

3

Extended facing

The mirror image of the garment front, cut in one with the main shape, and interfaced.

1 Interface the garment front within the fold edge of the extended facing. Finish the edge of the extended facing with a narrow hem, or binding, or by another suitable method, except if the lining is to be hemmed onto it. In this case it should be lightly catch-stitched to the material first. Before completing the facing, refer to your pattern in case there is any other sewing job to be carried out at this stage, such as bound buttonholes to be made.

2 Turn the extended facing back along its fold line, onto the outside of the garment, right sides facing. Pin it to the neck edge, and tack. Remove the pins and machine with straight stitching where tacked. Remove the tacking, and press. Clip the seam allowance outside the stitch line along the curved edge, so the facing will lie flat when turned.

3 Turn the facing onto the wrong side of the garment, wrong sides facing, and press.

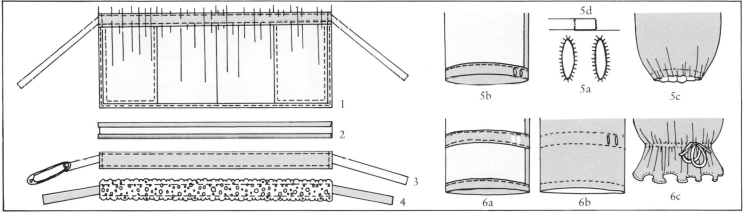

1

2

3

4

5d

5b

5a

5c

6a

6b

6c

CASING

Casing is a strip of material which is attached to a garment on the right or wrong side, as a carrier for a drawstring or elastic. Hems or facings are often used as casings. The position of the casing will be shown on your pattern, and a pattern included for the casing strip. Or use binding, ribbon or bias strips of material etc.

1 Casing strip is shown stitched to the wrong side of the jacket and belt.
2 Stage one: the casing strip before sewing, with its ends hemmed, and sides turned in.
3 The casing strip is stitched to the reverse side of the jacket, with the tie belt being drawn through the length.
4 Broderie anglaise casing like this would be top-stitched along both edges to the right side.

ELASTICATED SLEEVE HEM

5a Embroider a pair of buttonholes side by side, close to the sleeve seam, above the hem edge, before turning up the hem.
5b Turn up and machine the hem.
5c Thread elastic through the hem, using a bodkin or safety pin.
5d Trim the elastic to the right length for a good fit, then turn over the ends and place them over one another, then hem together.

CASING INSIDE A SLEEVE

6a Measure and mark the position of the casing lines on the wrong side, from the sleeve lower edge, taking the hem turning into account. Sew two button-holes where desired between the lines on the sleeve. Machine the binding to the sleeve along both edges.
6b Turn the sleeve right side out.
6c Thread a drawstring through the buttonholes. Tie the strings.

ELASTIC

Elastic can be stitched along the casing line instead of casing. Decide the appropriate length by trying the elastic on for size.
Pin at each end, and the centre, and between. Machine, at both edges if wide elastic, removing the pins, and stretching the elastic as you go. Use elastic stretch stitch or small straight or zig-zag stitches.

Buttons and button holes

Buttons and buttonholes need to be positioned and marked accurately (with pins, dressmaker's carbon or running stitches) from your pattern or to your plan. A dressmaker's ruler is helpful for this job.

Buttons are positioned first, on the centre line of the garment or in relation to it, and buttonholes are placed in the overlap to correspond. While a top button may be placed on the neck fastening, about 2cm. ($\frac{3}{4}$in.) from the edge, the lowest button would normally be a distance from the lower edge, from 7cm. (2$\frac{1}{2}$in.) on a blouse, to 30cm. (12in.) or more on a coat. They could be spaced in ones or groups, equally and equidistantly from the edge. Buttonholes are cut fractionally wider than the button. A horizontal buttonhole would have one end centred over the button, and when embroidered, this would be the round end, and a bar end at the other end. Vertical buttonholes, centred over the buttons, would have either two round ends or two bar ends.

It is important to trim away bulky seams inside before making buttonholes, especially at the neck.

BUTTONHOLE STITCH

1 Begin with backstitches on the wrong side, at the left. Push the needle through the material in front, with the needle upright, a stitch length below the buttonhole cut.
2 Wind the thread under the needle from the left, up to the right.
3 Pull the needle through the loop formed by the thread under the needle.
4 Draw the thread up evenly and tightly to form a knot on the edge of the cut. Make stitches close together to form corded row on the cut, and take care to push the needle neatly through all layers every time. Finish with backstitches.

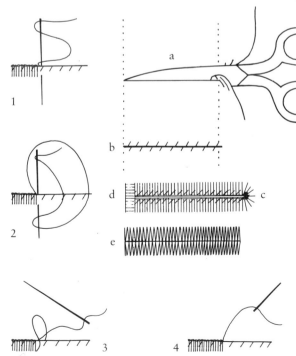

EMBROIDERED BUTTONHOLE

(a) Use buttonhole or small sharp scissors. Start with a level snip on the buttonhole mark and make a smooth cut through all layers.
Choose an appropriate size needle, and thread type for the fabric.
(b) Oversew round the buttonhole through all layers, avoiding fraying the cut. Embroider buttonhole stitches close together, of equal depth along the side.
(c) *Round end:* wheel close together oversewing stitches. (d) *Bar end:* satin stitch three or four rows across then buttonhole stitch along over them, with an odd number of stitches to centre one.

MACHINE STITCHED BUTTONHOLE (e)

A machine stitched buttonhole is made using zig-zag stitch closed up to form a satin stitch, snipped through the centre space. Some machines carry out this operation automatically. One tip for success:– take the zig-zag stitch round the buttonhole twice. Consult your machine instruction book for how to sew on a button and make a buttonhole using your machine.

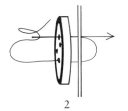

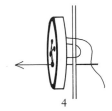

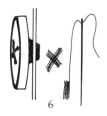

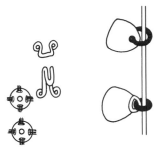

2

4

6

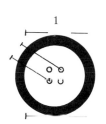

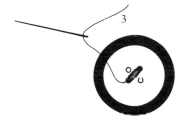

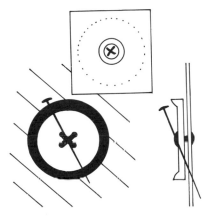

1

3

5

SEWING ON BUTTONS, PRESS
FASTENERS, HOOKS AND EYES
Use button thread, or
suitable regular thread.
Mark the position of the
buttons carefully from the
pattern.
1 Pin the button in
position under the
proposed buttonhole,
towards the round, button
end, or centred for a
vertical buttonhole.
2 Anchor the thread on the
wrong side with small
backstitches. Bring the
needle and thread up
through the button out of
the surface. Put the needle
straight down again
through button and fabric,
and draw the thread right
through, evenly and
without pulling. Allow for
a thread shank by holding
the button in your finger

and thumb to keep it
slightly off the material.
Or sew over a needle
across the top of the
button.
The side view of the thread
going through the button
and the material is shown
in 2 above.
3 Shows the same from
above. The threaded needle,
is taken over, down through
the material, brought back
up, then through the
opposite hole, and back
down again. This is
repeated two or three times
each way. Aim at making a
cross of an equal number
of threads through a
button with four holes, or
two parallel bars of
threads. See 4 and 5.
This extra thread between
the button and material is
called the shank.

6 Wind the thread round
the shank evenly, then take
the thread through to the
wrong side of the fabric,
and secure with small
backstitches.
7 SHANK BUTTON and
PIERCED BUTTON: A button
with a metal shank has
strong button thread
stitches sewn over and
over the shank, begun and
finished by small back-
stitches on the wrong side.
Metal, heavy shank
buttons do tend to cut
through thread, so sew on
with an extra number of
threads.
The pierced button is
sewn on in a similar way,
but with a fine needle
passed through the holes.
Strong button thread is
not so essential, depending
on the button.

REINFORCED BUTTON
When a button needs
strengthening, on an
overcoat say, a small
second button over a patch
of material is sewn on
under it on the wrong side
of the coat or fabric.
The threads are taken
through the small button,
up through the material
and large button, and down
through again until both
are sewn on.

PRESS FASTENERS
The half with the knob
goes on the underside; the
fastener is centred exactly
over it. Begin and end with
small backstitches on the
wrong side, and sew three
or four neat oversewing
stitches through each hole
in turn. Remember that

press fasteners clipped or
hammered on with pliers
are available. Some even
have buttons on the
surface.

HOOKS AND EYES
Usually the hook is on the
upper side, and the eye on
the under side, unless the
hook needs to be faced
away from the skin. Begin
and end with small back-
stitches, and oversew the
rings of the hooks to the
material, with stitches
across the bar of the hook
just above the rings.
Oversew the rings of the
eye in the same way.
Buttonhole stitch can be
used for large hooks and
eyes.

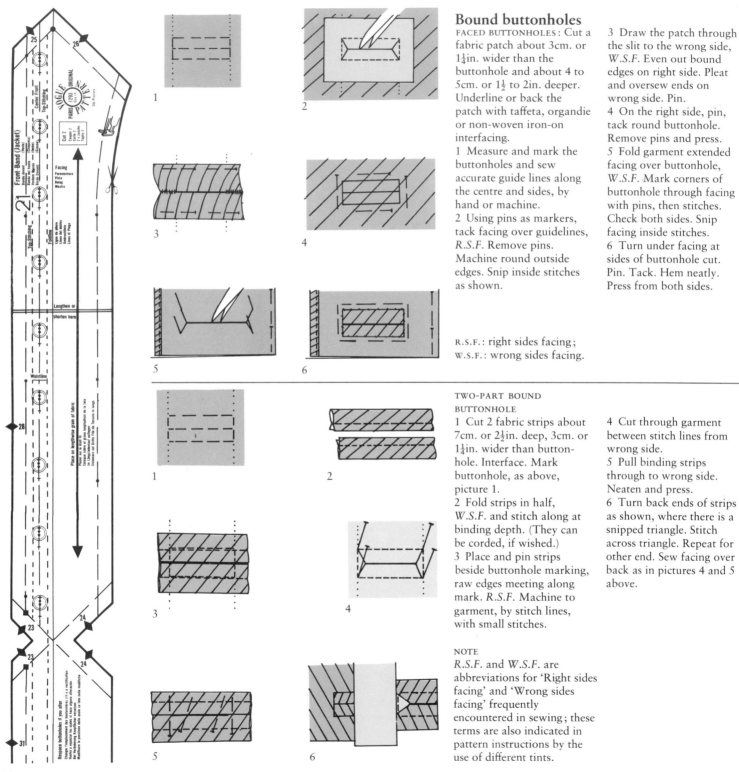

Bound buttonholes

FACED BUTTONHOLES: Cut a fabric patch about 3cm. or 1¼in. wider than the buttonhole and about 4 to 5cm. or 1½ to 2in. deeper. Underline or back the patch with taffeta, organdie or non-woven iron-on interfacing.

1 Measure and mark the buttonholes and sew accurate guide lines along the centre and sides, by hand or machine.

2 Using pins as markers, tack facing over guidelines, R.S.F. Remove pins. Machine round outside edges. Snip inside stitches as shown.

3 Draw the patch through the slit to the wrong side, W.S.F. Even out bound edges on right side. Pleat and oversew ends on wrong side. Pin.

4 On the right side, pin, tack round buttonhole. Remove pins and press.

5 Fold garment extended facing over buttonhole, W.S.F. Mark corners of buttonhole through facing with pins, then stitches. Check both sides. Snip facing inside stitches.

6 Turn under facing at sides of buttonhole cut. Pin. Tack. Hem neatly. Press from both sides.

R.S.F.: right sides facing;
W.S.F.: wrong sides facing.

TWO-PART BOUND BUTTONHOLE

1 Cut 2 fabric strips about 7cm. or 2½in. deep, 3cm. or 1¼in. wider than buttonhole. Interface. Mark buttonhole, as above, picture 1.

2 Fold strips in half, W.S.F. and stitch along at binding depth. (They can be corded, if wished.)

3 Place and pin strips beside buttonhole marking, raw edges meeting along mark. R.S.F. Machine to garment, by stitch lines, with small stitches.

4 Cut through garment between stitch lines from wrong side.

5 Pull binding strips through to wrong side. Neaten and press.

6 Turn back ends of strips as shown, where there is a snipped triangle. Stitch across triangle. Repeat for other end. Sew facing over back as in pictures 4 and 5 above.

NOTE
R.S.F. and W.S.F. are abbreviations for 'Right sides facing' and 'Wrong sides facing' frequently encountered in sewing; these terms are also indicated in pattern instructions by the use of different tints.

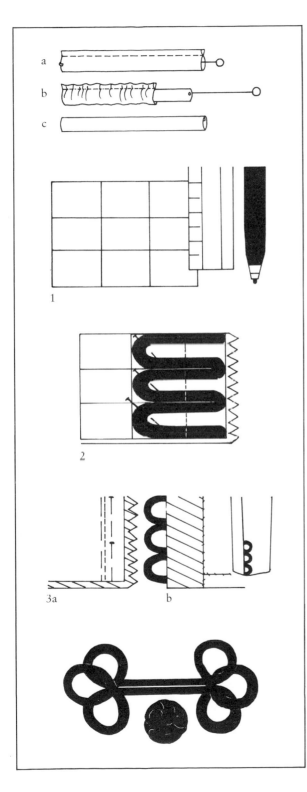

ROULEAU STRIP

(a) To make a rouleau strip, fold a bias fabric strip in half along its length. Tack, and machine with small stitches fairly close to the raw edges. (From the fold edge to the stitch line makes the finished rouleau width.)
(b) Using a strong needle and double button thread securely stitched to one end, pull the rouleau through its own length until turned right side out.
(c) *The rouleau tube:* can be used pressed or unpressed, for ties, button loops, drawstrings, with open ends turned in and oversewn; frogging, fancy borders sewn on by faggoting (page 99) loops along the finished edge, hand stitched on; raised designs machined to garment etc.

BUTTON LOOPS

Use cord or rouleau; tissue or greaseproof paper, ruler, pencil, pins.
1 Cut paper to the depth and width of the button loop plan. Divide with horizontal lines to each loop width. Rule a dotted stitch line parallel to the paper edge, and the loop depth in a solid line beside it. Pin plan to garment right side, the loop end spaces parallel with the seam edge.
2 Bend the rouleau round each space as shown, in continuous loops* close together on the divide lines. Pin. Machine through loops and paper along the stitch line. Tear away paper.
3 (a) Sew a facing strip over loops, *R.S.F.* matching seam raw edges.
(b) Turn strip back, *W.S.F.* over loop ends, now inside garment, and hem. Sew on ball buttons opposite loops.
* Loops may be cut separately and sewn on spaced apart, if wished.

FROG FASTENING

Draw shape, as for button loop plan, on paper for fancy loops, linked by two parallel rows of rouleau. Place a similar loop at each end. Wind the rouleau round over the plan, and pin. Hand sew to garment with small, concealed stitches. One loop is placed over edge for the button where necessary.

CHINESE BALL BUTTON:

Made of interlaced corded frogs, drawn up tightly, the end sewn inside.

Pressing

Throughout the making of your garment you will constantly be instructed to 'press' it. The final pressing can now take place, and the garment will be ready to wear.

IRONS: You may have a dry iron, or a steam-dry iron, or a steam-spray-dry iron. All the steam pressing can be done with a dry iron with the aid of dampened press cloths, though a steam iron is an added convenience. If your iron is marked with the older style code for heat settings (numbers and/or words) it will look like this:

> Code: 1: cool
> 2: warm
> 3: medium hot
> 4: Hot
> 5: Very hot

The setting for steam ironing is shown by a picture of steam.

If, however, it is marked with the new International Textile Care Labelling Code, it will carry dots indicating temperature variations as in the chart on page 89 opposite.

FABRIC SETTINGS: *Always*, but always, test press some of the fabric, a scrap, or a piece out of sight inside. Even cotton or linen, which can be ironed very hot, may be combined with a fibre which requires a cool setting ... and care accordingly should be taken with the heat adjustment. Synthetic fibre knits will require a cool, dry iron if any.

1 Acrylic, e.g. Acrilan, Courtelle, Orlon (cool).
2 Acetate, e.g. Dicel, Lansil; Triacetate, e.g. Tricel, Tricelon; Polyester, e.g. Terylene, Crimplene, Terlenka, Diolen, Trevira, Polyester mixtures; Nylon*, e.g. Bri-Nylon, Enkalon, Celon, Blue C Nylon; Wool; Silk (warm).
3 Rayon or modified Rayon, e.g. Vincel, Sarille (medium hot).
4 Cotton, Linen (hot).
5 Very wet cotton and linen articles (very hot).
* Nylon fabrics vary considerably in texture. Lightweight nylon is best ironed on setting 1. Do not iron fabrics containing Rhovyl, Thermovyl, Dynel or Ulstron. (Coding information by courtesy of Hoover Ltd.)

DRY IRONING: Some fabrics spot or may otherwise be spoiled by damp pressing. Dry iron Courtelle and other acrylics; chiffon, georgette and silk. Metallic fibres may tarnish, or even be damaged by heat or steam pressing, so test first and press with extreme caution.

EXTRA HOT DAMP PRESSING: For linen or close woven *non-synthetic* (look out for mixtures or blended fabrics) fabrics. Use a damp cheesecloth, press cloth, or *cotton* sheeting. *To dampen:* Wet a corner of the press cloth, and wring it to spread the moisture evenly. *To press:* Press under pressure, with the cloth spread on top of the fabric, and keep it moving, to avoid iron indented pressure marks forming. Place brown paper under seam and dart allowances, to avoid an edge impression in the fabric right side.

WOOL DAMP PRESSING: A strong cotton sheeting press cloth may be suitable for very closely woven smooth surface wool fabrics. Guard against the quick drying of the fabric under the hot iron, which could flatten the material too intensely, and make it shine.

FOR WOOL WITH ANY SORT OF SURFACE TEXTURE, NAP OR PILE: Preferably use dampened drill, calico or dressmaker's (undyed) canvas pressing cloths, as these will not crush the pile quite so heavily. (A way of taking out shine too.)

FOR FABRICS WITH RAISED DESIGNS OR NAP: Lightly pressing right side down on a crisp Turkish towel can help prevent flattening the design. This is also a tip for lightly pressing velveteen.

VELVET: Use a velvet pressing pad, or a home-made alternative such as a Turkish towel or a stiff clean clothes brush. Press very lightly.

STEAM PRESSING: Woollens can be steam pressed on the *wrong side* without the use of a damp cloth, except for hard finished weaves such as suitings, which should be pressed on the right side with a muslin or cheesecloth press cloth.

Pressing your dressmaking

FIRST STAGES: Press the seams and darts, and any pleats etc., of each unit section as it is completed, keeping fabric shapes smooth pressed.

SECOND STAGE: As the unit sections are added up to make each completed unit, contour pressing will be required. Press shoulders, bust, rounded shapes over the tailor's ham, and sleeve seams etc., over the roll shape presser. Use your tailor's mitt for pressing gathers, and the ironing board for the larger level areas. Use a sleeve

board to press sleeves.

THIRD STAGE: The completed garment. *Hem:* Press with a crisp fold edge, but avoid pressure over the stitching, as this may indent the tape and stitch marks on the right side. Use the 'banger' over bumpy areas of tailored garments. Steam press them and while they are still damp, bang them flat. This can be applied to buttonholes, lapels, pocket flaps, but not where it could cause any damage to buttons or zippers.

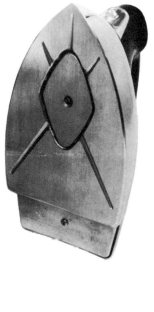

IRONING

 There are four variations of the ironing symbol. The first three have dots to indicate variations in temperature and the fourth, the symbol crossed out, indicates that the article should not be ironed. The temperatures shown in brackets are the maximum sole plate temperatures indicated by the dots in the symbol.

	HOT (210°C)	Cotton, linen, rayon or modified rayon.
	WARM (160°C)	Polyester mixtures, wool.
	COOL (120°C)	Acrylic, nylon, acetate, triacetate, polyester.

DO NOT IRON. (This symbol should only be used in cases where ironing would be detrimental to the fabric and NOT on easy care fabrics to indicate that ironing is not necessary.)

Women's trousers

Trousers . . . so contemporary, convenient and comfortable – and good looking when well cut and fitted. There is no garment more difficult to find to fit you perfectly, and few more simple to make. The problem of achieving a good fit can be solved by taking time and care at the stage of altering the pattern to your exact size, and especially by making up a trousers' basic fitting pattern for reference.

Shape and style

The shape depends on fashion, but may be wide or narrow legged, flared or seamed across below the knee. The same applies to the waist fitting which may be a simple waistband, elasticated, or have a high cummerbund, or a bib and/or braces. Patch pockets; seam pockets; topstitched seams; buttons, embroidery and cuffs – all are details which attract admiring looks. Most of all, however, it is the fit and cut which will count, and this must be emphasised again and again.

These factors also apply to culottes, knee-length trousers (which are often disguised as a divided skirt and worn for walking or cycling), shorts, and Bermuda shorts, which are tailored and cut to thigh or above-knee length. Spanish-style culottes are calf-length wide, flared trousers, which look superb embroidered, with buttons up the side seams, made in black material and worn with boots. For pants' jump suits, don't forget to allow extra length in the body for bending and stretching.

Fabrics

Choose firm, light fabric which will retain its shape without stretching or bagging at the seat and knee, and which will be smooth to wear against the skin. Scratchy tweed and thick wool cloth will rapidly prove too uncomfortable to wear, like shoes that pinch.

For summer, trousers look good made of crease-resisting linen or slub; polyester, cotton, and blends of the two; Terylene; twill or gaberdine fabrics. Nylon or Crimplene or polyester or plush velvet jersey are fine, but should be of fairly substantial quality to ensure a stable shape. Acrylics and double-knit jersey are excellent for colder weather, as well as fine plaid, velveteen, needlecord and corduroy. Soft knits are seductively comfortable but are liable to look happy rather than slimming on the overweight! You can also make trousers out of sheer materials for evening wear – flared, wide, pleated or harem trousers gathered into the ankles. Sheer fabric would need to be lined with silk, left unattached at the leg hems for wide-legged trousers. Crêpe and satin are ideal fabrics for afternoon or evening wear, as are ciré or silky jersey, and, of course, velvet.

If you take time and trouble at the outset to make sure you have the trousers absolutely right for you, and then treasure your arduously achieved perfectly fitting basic pattern, you will soon have an enviable wardrobe of expensive-looking trousers and trousers outfits, which were in fact made by you at bargain cost.

Patterns for trousers

When buying your trousers' pattern, read with care the measurements on the reverse side of the pattern envelope, or in the pattern catalogue. Normally you would buy a pattern by the waist measurement, but if your hips are extra-large in proportion to your waist size, you may need to buy a larger pattern and adjust it at the waist.

A trousers' pattern usually consists of back and front pieces, and two of each are cut out, normally with the straight grain of fabric symbol placed down the length when cutting out. Also waistband, pocket and patterns for other features of the design. You will notice that the back crotch seam is longer than the front, and that the curve and overall shape differ too. This is to give more length and width to accommodate the hips and allow for movement.

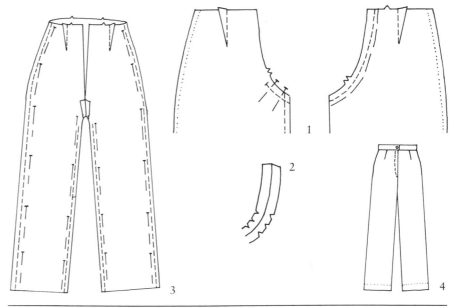

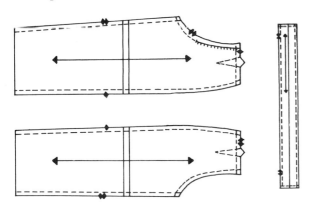

MAKING THE TROUSERS

Work from a pattern carefully adjusted to fit you. If possible one tested on a prototype pair of trousers made up from a basic fitting pattern in muslin or cotton, and already adjusted to your size and shape

IMPORTANT: try to keep any alterations in line with your original pattern shape, taking in a little, or letting out a fraction, but not re-styling too fundamentally. The latter could lead to trouble, and is difficult to do successfully. Work with trousers level on the table.

1 TROUSERS WITH CENTRE FRONT ZIPPER AND WAISTBAND: Complete the darts. Matching notches and right sides facing, place the front shapes over one another, and join the crotch seam as far as the zipper opening. Repeat for the back shapes, but with a full length crotch seam.

2 Clip the curved part of the seams outside the stitchline.

3 Sew on any seam pocket shapes here. Matching notches, and right sides facing, place the front over the back of the trousers. Pin them together down the inside leg and side seams, taking in the pockets in the seams, if any. Tack. Remove the pins. Try on the trousers for fit, both standing and sitting. Pin the zipper opening to close. Standing up, check the waist. Does it fit well? Or pull unduly out of place when you bend? Leave a gap at the middle of the back? Is the crotch neatly fitting (neither too tight nor elephant-seat baggy), giving you a long-legged but comfortably roomy and tailored appearance – a real Savile Row cut? If tailored, try this test. Stand up, and hold the trousers at both sides. There should be about 2 to

3cm. (1 to 1½in.) ease at each side, or about an inch plus, below the waist, across the abdomen. Standing up, bend up your knee. Does the material drag across the front of the thigh? The hips may be too short, or the leg too tight somewhere. With the leg hems turned up, look at the length in a cheval mirror. Does the edge lie over the upper part of the shoes, and rest just above the heel? It could be shorter than you like if above this level. Evening trousers should be floor length.

IMPORTANT: look at the line. Are you satisfied by the flare, or the position of the seams? The shape?

4 When you are happy about the fit, sew in the zipper, if not already in place, and attach the waistband and button and buttonhole. Or complete otherwise as directed in your particular pattern. Press.

Pockets in seams

Pockets can be stitched into seams, more or less anywhere there is a seam. Sometimes they are ordinary trousers pockets like those shown here, which are cut long and wide enough to fit the shape of the hand, and are stitched into pants side seams.

Similar pockets can be sewn into the seams of a skirt, or crescent-shaped ones concealed in bodice stitch lines. They can be hidden under pleats, or topstitched yokes, and sewn horizontally, vertically, in a curve, at an angle, constructed in much the same way as the ones on this page.

Trousers' pockets

Use the pattern shapes given with your pattern (and refer to your own pattern instructions of course). The outline provided here gives general advice, which might differ in some particulars, depending on the design of your garment, in your pattern.

SEAM POCKET

1 Cut out two identical pocket shapes in taffeta or some other sturdy lining material. Pin each shape separately to the extended seam allowances provided for them alongside the pocket opening in the trousers' seams, right sides facing. Tack. Remove the pins and machine. Remove the tacking. Press.

2 When joining the trousers' side seams, at the same time, place the pocket shapes together, right sides facing, and continue the side seams round the pockets, and on down the outside leg. As the pockets usually have hard wear, add a second row of machine stitches.

3 Turn the trousers right side out, and place the pockets forward. Press.

CUTAWAY JEANS STYLE

1 Cut out the lining in white calico, for the pocket inside front, and the larger denim or fabric shape, for the pocket backing, following the pattern pieces: (or a tracing from your jeans pocket, for a home-made pattern, with extra allowed for seams).

2 Match and pin the calico shape wrong sides facing to the curved cut-out shape of the trousers front. Pin them together along the curved edge and tack. Trim away the seam allowance from the calico round the curve, then turn the denim edge over onto

it, in a narrow hem. Machine twice.

3 Place the fabric backing, right sides facing to the calico lining, so the shapes match. Pin and tack together round the long curved edge as shown. Remove the pins. Machine and remove the tacking. Repeat for the second pocket.

4 Right sides facing, place the trousers front on the trousers back, and join them together down the inside leg and side seams as already described. A fitting dart can be made in the waistline edge of the pockets too, if wished, before the waistband is sewn over the top.

5 The completed pocket.

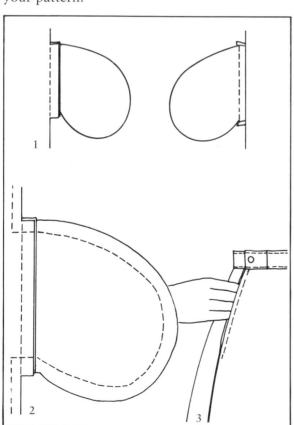

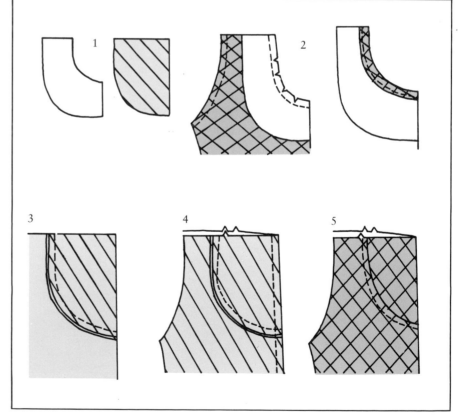

Zippers on trousers

Zippers on trousers are usually inserted in a fly-front fastening. A strong metal trousers' zipper is used, but if the fabric is thin, sometimes a nylon lightweight zipper is more suitable.

The zipper is sewn between an underlap and an overlap. One zipper tape is stitched between the side of the trousers' opening and the underlap; the other tape is sewn under the overlap, concealing the zipper completely.

It is important to have a zipper of the right length for the opening. When it has been stitched in place, the waistband is added, taking in the zipper tapes. The waistband overlap is fastened by one or more buttons or by a flat trousers' hook fastening.

A fly-front is used for jackets and overcoats too, when a strong separating zipper would be needed. Buttons can be used instead, but then a double overlap is required, with the buttonholes in the under layer.

1 Using pattern pieces, you will find that one is for a strip of fabric, curved at one end, to be faced with lining material, or machine over-edge stitched, or otherwise finished. This shape is called the 'underlay'. Open the zipper and pin the left tape to the underlay, along the seam allowance. Tack the zipper in place from the top edge down, keeping the tape flat with the underlay. Remove the pins.

2 Turn under the seam allowance at the edge of the trousers along the left side of the front centre opening. Pin this turned-under edge over the zipper tape on the underlay, starting from the top and working down. Tack. Remove the pins and press, keeping the three layers of underlay, zipper tape and trousers front (with the trousers front right side out) level and smooth together.

Attach the zipper foot to the machine and straight machine stitch through all layers, close to the edge of the turned back trousers' seam.

3 Turn back the wider hem allowance in a single turning, on the right side of the centre front opening, wrong sides facing. With the zipper open, pin the second tape down the inside of this wider hem, close to the turned-in hem raw edges, working from the top, keeping them level and smooth together.

4 Turn the zipper right side up, and move the slide fastener up and down to make sure it is running freely. Tack the second tape to the overlap where pinned. Remove the pins. Machine where tacked, curving the stitch line at the lower end, with the zipper open. Be careful not to stitch through into the underlayer when machining the tape on the overlap.

5 Close the zipper and sew on the waistband, button and buttonhole.

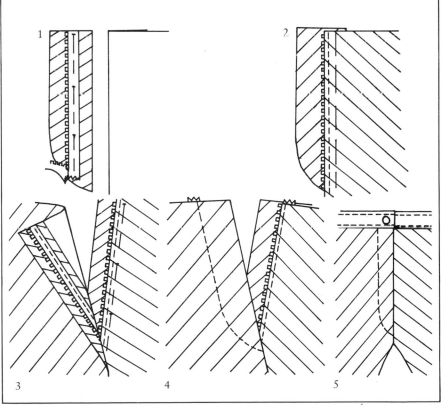

Sewing fancy 13

Braid

Braid is a feature of sewing to be used uninhibitedly. A garment, heavily buttoned and braided has a striking effect. Think of the style of a full-dress military, or braided naval, uniform, or the charm of a velvet jacket bordered with corded ribbon, or a girl's peasant shirt with rows of embroidered tape round the neck and sleeves interspersed with broderie anglaise frills. Of gold braid or bands of velvet ribbon, discreetly or lavishly applied; or leather bands emphasising seams of a wool garment. Carefully sewn on they all add incomparably to the romance and glamour of clothes.

IN GENERAL: Braid should lie flat on the fabric and be exceptionally neatly topstitched and mitred. If placed away from the edge, its position should be carefully measured and marked, before sewing on. With knitted braid, make sure it is not stretched when sewing on, or it could have a wavy effect. Use a stretch stitch for knits or zig-zag, along each edge, or tiny straight stitches. Cord sewn on with concealed stitches and frogged, or fine fancy soutache braiding, combine well with braid.

TO FINISH OFF BRAID ENDS: Turn under neatly and hem to the braid other end, or machine across. If possible sew in with a seam, or cover with a second braid band. Frill raw edges can be concealed under braid in this way.

TAILORED BRAID: Use folded-over knitted or twill braid; frogged or corded braid; grosgrain, velvet or satin ribbon; stiff corded petersham or twill tape. Sometimes bound over the edge; sometimes built into the seam like corded piping; sometimes stitched flat along the edges. Leather bands along seams.

Remove bulk by trimming away the seam allowances outside the stitchline before turning and pressing, for sewing on braid later.

SOUTACHE OR RUSSIAN BRAID: Pretty, frogged, borders of fine, often black, corded braid. Draw the design on paper, then pin to the border. Sew through the design onto the fabric with tiny stitches or use a tailor's chalk dressmarker on the right side. Pin the braid all round the design, keeping the cord flat on the fabric, then handsew neatly in place. Reinforce with machine stitching if wished.

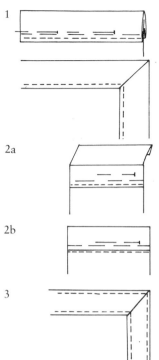

1

2a

2b

3

1 FOLDED BRAID Fit the garment edge right into the crease of folded braid. Keep the braid level and even, and pin and tack to the edge, through all layers. Mitre corners. Take ends into seams where possible. Remove pins. Machine topstitch in place through all layers. Press.

2(a) Open the braid, and pin level round the garment edge with the material edge in the braid crease. Tack, and machine top stitch braid in place.

2(b) On wrong side pin and tack braid just above the stitch line. Hem. Press. Finish ends as before.

3 FLAT BRAID: Pin, tack and machine along both edges to the edges of the garment, as for embroidered braid. Pay special attention to mitred corners, and sew braid ends into seams or hem over seam joins. Topstitch extra neatly.

BOUND EDGES: As well as braided edges, tailored garments can be bound with bias strips cut from satin or corded silk etc., and sewn over the edges as for other binding. Mitre corners on the right and wrong side with stitched down folds. Turn in the binding ends at seams slip stitched onto the garment edges on the right side, then doubled over and slip stitched onto the wrong side. Mitre the corners and fold in the ends at seams and hem down.

Topstitch if wished.

1 EMBROIDERED BRAID, RIBBON OR TAPE: Mark the braid position on the garment. Pin and tack the braid flat where marked. Machine close to both edges.

2 RIC-RAC: Zig-zag woven braid. Pin and tack to marked position. Machine with straight stitching along the centre, or have half braid showing above an edge and machine close to edge.

3 BRODERIE ANGLAISE FRILL

(a) Broderie anglaise trimming, raw edges at the top.

(b) Gather the upper edge with two rows of gathering stitches. Draw up into a frill.

Mark the position of the frill on the garment as for braid. Pin the raw edge along this mark, adjusting the gathers. Tack. Remove pins. Machine.

(c) Cover the raw edges with braid stitched along both edges. Broderie anglaise trimming is available with two woven or fancy selvages and narrow to very wide.

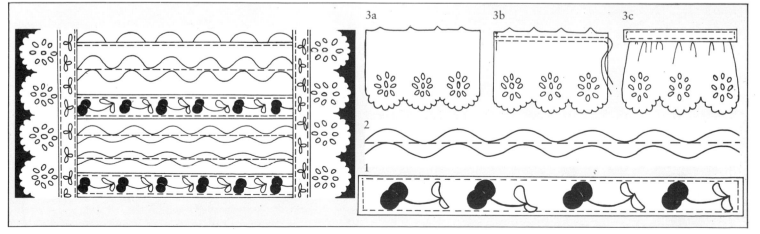

3a   3b   3c

2

1

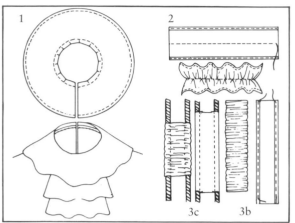

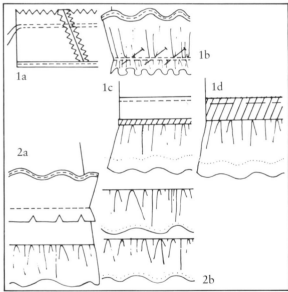

CIRCULAR FRILLS (1):
Glamorous, flared ruffles usually made of soft, supple material such as chiffon, georgette or crêpe. Circular frills can be sewn round sleeves or skirts, or cover an entire garment. A circular frill should be roll- or narrow-hemmed at the outer edge, or if made of two circles, plain seamed together, right sides facing, round the outer edge, then turned right side out and pressed. Stay stitch round the inner raw edge and clip in seam allowance.
The frill can be attached by bias facing or a plain seam.

RUFFLES (2) AND RUCHING (3)
(a) A ruffle is made out of ribbon, or a hemmed, lace edged strip, gathered up the centre. The gathered strip is drawn up to the right length, and attached to the garment with straight machine stitching along the gather line.
(b) First ruching method (see 3 above): Ribbon, or a strip of fabric, can be gathered at both edges, and pinned at each edge between ungathered, turned in material, tacked, and topstitched close to the plain edge, or joined by plain seams as for inserting lace.
(c) Second ruching method: Turn in the edges of a fabric strip onto the wrong side over cord, and machine using the zipper foot.
Pull up the cord to gather the band. Sew on where wished.

FRILL 1 (a) Hem or otherwise finish, such as by additional lace trimming of the frill edge.
(b) Sew gathering stitches along the top edge. Gather the frill to the required width. Right sides facing, match frill raw edges to garment raw edges. Pin. Tack. Machine.
(c) On the wrong side, sew bias binding for facing round the seam allowance of the frill join, outside the stitch line. Machine.

Press facing. Turn up onto garment over gathered and seam raw edges. Tack, and slip hem or blind stitch to garment. Press.
FRILL 2: For frill on garment not at edge.
(a) Right sides facing, frill above placement line, pin frill to material marking along gathering line. Adjust gathers and tack. Remove pins and machine.
(b) Lower frill and press. The upper edge may be topstitched if wished.

Frills and flounces

TO MAKE A FRILL PATTERN: Measure the depth of the frill, and add the seam and hem turning amounts. Frill hems are usually narrow. Where a frill is ruffled above as well as below the gathering line, add the extra depth required for this.

For the width, allow one and a half times the basic width for heavier materials; twice to two and a half times the width for medium, and three times the width for flimsy materials.

Lace, sheers and sequins

* Pre-shrink lace made of natural fibre, especially cotton lace.
* The lace pattern may go one way only; if yours is like this, choose a 'with nap' pattern.
* The lace pattern, like plaid or border prints, needs to be matched at the seams, and balanced too. Place the pattern shapes over the centre of a pattern in the lace, to make the best of it, and to avoid it looking lop-sided when made up.
* As lace is partly see-through, it may need a special underslip. Underlining is suited to lace. Use silky fabric, such as crêpe de chine, taffeta, or silk itself, for a lustrous background, or lawn for coarser cotton lace. To retain the sheer look, back with net, organdie, organza or tulle. Leave lace sleeves unlined.
* For sheer lace, fine darts and seams are needed. Make a plain seam and *double stitch* it, that is, sew a second machine row close to the first, then trim the seam allowance outside away. Do the same with darts.
* Appliqué lace seams will join lace almost invisibly. Align the lace pattern, as for plaid, overlapping at the seams, and pin and tack it. Snip round the edge of the design carefully, then whipstitch or machine it to its counterpart exactly. Trim the underside surplus, and sew these edges down with tiny stitches too.
* Try to place the hem fold edges against the fancy lace edge, so no hems are needed. For other hems, face them inconspicuously with net strips, or stiff horsehair braid. Lace can be edged with similar lace narrow trimming, topstitched under a single turning.
* Back fine, sheer lace onto tissue paper and sew as one, gently tearing the paper away afterwards.

1 LACE INSERTION *First Method*: Mark position for insertion for fabric right side. Pin lace with two woven edges right side out, over the insertion mark, machine with fine straight or zig-zag stitches along both edges. (Be sure that the tension of machine stitching, lace and fabric result in an unpuckered insertion, by testing through all layers on a spare piece of lace and fabric.) Very carefully – so as not to cut through the lace – Snip through the fabric between the stitch rows on the wrong side.

Second method: Cut along marking for insertion and turn under the raw edges of the two pieces which result from this. Tack and press. Pin a lace band behind it, taking care that the lace is equal width all round the insertion. Tack, remove the pins, and machine topstitch the lace in place all round. Or join lace to fabric along either edge with plain seams, with inserted frills if wished, and press the seams away from the insertion when completed.

2 LACE TRIMMING: Can be sewn under or over a narrow hem using the machine narrow hemmer, or lace insertion, or otherwise be edged with lace.

3 LACE APPLIQUÉ: Snip a design out of the lace. Pin and tack it to the background material and whip or hem or machine satin stitch it in place round the edge. Sew the inner outlines too unless the background fabric is to be cut away. In this case snip away background fabric close to stitching.

4 Whipstitch is neat, tiny overedge stitch, close together. Use a fine thread and small needle, such as a 'between'.

5 SEQUINS: Begin with several small backstitches on the wrong side. Using a fine or beading needle and thread, pick up a sequin on the needle. Make a backstitch into the material and bring out the point for the next sequin centre. Sequin strip is sewn on by hand from the wrong side, lightly slip stitching the edges with long stitches. Sew pailletes (large sequins with a side hole) in the same way.

BEADS: Trace the design on tissue paper, and transfer through it onto fabric with tiny running stitches. Remove the tissue paper. *Bead motif*: Back onto organdie and use an embroidery hoop.

SEW ON THE BEADS: Using a beading needle and beeswaxed, fine strong thread or nylon thread or bead cord, sew each bead or rope of beads in place with small backstitches. Begin and end with two or three backstitches on the wrong side.

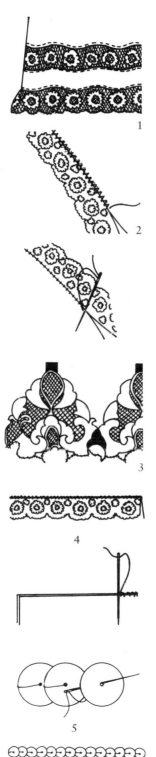

Embroidery

Embroidery has always been one of the great pleasures of sewing.

Here is a selection of popular embroidery stitches. If you would like to try some others you can often find inexpensive booklets on the needlecraft counter, published by the embroidery yarn manufacturers; one favourite is *100 Embroidery Stitches* published in the 'Anchor Embroidery Stitches' series.

Equipment

EMBROIDERY HOOP: A double wooden ring with a screw adjustment over the outer ring. The material is stretched over an inner hoop, and the outer ring slipped over the top and tightened.

Hoops come in different sizes. Use to embroider small areas; monograms; bead embroidery. Also for embroidery and other free-motion stitching on your sewing machine.

EMBROIDERY FRAME: A rectangular frame on a stand, or held on the knee. The embroidery is stitched over the fabric strips on the frame, and laced tight at the sides. Used for larger pieces such as embroidered pictures, cushions or seat covers.

THREADS AND YARNS: Stranded cotton; soft embroidery thread; tapisserie wool; crochet cotton; machine embroidery thread No. 30.

NEEDLES: Crewel; tapestry; chenille; darners; wool embroidery; beading.

TRANSFERRING DESIGNS: Commercial iron-on transfers are available, or make your own designs, through dressmakers's carbon onto material, by pinning material, right side up, dressmaker's carbon face down and design above, and drawing through with a ball-point pen. Or use a tracing wheel in conjunction with tailor's chalk or chalk pounced through perforations in the design, in each case supplemented by tiny running stitches over the design outline.

Types of embroidery

CREWEL: Fancy-stitch embroidery of elaborate designs in rich colours, often flowers, leaves and birds on linen or other fine fabric. Use a *crewel needle* and fine embroidery wool or yarn.

CANVAS WORK: Various tapestry or cross stitches worked over canvas or fine linen, using wool or cotton embroidery yarns and a blunt tipped *tapestry needle*.

CUTWORK: Eyelet holes as in broderie anglaise, or in other designs, often leaves and flowers, with the spaces between cut out. To work, transfer the design first. Stitch round the edges with one or two lines of small running stitches, then snip away the cut-out areas. Satin stitch overcast round the cut edges and along the design outlines, or use machine satin stitch.

DRAWN THREADWORK: Threads are drawn out from woven material in bands and the edges hemstitched in various patterns.

Appliqué, patchwork, quilting and smocking are other embroidery methods described in detail later.

HEMSTITCH (a): Use plain woven fabric. Draw several threads out next to proposed fold edge of hem. Turn and tack the hem, if desired, close to the drawn thread band.

METHOD: Work from the wrong side and right to left. Secure the thread, then bring it through the material a stitch length from the drawn thread edge. Push the needle in between the threads immediately below, and take the point to the left, behind the threads, bringing it through forward between three or four threads along. Take the needle back to the right, and put it through to the right side again in the first place. Bring the needle through towards you a stitch length above and draw the thread nearly round the base of the drawn threads. Repeat along both edges, for the hem through the fold edge.

FAGGOTING (b)

Used for attaching rouleau or other bands to an edge. Pin and tack the garment edge on paper, and the rouleau or band just above it. Start from the left, and bring the thread through the edge of the garment and push it into the edge of the rouleau at a slight angle to the right. Bring the thread forward, passing the needle under the thread. Push it into the edge of the garment again, to the right, and at a slight angle. Take it to the right into the rouleau again, taking the thread across in front of the last stitch. Repeat until the rouleau is stitched to the garment all round. Remove the tacking and paper. Press.

Embroidery stitches

* Use the appropriate needle and yarn for the type of stitch, fabric weight and design.
* Mount the fabric onto organdie for motifs and monograms, also for bead embroidery. Leave plenty of fabric surrounding the embroidery, for cutting out, seam turnings, hems etc. later.
* Back sheer material onto tissue paper and gently tear away after stitching.
* Test-iron the transfer on a spare piece of the fabric first. Cut away

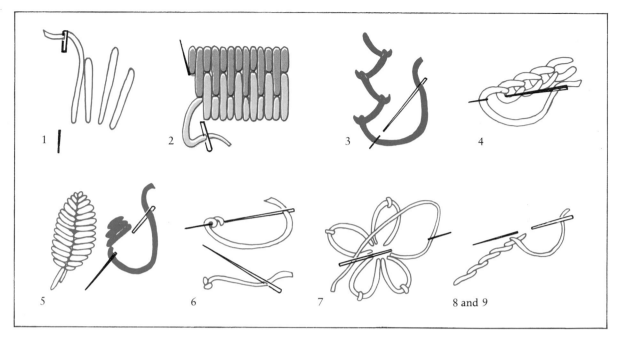

trade names etc. from the transfer before pressing.
* If possible, work with the embroidery stretched over a hoop or frame.
* Avoid puckering the fabric with tight stitches by not drawing the thread through too tightly. Stitches should lie evenly on the fabric surface.
* Begin with a knot on the wrong side and weaving the needle and thread through the back of the embroidery. Finish by the same weaving, and two or three small concealed backstitches.

1 STRAIGHT STITCH: Sew long straight stitches over and over, arranged in 4 flower wheels of equal length or random lengths.
2 LONG AND SHORT STITCH: Make a long stitch as for satin stitch, and a half stitch beside it; a long stitch again, then a half stitch. Below, a half stitch, then a long, then a half, then a long. The outside stitch can be dark, the next row lighter, to form a shaded surface.
3 FEATHER STITCH: Bring the thread forward, and put the needle in a stitch below to the right. Bring the needle through from the back of the stitch, over the thread. Draw the thread through and repeat, always in the reverse direction to last time.
4 CHAIN STITCH: Bring the needle out at top left, and put it in again beside the same spot without tightening the thread. Bring it through a stitch below, over the thread, which forms a loop round it. Draw the thread through, and put the needle in beside where the thread came out, but this time inside the loop. Repeat to form a chain.
5 SATIN STITCH: Outline the design in tiny running stitches, and if raised satin stitch is desired, fill in the design all over with running stitch first. Bring the needle through to the front, at the outline of the design, and take it back and put the point in again at the other outline. Bring it through again, beside the end of the first stitch, then back in beside the other end. Repeat, over and over, forming a smooth surface with stitches that fit the shape accurately. Stitches may be horizontal or slanting.
6 FRENCH KNOT: For rosebud dotted edges on organdie collars etc. Bring the thread through. Wind the thread twice round the needle point, holding the thread steady with your left thumb as you do so. Pull the needle through to form a knot, close to the fabric. Put the needle in again where the thread

came out, and sew off the knot on the wrong side with a backstitch or two, and trim, or carry the needle along under the fabric for the next stitch.
7 LAZY DAISY: Make a wheel or spray of chain stitches, in which the thread is taken over the end of each stitch and back to the centre or starting point for the next stitch.
8 STEM STITCH: A line of slanting stitches overlapping one after the other. Put in the needle a stitch along at a slight angle, then bring it through half way back along the last stitch. Take the stitch half a stitch ahead at a slight slant. Repeat for stitch line.
9 OUTLINE STITCH: Made in a similar way, but with the needle brought out just beside the last stitch, and taken forward at a less acute angle, to form a finer line.

Cross stitch

Cross stitch is simple to sew; indeed, after running stitch, it is one of the first embroidery stitches happily tackled by young children. A repetitive stitch used in canvas work, it is enjoyable to do, and can be marvellously attractive when made into such beautiful items as traditional Basque embroidered household linen, with its deep, solid ornamental cross stitch borders of dark blue or some other plain, vivid colour, on white.

It is delightful, too, when applied in geometrical snowflake-like patterns, to colourful toy town pictures of birds, flowers and houses, or to decorate a wide variety of things, from gingham aprons and blouses, to table mats, cushion covers, even framed samplers.

IN GENERAL: The stitches should lie evenly on the fabric. Also the threads of each stitch should be sewn in the same direction as other similar stitches in the row or block. That is, if the first cross stitch has its under stitch going from the upper right to the lower left, and the other stitch crosses it from the upper left to the lower right, this order should be retained throughout. Otherwise the surface effect will not be regular.

MATERIALS: To help achieve equal-sized stitches easily, material in which the threads can be counted readily is usually used, either canvas, or cotton mesh fabrics which have a certain number of threads or holes to the inch or centimetre. When sewing the number of threads or holes to each stitch either way is counted, ensuring even stitches.

Check material, such as gingham, is also ideal for cross stitch, and they are often combined. For finer work, linen or other plain woven fabrics are used, often combined with minutely small stitches. Cross stitch goes well with felt, sewn in wool or thick cotton yarn, though here the embroidery has to be freehand.

THREADS: The most readily available and effective threads and yarns to use with canvas or gingham are stranded embroidery cotton, soft embroidery cotton or tapisserie wool. Crewel stranded wool or pearl cotton are obtainable from specialist needlework materials suppliers, such as the Needlewoman Shop in London, or similar stores in your nearest city.

FOR YOUR OWN CROSS STITCH DESIGN, use squared graph paper. Count each graph paper square as a single stitch on the canvas. Draw the outline and design shapes onto the graph paper, and repeat the number of rows and squares in stitches. You can draw in a colour key too. Or draw direct on the canvas.

WHEN COMPLETE remove the canvas from the frame, and cut out the shape required for the embroidered part, leaving a seam allowance round it. Press, from the wrong side.

Always sew the under and upper crossed stitches in the same direction, i.e. the under from below right to upper left each time, for an even appearance.

Two-journey cross stitch. (a) Bring the thread through at A. Put the needle in at B. Bring it through at C. Repeat for row from B.

(b) Start again at the upper left end of the row. Bring the thread through at A. Put the needle in at B. Bring it out at C. Repeat for row from B.

SINGLE CROSS STITCH: Bring the needle out at A, down right to B. Bring it out above at C, and in at D. Bring it out again at C. Repeat for other stitches.

DOUBLE CROSS STITCH: Make a cross stitch, but after D bring the needle out at E, go from E to F, out at G up to H and back to A.

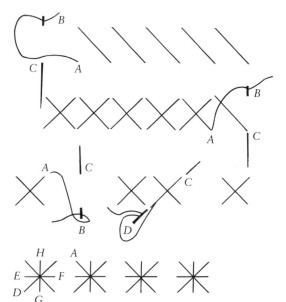

Appliqué

Appliqué consists of shapes cut out of material or leather, sewn or glued onto a fabric or skin background. This is the method you use if you wish to stitch a pink check elephant shape on a child's pinafore, or an alphabet or felt flowers on a wall hanging.

These days, appliqué can be an exciting form of sewing, with an entire fabric landscape or still life stitched all over a long skirt or floor length evening coat, the picture built up in layers stitched round the edges of each material shape, sometimes additionally decorated with embroidery, beads, trimming etc.

Firm, closely woven fabrics are easiest to use for sewing appliqué. You can mix printed cotton and silk with satin and velvet, and fine metallic tissue. Do avoid stretch fabrics, even such light-stretch materials as moss crêpe. Otherwise you will have an impossible time trying to persuade the shapes and background to stay flat without bubbling round the edges of the stitching. To test, pull the material, or press it with your finger from the wrong side. If it gives at all, don't use it.

Fabrics which fray easily can be a nuisance too, but may be the right texture or colour, or reflect the light in just the way you need for part of the picture. If so, try cutting a narrow seam allowance round the edge (clipping any curved edges) and turning and gluing it under, or backing the shape with its turned edges, onto a non-woven sheer iron-on interfacing. The edges can also be turned and tacked over organdie.

Another important factor to watch is whether the fabrics applied can be cleaned or washed, are dye-fast and non-shrink. This is not so important with a framed picture, but for children's clothes it is a vital consideration. Ordinary felt, so perfect for appliqué because of its firm surface, non-fray edges and brilliant colours, can be a snare, because with the type of felt at present available, colours usually run and it loses its looks when washed.

PATTERN: Trace the shapes, or where needed enlarge them onto squared paper. Cut out. Appliqué with non-woven fabric is cut round the exact shape; for woven fabric, turnings to neaten raw edges need to be added.

BACKGROUND: Join main seams to be appliquéd over together, keeping the work flat. (For a garment, shoulders would be left open.) Hems may be turned up first and appliquéd over, or faced onto the right side as part of the appliqué design.

The work is lined when the appliqué is completed.

APPLIQUÉ STITCHES: Any flat decorative stitch such as hemming; blanket stitch; herringbone; satin stitch by hand or machine; machine zig-zag or embroidery stitch.

APPLIQUÉ PICTURE (a motif should be backed on organdie but is carried out otherwise in the same way); Either draw a design for a picture based on the selection of fabric oddments available, or design the appliqué picture, and measure the shapes, deciding on the colours you wish for. Shop for the pieces of material required, or match them up from your scrap-bag. The picture is built up in layers, with the lowest layer of background shapes arranged first. Try out all the shapes, before you begin to sew them in place and make any adjustments needed at this stage. Turn in the edges of woven fabric shapes, clipped so they lie flat where necessary. Embroider round the edge where the stitches will show when finished. Where they come under another layer of appliqué use running stitch or slip hemming, or machine straight stitch or zig-zag, so the stitch line will not show through the shapes above. Complete each layer in turn. Flat bias binding or ribbon borders, or lace etc. can be included in the design, as can buttons, beads and sequins. Satin stitch details afterwards, or otherwise embroider such finishing touches as leaf spines and stalks.

BLIND APPLIQUÉ is carried out rather like patchwork, using printed or woven cotton fabric shapes, turned in and concealed slip-stitched to the background. Embroidered and patchworked Blind Appliqué of flowers and other designs are features of American quilts.

GLUED APPLIQUÉ: All this can be carried out with glue, for such materials as felt, P.V.C. or leather. Be sure to use suitable glue, and tap the appliqué in place.

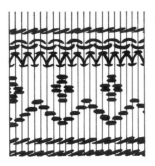

Smocking

Smocking is embroidering across gathered material. If a fabric can be gathered readily, it is probably possible to smock over it. Good smocking is founded on an evenly gathered surface, and about three times the width material is needed for it To help form level, regular spaced rows, a smocking transfer is often used, rows of dots ironed onto the wrong side of the fabric. Gingham checks lend themselves to even smocking too. Fine wool, lawn, silk or Viyella are ideal for smocking.

GATHERING THREADS: *Method:* Use knotted thread and begin at the top right of the top row on the wrong side of the material. Make level equally spaced running stitch rows of gathering thread from one side of the smocking area to the other, and out behind the dots. When all the rows have been gathered, draw them up to the desired width and wind the thread round pins.

Stroke out the gathers with a needle to form a finely pleated surface on the right side. Cut out a sheet of paper to the correct finished dimensions of the smocking area, and pin and tack it across the gathers on the wrong side. Remove the pins.

SMOCKING: Work from the right side. Bring the thread through at the end of the top row on the left, and begin to smock. Stitches should be light and even on the gathered surface. Designs are usually two-way bands, with firm outlined borders to keep the smocking in shape, except for all-over honeycomb stitch.

FINISH: Finish a row of smocking stitches, or for a new thread, with one or two small backstitches on the wrong side. When complete, gently remove the paper and gathering threads.

MACHINE SMOCKING, using rows of machine embroidery, can be taken across the gathered lines. Use machine embroidery thread. Remember, machine smocking will not have the elasticity of hand smocking.

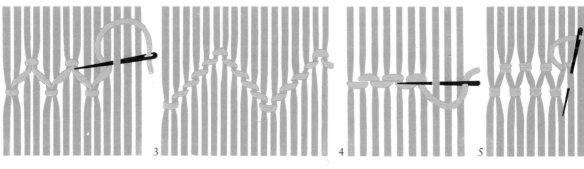

1   2   3   4   5

Stitches

1 OUTLINE STITCH: Used to give smocking a firm outline. From the left, take the needle a stitch across the next pleat to the right, *slightly* slanting, and put it back through the pleat, just inside the last stitch. Draw the thread through. Repeat.

2 CHEVRON STITCH: (a) Bring the needle out at the top left end of the row. (b)Take it across two pleats level, under the thread, and put it back in through the last pleat. Draw the thread through between the pleats.

(c) Take the thread down to the right across the pleat, and put the needle back through the pleat, level, above the thread. (d) Take the needle across two pleats level, above the thread, and put it back through the last pleat. Bring it through between the pleats and above the thread, level. (e) Take the thread up to the right across the pleat and put the needle back through the pleat, level, below the thread. Repeat from (b).

3 WAVE STITCH: Begin at the left. Take the stitch across two pleats, and put the needle back through the pleat, bringing it out above the thread, level, between the pleats. Repeat for the required number of steps up. For the top stitch, take the stitch across two pleats, and put the needle back through the last pleat with the thread *above* the needle, and the needle pointed one step down. Repeat for the required number of stitch steps down. For the lowest stitch, take the stitch across two pleats, and put the needle back through

the last pleat with the thread *below* the needle, its point one step up. Curved wave rows can also be made this way in more softly graduated steps.

4 CABLE STITCH: Take a level stitch across two pleats, and put the needle back through the last pleat, level, below the thread. Take another stitch across the next two pleats, and put the needle back through the last pleat above the thread. Repeat for row. (Another outline stitch.)

5 HONEYCOMB STITCH:

Make a back stitch across two pleats.

Make a second backstitch over the same two pleats close by the first, and draw the stitches tight. Point the needle up vertically at the back of the last pleat, and bring it through on the left at the row above, in the same pleat. Make a double backstitch across this and the next pleat, then take the needle, pointing down, back down a row, and bring it out on the left of the last pleat. Repeat for row.

Shirring

SHIRRING is the name given to a ruched surface. The extra material width required would vary more than for smocking, depending on the thickness of the material as for frills.

Leave the seam allowances ungathered. Gathering rows are level, spaced as for smocking, but the stitches do not necessarily have to be so rigidly equal. Rows can be machined and fixed in place, including with machine embroidery stitches, or be decorated with bands of ric-rac or broderie anglaise or ribbon. Or they can be stitched with elastic thread, giving them a stretch surface.

Shirring is suitable for all light materials that will gather and drape, such as nylon jersey, crêpe, satin, chiffon or panne velvet, lightweight wool, georgette, silk and similar synthetic materials. It is often used for blouses, waist-lines and cuffs.

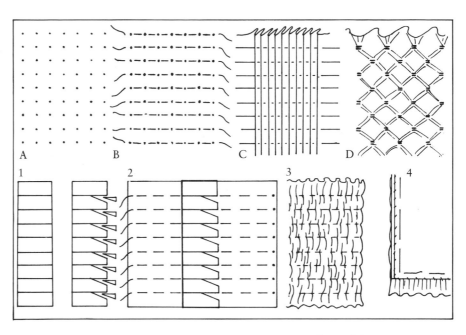

Shirring

MEASURING THE ROWS: For speedy measuring of shirred rows, make a gauge, from a strip of cardboard cut to the depth of the shirring. Mark the gauge with all the rows you intend to sew, by lines drawn at the desired intervals, in pairs, or threes, or singly and equally spaced as the case may be. (1)

(2) Cut the notch out under the end of each line, so the spacing of the stitch rows can be checked with the gauge at a glance, during and after sewing the gathering lines or elasticated shirring guidelines. (3)

(4) For fixed shirring, make running stitch gathering rows and draw up to the required width, as for smocking. Anchor the threads round pins, adjusting the gathers. Machine the rows level with straight, zig-zag or embroidery stitching, then fasten off the thread ends of the machine stitching.

A stay or underlay (5) can be made to line the shirring on the wrong side. Cut a panel of lining material to fit the shirred areas, plus seam allowances. Turn in the raw edges, and pin and tack the panel over the shirring round the edges. Hem or slip-stitch in place.

ELASTIC SHIRRING: Use about twice the fabric width for elasticated shirring. Mark the rows accurately with tailor's chalk or tacking guidelines, using the gauge as a guide. Wind elastic thread, stretched round the bobbin, by hand. Use a long stitch with normal sewing thread on top of the machine. Or follow directions given with the elastic thread.

Smocking

A Transfer the dots, aligning exactly to the straight and crosswise grains, onto fabric wrong side.

B Knot long thread, and run gathering rows of running stitch between the dots.

C Gather smocking area to desired width. Anchor threads round pins. Stroke gathers. Back onto paper underlay.

D Smock on right side from left to right. When completed, remove threads and underlay. Honeycomb smocking shown here.

Belts

A belt is an accessory worth taking some trouble to make. Good ones are increasingly expensive to buy, especially when well-detailed or made of leather, and then, there is always the question of getting just the one you want. To make one successfully at home is more and more within the scope of the do-it-yourself dressmaker, and there are various aids to help give it a professional look

A belt can be made from the same fabric as the garment; printed cotton, wool, P.V.C., imitation leather; suedette, broad elastic, braid, webbing, ribbon, lace or broderie anglaise.

Plaid, polka dots, brocade. Leather or suede, dyed or natural cured skins. You can even use fake fur, pony skin or leopard skin. Not to mention metal links, rings or fabric.

For the belt's construction, from the haberdashery counter you can buy strong belting or corded petersham ribbon, sometimes boned, or belt weight interfacing. An eyelet punch to clip lacquered metal eyelets on the belt holes is not at all costly. Buckles, linked fastenings, metal studs. From the hardware shop, all-purpose glue such as Bostik for plastic; pure rubber adhesive like Copydex for natural materials.

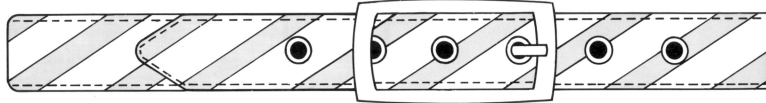

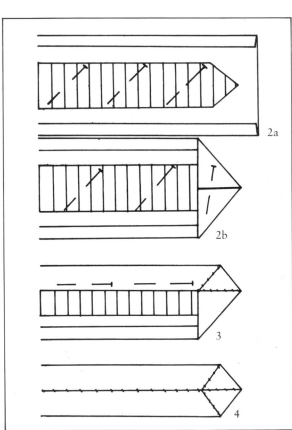

TO MAKE BELT: Attach any braid or ornament to be sewn on first. Iron-on an interfacing strip, cut to the finished width of the belt, and shape, at this stage. Turn in one end and one side of the belt seam allowances. Pin, tack and remove the pins. Press. Trim the belting strip to a point.

1 Place the prepared belt strip right side down on the work table.

2 (a) Centre the belting along it. Pin the belting to the belt strip lightly to anchor it, while you turn (2b) the corners of the belt over the pointed end of the belting, sides to middle, and oversew down the centre. Remove the pins.

3 Take the side of the belt without the raw edge turned in, and fold it over onto the belting, so it fits closely over the belting edge. Include the belt point in this turning, which

would result in a second fold. Pin.

4 Take the other side of the belt with the raw edge turned in, and fold it too onto the back of the belt, including at the point, so that it overlaps the other side down the centre. Pin. Oversew this side of the belt onto the other, as well as along the point and folds. Press.

5 TO MAKE A BELT WITH A ROUND END, OR CURVE, begin with the decorated strip. Fold it in half, right sides facing, and join it down its length with a plain seam. Refold it, still right sides facing, so the seam lies down the centre. Trim, pin, tack and machine across the end in the shape desired; a curve as shown here, or a semicircle, or angle. Clip outside the seam on a curved shape. Trim the end of the belting to match. Turn right side out

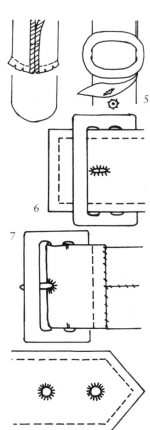

Take a little care to assemble the correct materials and tools, and next time, instead of going out to search for a new belt, try making one.

The plan given here for making a simple belt can easily be adapted for other designs in different materials. Either you can cut the belt material shape from your dress pattern, or you can cut out your own. To begin with measure your waist, and for a belt which slots through a buckle and overlaps like this one, allow about 18cm. to 20cm. (7in. to 8in.) extra for the buckle and belt overlap, plus seam allowances. Cut the strip twice as wide as the belting, plus seam allowances.

In addition buy the same length belting, or use iron-on or non-woven interfacing; a buckle to fit the width of the finished belt (taken across the buckle bar with a fraction of room to spare on either side of the belt). Braid or other ornaments for the belt. Eyelets and eyelet tool, or the eyelets could be machine or hand embroidered. An awl for piercing the belt for the buckle prong, or a press fastener or short strip of Velcro where the buckle has no prong. Thread, needles, pins scissors. Sewing machine.

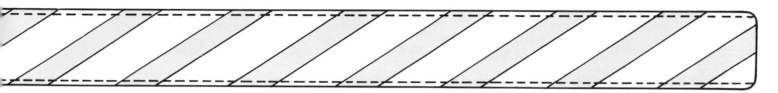

and *pull* over the belting. Press. The rest of the belt is made following the same steps as for the other. Top-stitch all round the belt except at the buckle end, if wished.

6 FOR A BUCKLE WITH A PRONG: Sew eyelet holes for fastening the belt at the pointed end over the prong and a longer eyelet hole for the buckle prong, about 5cm. (2in.) from the buckle end.

7 Slot the buckle into the belt, and the prong through the eyelet. Turn the belt end onto the wrong side and turn under the raw end, and hem or machine to the belt. Oversew several stitches on either side to hold the buckle in place. For a buckle without a prong sew a press fastener or strip of Velcro to fasten the end.

(a) EYELET HOLE: Mark the eyelet hole on the belt and stitch round it with tiny running stitches. Make a hole with an awl, and buttonhole stitch or machine round the hole. Or add metal eyelets with eyelet pliers.

(b) BELT CARRIERS: Cut strips as wide as the belt plus about 3cm. (1¼in.). Make the strips about 4cm. (1½in.) wide. Turn in one edge, and overlap the strip sides to middle. Oversew down the centre. Press. Turn in the raw ends. Pin in position on the garment and hem or machine in place. Belt carriers may be topstitched if wished.

(c) A BELT LOOP: To hold a belt end in place, make a belt carrier twice the length of the belt width, plus 2.5cm. (1in.) overlap, and oversew the ends together. Slip onto the belt. PRESS FASTENER OR VELCRO ANCHOR FOR BELT END: If you do not make a belt loop, sew a press fastener under the belt end, and the other side of the press fastener onto the belt as an anchor. To do this, first mark the position to fit you, when wearing the belt. Or add a Velcro strip.

(d) For a BUTTONHOLE STITCHED THREAD CHAIN BELT CARRIER: Use button thread. Mark the belt width on the side seam, above and below the waist seam. Begin with several backstitches on the wrong side, and take a long stitch to the opposite mark. Secure with a backstitch. Make four or five similar long stitches in the same way. Start close to the top, and buttonhole stitch closely along these five threads, with the knots in a ridge to one side. Finish with backstitches. Make a button loop in the same way but in a semi-circle to loop over a button sewn to the edge of the garment.

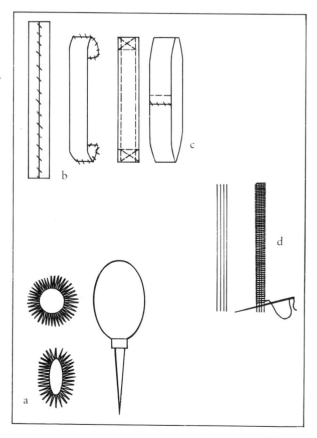

Shaped and sash belts

A contour belt has all the elegance of a subtle shape, which fits gracefully round the body. To achieve a belt with the correct line, either it would be advisable to have a pattern, carefully adjusted to your size, or better still, if you have a favourite shaped belt in your wardrobe, to take this as your model.

TO MAKE THE PATTERN: Use dressmaker's squared or other paper; Sellotape; a ruler; dressmaker's ruler or T-square; a pencil.

Fasten the belt down flat on the paper with Sellotape. Draw round the edges then remove the belt. Using your dressmaker's ruler at right angles to the outline, add about 1.5cm. ($\frac{1}{2}$in.), all round the edges for seam turnings.

FOR A LINKED BELT: Make two 4cm. to 5cm. overlaps ($1\frac{1}{2}$in.) if needed, at each end.

FOR A BUCKLED BELT: Allow 5cm. (2in.) extra at the buckle end, and 13cm. to 15cm. (5in. to 6in.) extra for the belt overlap.

TO MAKE THE BELT: You need fabric; non-iron or other interfacing; lining material, cut slightly smaller than the belt shape. For light or sheer material, underline the fabric with organdie, silk or taffeta or transparent Vilene, then interface and line the belt. Leather is dealt with separately.

Method: (1) Mark the stitch lines on the fabric wrong side. Pin the interfacing within the stitch lines onto the wrong side of the belt. Snip the edges where curved outside the stitch line, so they will lie flat when turned. Press the edges onto the interfacing. (1b) Tack then catchstitch in place. (2) Turn in and pin the lining shape onto the belt on the wrong side. Tack then remove the pins. Hem the lining to the belt all round. Remove the tacking and press. Attach the buckles.

LEATHER BELT: (3) To make a leather belt, cut out the shape from a skin, following the methods for working in leather given on pages 110–111. Join several sections together to make up a full length if necessary. (a) Cut out the interfacing to the finished belt shape and glue it in place on the wrong side of the belt. Snip the curves so the edges will lie flat when turned, cutting out in notches to avoid bulky overlaps if need be. Turn and glue the seam allowance onto the belt, and tap lightly in place. (b) Snip the curved edges then turn in the seam allowances on the thin leather lining and glue. Glue the lining onto the

belt and tap and smooth in place. (c) Attach buckles and stitch down. Machine topstitching may be added to the belt. Punch eyelet holes if needed.

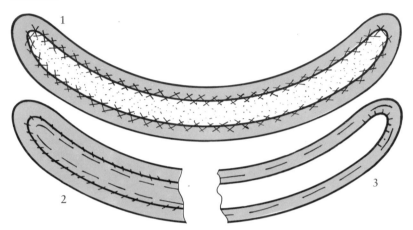

SASH BELT: A sash belt consists of two pieces of material or soft leather, or soft leather-fabric. Interface the belt shape with flexible interfacing. The belt should be cut to your waist size, plus about 18cm. to 20cm. (7in. to 8in.) for the buckle turning and belt overlap, and to the width desired – about 9cm. to 13cm. at the widest point ($3\frac{1}{2}$in. to 5in.) is a good width. Add seam and hem allowances. Cut one end wider, at an angle.

SASH BELT: The lining is cut narrower than the belt so that when stitched together and turned right side out, the belt turns over on the lining side at the edges for about 0.5cm. ($\frac{1}{4}$in.).

1 Place one long edge of the belt against the equivalent long edge of the lining, right sides facing. Pin and tack for fabric; paperclip or Sellotape for leather. Remove pins and machine. Repeat for the other long edge.

2 Adjust the belt with the lined side on top. You will see some of the main belt along the long edges. Place the angled short edges together and pin, and tack. Remove the pins and join with a plain seam. Trim away the corners, remove the tacking and turn right side out. Press for fabric. Pinch out for leather.

3 Turn under the raw edges of the short straight belt end, and oversew them together for material, or glue for leather. Pleat, then push through the buckle and hem onto the wrong side.

4 Sew on a press fastener or Velcro under the loose end of the belt to hold it in position.

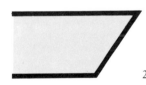

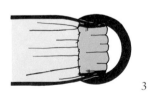

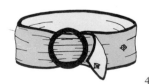

BIAS SKIRT: The pattern is placed diagonally on the material, though the straight grain of fabric symbol is still placed parallel to the selvage. Before attempting to level a bias cut skirt it should be hung up for at least 24 hours to allow it to drop first.

A fairly narrow hem is easiest to make successfully.

Sheers and beads
* Line sheer materials with silk, lawn or similar synthetic fabric.
* Pin and tack sheer material to tissue paper and work as one. Tear paper away gently later.
* Use fine French seams.
* Sheer material bias binding should be used double thickness.

HEMS: Make handstitched rolled hemmed edges, face with transparent fabrics, or use iron-between non-woven fabric such as Wundaweb, to eliminate stitching. Or picot the edge.

* Stiffen a hem with horsehair braid, organdie or transparent iron-on Vilene.

NET: Choose non-flammable net. Use double-stitched plain narrow seams. Hems are not needed. Net can be exciting used imaginatively, smocked, stitched with ribbons, sequins or chain stitch embroidery etc.

BEADS: Sew beads on individually, or close together in infilled designs, or in little ropes or tassels or loops. (See also page 97)

Lacquered wood beads can be combined with wool embroidery.

Beaded or sequinned fabric
As this is costly, work from a carefully adjusted basic fitting pattern or make a muslin toile first, for a perfect garment fit before cutting out in the fabric. Unpick the sequins from seam allowance and stitchline and finish edges with shaped facings.

Rolled hem
For a finely finished edge on sheer material, use a handstitched rolled hem:

1 Straight machine stitch or hand running stitch about 0.75cm. ($\frac{1}{4}$in.) from the raw edge. Trim away close to the stitch line.

2 Roll over the material edge by hand a little at a time, and tiny hem, slip hem or whipstitch (the latter overedge). Repeat for all the rolled hem edge.

Fringe

Fringe may be made by drawing threads out from the raw edge of plain woven fabric, such as coarse woven wool, linen or rayon, and hemstitching the fabric edge, or at least stay stitching it. A simple way of making a separate woollen fringe from your own spare knitting wool or other yarn, is to make a *knotted fringe* round the edges of a finished hem. (See opposite.)

Fringe of every kind can be bought ready made, from deep, glamorous wool fringe for a mohair winter cape, to tufted white cotton fringe to stitch round a towelling beach tunic. Explore the trimmings section in the haberdashery department. You will find long, short, fancy, simple versions . . . fringe with bobbles, tassels, cords . . . silky lampshade fringe. Don't be inhibited about whether it was intended for furnishing or dressmaking, though do check that it can be laundered or cleaned when attaching it.

SEWING ON FRINGE: The commercial variety of fringe usually has a braided edge, or looped machined-across edge. To sew it on the garment, *finish the hem first*, narrowly, so that the stitch line won't show above the fringe. Fringe can be topstitched on a faced or lined edge with no hem.

FOR BRAIDED FRINGE: Place the braided edge, right side out, on top of the right side of the hemmed edge. Begin at one corner, preferably by a seam, and working with the garment level on the work table, pin the fringe all the way along the edge. Mitre the corner, and continue along the next side. Turn under the ends of the fringe braid at the end of a seam, and machine them, when stitching with the rest of the stitch line. If they are being joined half way along a seam, turn under one end, and overlap it onto the other, and machine and hand finish if necessary.

TO SEW ON FRINGE: When pinned, tack, carefully avoiding any wavy joins, and keeping fringe and garment edge flat together, and neat at the corners and joins. Remove the pins and machine straight stitch all round. A single row of stitching will be enough for narrow braid, but machine wide fringe braid along both edges. Zig-zag or other stitches can be used. *For looped braid:* Attach in the same way as for braided fringe, but on the wrong side of the finished hem. Machine topstitch from the right side, for a good appearance to the stitch line.

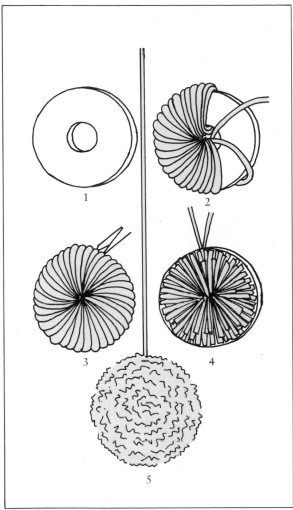

TO MAKE A TASSEL: Have cardboard; wool or embroidery thread, a needle and scissors.

1 Measure and cut a rectangle of cardboard to the overall depth of the tassel. Wind wool or other yarn over and over the card.

2 Pass a threaded needle under the top of the wound wool, and take several stitches over and over it, leaving long ends. Tie off these ends tightly.

3 Snip along the lower edge of the tassel. Remove the cardboard.

4 Wind thread round the tassel below the top, and trim the tassel end.

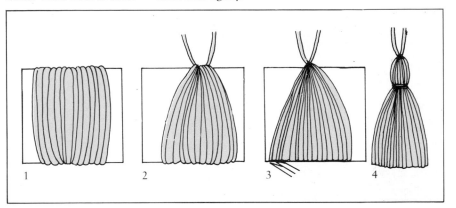

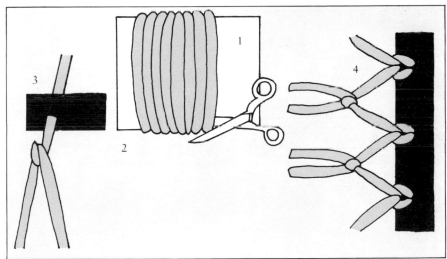

TO MAKE A POM-POM: Have cardboard; a compass or round object such as a jar, the size required for the pom-pom circle; a felt tip pen; paper scissors. Wool; wool needle.

1 Draw two circles on cardboard to the size required for the pom-pom. Make a smaller circle in the centre of each larger one. Cut out round the inner and outer circles.

2 Place the cardboard rings together. Thread a wool needle with wool and begin to wind the wool over the rings, through the centre holes evenly all round. Repeat.

3 When the rings are filled, carefully snip the wool between the edges of the two cards round the outside.

4 Wind a length of wool tightly round between the cardboard rings, and knot tightly, leaving two long ends for the string.

5 Cut away the card, and you will have a wool bobble. Trim away any uneven strands on the outside.

TO MAKE KNOTTED FRINGE: Materials: A strip of card cut to the depth fringe required. An awl or steel knitting needle. A crochet hook. Wool or yarn.

1 Wind the wool or yarn round the card as for a tassel, and count the number of turns, so each knot in the fringe has the same number of strands, say four strands each knot.

2 Cut the lower end of the fringe on the card. Remove the wool folded.

3 Pierce a hole through the finished hem with the awl or knitting needle, or the point of your scissors. Push the crochet hook through from the wrong side, and hook the folded loop end of the wool through.

4 Pass the cut ends of the wool through this loop, and draw it up to rest on the fabric edge neatly, the ends hanging below. Space the loops equally apart along the row, and keep the knots and fringe ends equal sized. The ends can be knotted together to form a continuous looped fringe.

109

The Fur and Leather look

Today's uninhibited do-it-yourself sewing enthusiast is not likely to be deterred by the myths attached to handling some fabrics. Leather? Suede? Real fur? If you would like to try your hand at sewing these and their synthetic counterparts, here are a few general tips which you will find helpful.

TOOLS: To transfer pattern marks onto the reverse side of the skin: use blackboard chalk or a plain tracing wheel; for cutting the leather, flat on a cutting board from the wrong side: a razor blade in a knife holder such as a Stanley knife, and to use with it: a metal ruler. To secure the seams for sewing (skins are not pinned or tacked): Sellotape (or similar) and paper clips or plastic clothes' pegs. For sewing: extra sharp needles changed frequently or glover's wedge-tipped needles; wedge-shaped sewing machine needles, too. (Ask for leather needles.) Use with strong waxed thread, beeswaxed for skin; synthetic thread for synthetic P.V.C. Adhesive for hems and seams: rubber cement, i.e. Copydex, for natural fabrics; all-purpose, i.e. Bostik, for synthetics. To tap glued surfaces in place: the wooden clapper pressing tool, or a hammer or clean clothes brush back, padded, or used over a thin layer of padding.

SKINS: Select skins dyed to match each other: Inspect them for thin places and scruffiness. Pattern: choose a simple design with plain shapes, placed on the best part of the skins, in the direction of the nap. Use a 'with nap' cutting layout.

SEAMS: Single turnings only are required, as vinyl fabrics do not fray, nor do skins. Machine *plain seams* with medium to long straight stitches, and glue back the seam allowances. Overlap *flat fell seams* after lightly gluing and tapping in place. When dry, topstitch down both sides.

HEMS: Make narrow single turned hems, glued in place, and topstitched close to the edge if wished, from the right side. Use straight or zig-zag machine stitches for topstitching. Or cut the edge in a fringe.

BUTTONS AND BUTTONHOLES: Glue a reinforcing patch of calico or leather under the button and sew on through a small button on the underside. Use bound buttonholes. Or punch holes and lace with thongs.

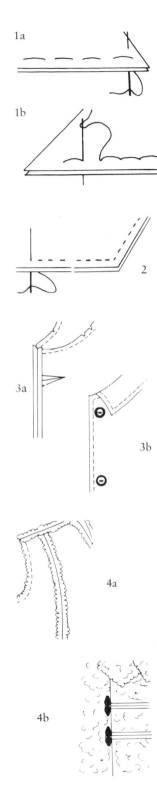

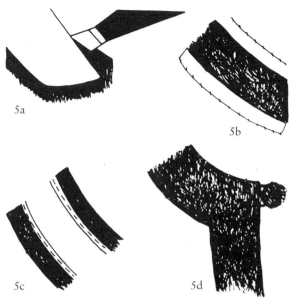

(1) SADDLE STITCH: Long heavy thread running stitch topstitching. Sew running stitches about 0.5cm. or ¼in. long taking the needle and thread through each time. A second saddle stitch row in the spaces can be used for securing leather joins.

(2) STAB STITCH: Tiny running stitch used for sewing sheepskin. Wear your thimble and use waxed button thread and a sharp or glover's needle. Match the two sheepskin edges, fur sides together. Take the needle and thread right through each time.

(3) P.V.C: If available for your sewing machine, use the roller or non-stick presser foot and a long straight stitch for the plain seams. Do not pin or tack P.V.C. fabrics, but use Sellotape, and paper clips or pegs as for leather. Cut darts down the centre, and glue back at the sides. Glue plain seams and hems too, but use suitable materials, *not rubber cement*.

Topstitched edges need only single turnings. CLOTHES: P.V.C. does not give, so have deep raglan sleeves or deep armholes and a roomy pattern. Reinforce easily torn seams which are likely to be pulled with wear, with twill tape. Sew buttons over a reinforcing glued-on patch and button, and use bound or faced buttonholes or buckles and straps; toggles and loops or press fasteners, especially the hammer-on or clip-on type.

(4) FAKE FUR: Fake fur is a most hardy material. Some of the fabric used for infant clothes will survive a punishing existence and constant machine washing.

PATTERN: Fake fur has pile, so use a 'with nap' pattern in a simple design.

CUTTING OUT: Use shears or a cutting tool and ruler with a cutting board as for leather. Plain seams, taped where vulnerable. For knitted fur, do not tape armholes so you retain the built-in stretch. Brush the fur to the right side when you tack the seams. Button loops and frogged fastenings or duffle coat type toggles and loops are easier to make on fake fur than buttonholes.

(5) FUR: (a) Place the fur side down on the cutting board, and chalk the pattern shapes on the skin, taking account of the direction of pile and any patterns in the fur. No seam allowances are needed. Cut along the pattern cutting line carefully, using a razor blade cutting tool and a metal ruler. Flick any loose fur into a newspaper. Place the cut fur edges together and Sellotape

them across to hold them together. Oversew with flat stitches taken across the edges, so the seam is almost invisible on the right side. (b) Face the edges with twill tape. Place the tape and fur side together, and oversew along the edge. Turn the tape onto the skin side, and glue felt on to the skin. (c) Oversew any joins. Line fur with muslin or taffeta, the lining turned-in to neaten and stitched round the tape edges. (d) A muslin lined fur collar can be hemmed to a garment collar round the edges. Link fur by a brocaded or fur button and button loop, or with a brocaded fur hook and eye.

(6) SUEDE PATCHWORK: Cut suede offcuts into patches. Overlap and join with zig-zag machine stitching, for a length of patchwork from which to cut a garment.

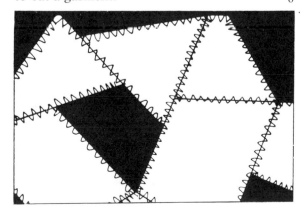

A tailored garment is one (such as a suit, or heavy overcoat), which has not been so much made as 'built', by skilful cutting, interfacing and lining of complicated fabric shapes, and by stitching, steaming and pressing. Here, then, are some helpful tips for those keen to accept the challenge of tailoring.

Materials

Wool, man-made fibres or blends in suit or winter weight; stable double knits; linen. Interfaced mainly with hair or fine canvas, or heavy-duty non-woven interfacing. Tailored garments are usually fully lined.

Seams, darts and stitches

Plain seams, and sometimes flat fell seams and welt seams are used. They can be reinforced with pre-shrunk twill or seam tape. Trim bulk from seam allowances and corners inside collars etc. DARTS: Slash darts in thick fabric down the centre and press open. In interfacing, cut away the dart fold so the sides meet or slightly overlap. Stitch with herringbone or catch stitch, or by seam tape sewn across the join.

Sleeves

Usually two part sleeves sewn in as for set-in sleeves (p. 68). Before joining second seam, tack, try on the sleeve for length, and mark hem fold. Untack the seam and sew a strip of interfacing along the hem on the wrong side, and inside a buttoned overlap, if any.

Shoulder pads

A folded bias strip of wool fabric 15cm. × 7.5cm. (6in. × 3in.) is slip stitched inside the top of the sleeve. Or use bought or made shoulder pads. Avoid too squared an effect unless part of the design.

Roll line

Where the collar and lapels turn over is called the *roll line*. To find this if it is not marked on your pattern, try on the unlined garment with the interfaced under-collar tacked in place, and with someone's help, mark with chalk or pins where the collar and lapels turn over. Separate the under-collar to *pad stitch* inside the *roll line*, holding it over your hand to shape it as you sew. *Pad stitch* lapels. Press over a roll presser.

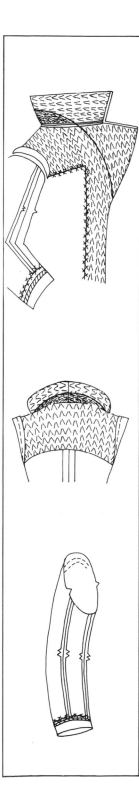

Collar

First method: (a) Place the under collar (made of two halves interfaced and seamed together down the centre) and upper collar together, right sides facing and matching notches. Machine together along the outside edge and down the ends. Trim the corners and seam allowances, turn right side out and press.

(b) Right sides facing and matching notches, sew the under collar onto the garment along the neck edge.

(c) Right sides facing, sew on the made-up garment facing along the top of the lapels and down the sides of the garment front opening, but to the unattached edge of the upper collar. Clip the seam allowance along curved edges. Turn facing right side out and press.

(d) Lift up the facing and slip stitch the under and upper collar together along the neck seam.

Second method: Join the interfaced under collar to the neck edge of the garment, right sides facing. Attach the upper collar to the facing, neck edge right sides facing. Place upper and under collar together right sides facing, and join along the outside edges, then on down the outside edges of the facing. Turn right side out. Clip curved seam allowances. Slip stitch the under and upper collar together along the neck seam as for the first method. Press.

Lining

Attach lining as shown on page 74. Some patterns recommend stitching the lining back shoulder edge onto the garment shoulder seam, and overlapping and hemming the front shoulder edge onto it.

Pressing

In tailoring use tailor's hams, the roll presser, press cloths and steam. Bang the collar and pocket flaps of bulky material during steam pressing, using the wooden clapper.

Vent

TO MAKE A VENT: interface the sides within the fold line as for a hem, and turn back the vent extension over the interfacing. Catch stitch or herringbone in place. Herringbone stitch the overlapped top of the vent, or it may be machined across as for inverted pleats. Turn up the lower edge hem corner as for a tailored hem, or mitre.

HEM CORNER:

1 *Lightweight material:* Turn back the facing raw edge, then the facing onto the hem. Hem down the side and slip hem along the lower edge.

2 *Thick material:* Cut away the hem and interfacing from the corners, leaving about 2.5cm. (1in.) catch stitched onto the inside. Turn back and herringbone stitch the facing raw edge onto the hem, and slip hem the lower edge.

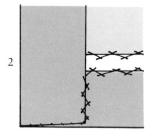

INTERFACING STITCHES: Slanted tacking for large areas; pad stitching for special closer sewn areas. Herringbone or catch stitch for joins which should meet or slightly overlap flat.

SLANTED TACKING:

3 Bring a slanted tacking stitch down to the left, and bring it out a short level stitch to the right, picking up the fabric lightly with the interfacing. Repeat. Reverse for the next row. *Pad stitch:* Shorter, more closely angled slanted tacking.

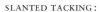

4 ARROWHEAD TACKS: Use silk buttonhole twist.

(a) Bring the needle out lower left and put it in a diagonal stitch up right to the depth of the tack. Take a tiny level stitch to the left and take the needle down a diagonal stitch to the right.

(b) Repeat until the triangular area has been covered with a flat, wigwam shape of satin stitches.

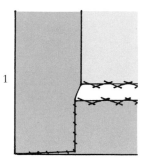

5 CROW'S FOOT TACK: Stitch the three sides of the triangle in turn. Used for reinforcing the top of pleats, and decoration.

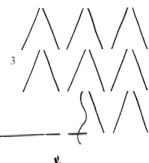

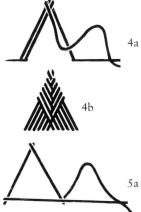

113

Sewing for children

Making clothes and other items for children is one of the great money savers in sewing. It is a splendid way of using a remnant, or left-over fabric pieces from dressmaking.

WHAT SORT OF THINGS CAN YOU SEW FOR CHILDREN? Practically everything they wear, and a good deal for the nursery too; such as cot furnishings or patchwork quilts, or pictures or soft toys.

CHILDREN'S PATTERNS: These begin from a size to fit an infant seven pounds in weight, to the teenage boy and girl with young adult clothes graded to their size and life-style requirements.

Between these two groups come 'toddlers', sizes two to six years, called 'Children's'. Girls' and Boys' is for youngsters aged about seven to twelve, and there is a useful extra size range for eight-and-a-half to fourteen-and-a-half-year old's called 'Chubbie's' or similar names, for the slightly plumper child, a common problem at this age, which gives a lot of clothing troubles.

SUITABLE FABRICS: Easy care fabrics are the ones to go for, for all ages. Frequent laundering is necessary for children's clothes, in view of their active, scrambling, jumping, mud-pie, tree-climbing, bicycling lives, and cleaning bills can be entirely avoided by choosing fabrics and linings which can be machine washed, drip dried, and which are crease-resisting, non-iron.

COMFORTABLE FOR BABIES, TODDLERS (AND OTHERS): Washable knits, stretch terry and plush towelling, cotton jersey, brushed nylon, brushed Courtelle, Celon etc.

FOR TOUGH TREATMENT WITH PRACTICAL VIRTUES: Denim, cotton canvas, drill, calico, twill, cotton gabardine.

COTTON FOR SHIRTS, SMOCKS, DRESSES, BLOUSES: Gingham, printed cotton. Liberty Tana lawn (especially smocked), poplin, voile, lawn, broderie anglaise.

FOR COLDER WEATHER: Needlecord, corduroy, Courtelle, washable double jersey, Viyella, Clydella, Courvella, brushed or woven rayon, such as Sarille or Vincel.

PARTY CLOTHES: Many of those above (party wear is informal for children too these days), velvet, satin, velveteen.

OUT OF DOORS: Quilted cotton (lined with cotton or Viyella) or quilted nylon, lined with nylon. Wet look or plain P.V.C. Fake fur. Wool cloth. Wool tweed with velvet collars for classic coats. Terylene and quilting.

NIGHTCLOTHES: Viyella, Clydella, brushed nylon, brushed cotton; Cotton and nylon stretch terry; cotton jersey; Winceyette; for dressing gowns: brushed Courtelle, quilted fabric or Teklan. See *safety*.

COLOURS: Children like bright, simple paintbox colours, red, yellow, blue, green. Though black, brown, navy, white and purple – even burgundy and camel colour – look good on them too.

PATTERNS: Checks, polka dots, stripes, plaids, and nursery designs suit children. Also flower or animal prints, or plain material with contrast bands.

DECORATION: Smocking, embroidery, bias binding, embroidered cotton braid, ric-rac, badges and motifs, large and small, and lace trimming.

SEAMS: Seams on children's clothes need to be strong and neat, and comfortable. Choose French seams or double stitched plain seams; flat fell seams; plain seams for thicker fabrics. Overedge or stretch stitch seams for knits.

FASTENINGS: Zippers or hammer-on press fasteners are good for young children, with Velcro as a useful alternative.

SAFETY: Safety is an important consideration for young children's clothes particularly. Draw strings are not advisable, especially round the neck. Rather choose a fixed gathered edge, a collar or an attached hood as a finish. Buttons which a baby could pull off and swallow, or plastic eyes on a toy, should be avoided. Fire-resistant properties, particularly of night-clothes and party clothes made of bunchy net, should be checked. Any fabrics with cotton or flammable fibres should be avoided for nighties. Teklan is flame-resistant material. Insist on flame-retardent fabric wherever possible.

Measuring children

Take the same measurements round the body in the way recommended for adults.

WAIST: Round the natural waist.

CHILDREN: BOYS: Round chest.
GIRLS: Round breast.

BACK WAIST LENGTH: From the knob of bone on the neck to the waist.

HEIGHT: Without shoes, feet level on the floor, stand straight against the wall. Place a ruler level across the top of the head, and mark where it touches the wall.

GIRLS: FINISHED DRESS LENGTH: For sewing also take: shoulder seam; arm length from shoulder to wrist with arm bent; neck, front waist length from collar bones to waist. For a yoked garment with smocking, take width across chest between arms. Allow ease.

BOYS AND TEEN-BOYS: In addition to waist and chest measurements:

Hips (seat): Round widest part.

Neck: Round base of neck.

Neckband size for shirt: Add 1.25cm. ($\frac{1}{2}$in.) ease.

Finished pants length: From waist down outside leg seam.

Toys

Save any fabric for possible stuffed toys or for making a collage appliqué picture for the nursery.

Calico and lining sateen are good for rag dolls. For features, embroider with stranded embroidery silk or soft cotton, or glue on felt shapes. Stitch down for young children.

For toys for children old enough not to try to swallow them, realistic linked glass or plastic eyes can be obtained. Hair on dolls can be made out of knitting wool or raffia.

FOR STUFFING: Kapok, foam plastic chippings, or cut-up old nylons are suitable. Sew children's toys strongly and keep safety in mind.

	TODDLER'S								CHILDREN'S												
Sizes	1		2		3		4		Sizes	2		3		4		5		6		6x	
	in	cm	in	cm	in	cm	in	cm		in	cm	in	cm	in	cm	in	cm	in	cm	in	cm
Breast	20	51	21	53	22	56	23	58	Breast	21	53	22	56	23	58	24	61	25	64	25½	65
Waist	19½	50	20	51	20½	52	21	53	Waist	20	51	20½	52	21	53	21½	55	22	56	22½	57
									Hip	—	—	—	—	24	61	25	64	26	66	26½	67
Approx. Height	31	79	34	87	37	94	41	102	Back waist length	8½	22	9	23	9½	24	10	25,5	10½	27	10¾	27,5

Sewing for men

Once upon a time men would have fainted away at the idea of having their clothes run up on the home sewing machine. They would have shunned flowered shirts, and as for having a suit made from a dressmaker pattern, it would have been unthinkable.

Today as home sewing equipment becomes as wide-ranging as that in a workshop, and with all the aids and advice available, such an improved professional finish can be given to garments, that the possibility of making other than the occasional shirt or pair of pyjamas for men at home is really beginning to be taken seriously, with a correspondingly dramatic improvement and increase in the variety of patterns available to sew for them.

To measure a man

The main body measurement given for a shirt is the neck size; for a suit, the chest size. For the latter especially, you would need a far wider range of measurements, and the points made about measuring yourself apply here too.

Measure

CHEST: across the back and round under the armpits, at the widest part.
WAIST: Round normal waistline.
HIPS: Round the seat.
HIGH HIPS: Round the hip bones below the waist.
NECK: Round the base of the neck, with 1.25cm. (½in.) extra allowed for neckband ease.
ARM: With arm extended and bent at right angles at the elbow, from nape of neck outside arm to wrist.
SLEEVE LENGTH (long sleeve): From shoulder bone to wrist, outside arm bent.
ARM CIRCUMFERENCE: Round bicep, about halfway between the armpit and elbow.
WRIST: Round wrist bone.

Until you get used to what suits a man, and develop the knack of fitting him, make a few of the more simple garments for practice – 'simple' meaning less important garments like shirts or waistcoats, or accessories such as ties, for which less expensive material is at risk.

Making a shirt

A man's sports shirt with short hemmed sleeves and a straight collar is as easy to make as a blouse. A tailored shirt is more detailed and here are some tips for success.

Use any fabric you would usually like for a shirt, from cotton and silk to fine wool or needlecord. Don't use too scratchy a material, and trim away bulk from inside the collar and neckband, and at inner corners.

BUTTON THROUGH SHIRT:

1 Sew an interfaced facing strip onto the right side of the left front opening, as a buttonhole band. (a)

2 Turn and machine a hem down the right hand front opening. Buttons (b) would be sewn down this.

3 Small pleats are usually made at the back where the yoke is attached, by matching black marker spots on the pattern. A fitted shirt may have contour darts or shaped seams, or the shirt may be cut straight or slightly shaped.

4 Two identical yoke shapes are cut out. These are attached with high front-of-shoulder and back-of-shoulder seams. Matching notches, pin the upper back edge of the shirt between the yoke shapes which are placed right sides against the shirt. Pin and tack together across this edge. Remove the pins, and machine through all layers. Remove the tacking. Fold up the yoke. Press and top stitch through all layers close to the seam.

5 The inside yoke is pinned to the shoulder edges of the garment front, right side of yoke to wrong side of shirt. Use a plain seam. Press the seam onto the yoke.

6 Turn under the front shoulder edges of the outside yoke shape, and tack and press. Pin this wrong side against the right side of the shirt fronts, over the stitch line of the inside yoke. Tack and topstitch in place close to the turned edge.

7 Make up the collar and attach it by a neckband to the shirt neck edge, following the pattern instructions. Also see *Making a shirt collar* on page 76.

8 Sew a tab facing in the sleeve above the shirt cuff as shown, or as indicated for your pattern.

9 Pin and tack the top of the sleeve, matching notches, to the armhole seam, which stretches from the front armhole edge, along the yoke raw edge, and along the back armhole edge. Use a flat fell seam, unless otherwise indicated.

10 Join the sleeve and shirt side in a continuous flat fell (or other) seam from wrist to lower edge.

11 Attach the cuff as shown here. If the cuff is cut to the same shape, but twice the depth, and buttonholes are sewn to correspond through all layers with the cuff turned back, the cuff can be worn with cuff links.

12 Make up and sew on the shirt pocket as directed for your pattern.

13 Sew buttons on the front hem and cuffs, and buttonholes to correspond. The buttonholes in the neckband and cuffs should be horizontal; in the front hem, vertical.

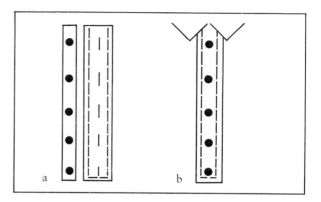

PLACKET

A tab facing for a placket is used for sleeve openings in shirts or tailored blouses.

1 Mark the tab opening. Machine stay stitch the sides and top, then snip the cut as shown.

2 Pin the two placket strips to the sides of the cut, *right side* against *wrong side*. Tack. Remove pins. Machine outside the stay stitch lines. Remove tacking.

3 Fold smaller strip through the slash onto the right side. Fold under, and machine close to edge.

4 Fold tab strip onto the right side. Turn in raw edges of tab and detached side. Tack in place. Machine the tab along this side and the sides of the top point, close to the edge. Repeat at the folded edge but when you reach the horizontal line placement, fully overlap the two sides, and continue to machine through all layers. Press, and machine across. Repeat for the second sleeve, but with the pointed tab at the left.

5 Attach a buttoned cuff.

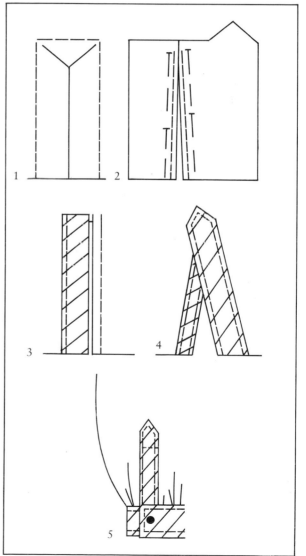

Renovations

Small items of clothing can be salvaged from the good fabric of a discarded adult garment. Such material can also be used for making accessories: a hat, a shoulder bag, a waistcoat. Replace a dull or worn part with new contrasting material. A new yoke, a different neckline, braid, pockets, buttons, a fresh collar and cuffs – all can work wonders in giving new life to a tired garment. Bear in mind when mixing and matching fabrics, old with new, to use similar fibres and thickness of material – and make sure they are compatible as regards dry-cleaning or laundering.

Begin by having the garment cleaned or laundered. Unpick the part to be replaced, or the entire garment stitch by stitch, the hem, darts, seams, tucks, pleats, etc. Press the material then select the best parts for the new pattern or decide on the partial renovations you would like.

Save zippers, buttons, hooks, eyes, press fasteners, but do use new lining, seam binding and tape.

For a new pattern: Place the pattern pieces on the material and cut out in the usual way, mixing in any contrast fabric if you need extra. The straight grain of fabric placement still applies. You can check this by the direction of the weave or knit in the fabric.

For partial changes: Use the original garment for the pattern, drawn on paper, with allowances for seams, darts etc. and any design alterations taken care of.

When altering a hem length: Always unpick the old hem completely. Remove any threads. Brush and press.

To lengthen: Face the edge. Or deepen with a lined facing or cuff of pleats or a ruffle etc.

To shorten: Mark the hem turning from the floor as you would for a hem on a new garment. Trim the hem allowance below and proceed as for a new hem.

TO SHORTEN OR LENGTHEN A BORDER PRINTED GARMENT OR ONE WITH A SHAPED LOWER EDGE, SUCH AS SCALLOPS: Make an extra seam on the garment as for a real seam (say for a bodice or yoke), and shorten or lengthen here. Take up at the waist or yoke seam. Or sew in decorative tucks, perhaps with a lace trimming.

For lengthening above the hem: Inset a decorative border, or lace insertion or a panel of different fabric.

1 ZIPPER: Replace a broken zipper by unpicking the stitches of the lining first, and part of the seam above and below, then the zipper stitches. Remove the broken zipper. Take out all threads with tweezers. Press the zipper opening and sew a new zipper into it following the original insertion. Sew back the lining. Press.

2 ELASTIC: Replace worn elastic by unpicking it with the seam ripper, and tweezer out the thread ends. Press where unpicked. Cut a new length of elastic for the old, plus end turnings. Place the end of the elastic at one seam. Pin the half-way fold to the opposite seam, and the other elastic end by the first. Anchor in between with pins, so the elastic will be evenly distributed round the edge when sewn. Set machine for elastic stretch stitch: multi zig-zag or with small zig-zag or straight stitches. Overlap and sew elastic ends together first. Take hold of the elastic and the edge of the garment underneath, and proceed to machine them together, stretching the elastic and removing the pins as you go. (For the anorak here, the elastic would be joined to the zipper tapes, and have the lining sewn over it afterwards.)

3 DARNS: Darns can be made by machine by random length rows of straight stitching, taken to and fro across the worn area. Or use the darner attachment, for free-motion darning, following your machine instruction book. A *hand-sewn darn*:

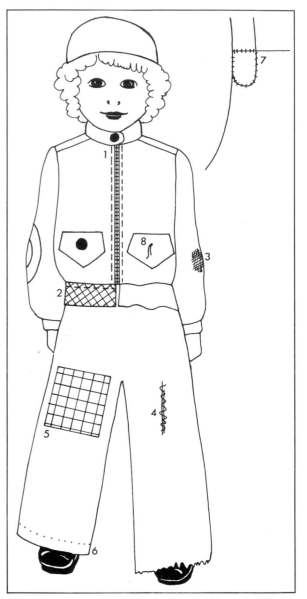

Thread wool or yarn in a darning needle. Hold a darning mushroom, with the part to be darned stretched firmly over it. Sew running stitches towards the darn area or trimmed hole, and take the thread across and for a few running stitches on the other side. Turn round and repeat from the opposite direction. Repeat until the hole is covered with threads. Now work across the darn at right angles to these threads, weaving the new threads in and out, and anchoring them at each side with flat running stitch. Weave in the thread end to finish. Press. The darn should look like neat plain weaving.

4 TEAR: Join a tear, after trimming the torn edges, by pinning the sides together over some thin backing fabric. Use stretch fabric and stretch stitch to mend stretch tears. Machine or running stitch to and fro across the tear along its length. Press.

5 PATCH: Trim away the torn, worn area to form a square or other tidy shape. Cut a piece of fabric to fit, plus seam allowances. Match any plaid and stripe patterns with the garment. Turn in and tack the patch raw edges, and place over the hole patch right side facing hole wrong side. Pin, tack and zig-zag, overedge or straight stitch along the sides. Turn the garment right side out. Turn under the raw edges of the garment onto the patch. Handstitch or machine in place. Or use a decorative fabric and make a feature out of the patch . . . such as an appliqué shape or fake pocket on the garment right side.

6 HEM: See opposite. Tape the inside of trousers' hems when they have to stand up to sturdy kicking about.

7 TAPE: To sew a new tape on an apron, unpick the old one and tweezer out any threads left. Cut new tape to the correct length, turn in the raw end and pin it to the wrong side of the garment in place of the former tape. Machine along the edges and across. Or hem in place by hand, and turn the tape back and oversew the folded edge to the garment edge on the right side.

8 BUTTON: Sew on a button of course!

Making a loose cover

Making a loose cover is not as difficult as might appear. The amount of material needed to cover an armchair may be formidable, but the cost of having the cover made professionally is even more.

MATERIALS REQUIRED:
Pattern: Large sheets of newspaper, brown paper or dressmakers' squared paper. A ruler; tape measure; upholstery pins; felt-tip pen or crayon or coloured tailor's chalk; large sheets of letter or drawing paper.
To make a fabric block pattern: a similar amount of calico to the material needed for the loose cover.
Loose cover: Fabric as required; strong thread; tacking thread; piping cord if used; Velcro, press fastener or hook and eye tape, or a furnishing zipper for the loose cover and each cushion, for an opening down one seam in each case. Pre-shrink all materials and cording.

1 First make a diagram with measurements, to enable you, preferably with the drapery assistant's help, to decide how much fabric you will need. Draw a very rough sketch of the chair (or other piece of furniture) and fill in the measurements from side to side and down the length. Allow any extra required for seams, hems and other fittings, and 11cm. (5in.) extra on all sides for tucking in the loose cover round the seat. Do the same for any cushion. Also, measure any seams where you wish to include corded piping to assess the length of cord required. Measure the length of seam openings for any Velcro or other fastening needed.
2 Draw shapes from your diagram full size onto the sheets of paper, plus seam and other allowances required. Write the name of each piece, and which is the top. Cut out.
3 Fit the paper pieces over the chair and draw where each seam runs. (Don't forget to leave the extra for tucking in round the seat, both along the inside back and sides round the seat shape.)
4 If you feel experienced enough to do so, you could go straight on to cut out the main material from this pattern. (Some wizards can even work direct with the material on the chair!) A safer way is first to make a fabric pattern in calico. Cut the paper shapes out in this material then make as perfect a block pattern as you can by fastening the calico shapes in the appropriate position on the chair, using upholstery pins to keep them in place. Work from the inside back seat tuck-in – up, over, then down the back, then forward down the front. Take the next stage over the arms, and end up with the panels which go down the front of the padded arms, and along the sides and front. Gathered or pleated frills may also be added round the loose cover lower edge. Allow extra material for this. Draw the outlines of any alterations on the calico, and mark each piece by name, and at the top. When you remove the calico shapes, add seam allowances etc. and tuck-in amounts, before shaping the pieces tidily. Double check the measurements are right, then pin this calico shape along the furnishing fabric length, roughly at first to make sure you have enough material (if you have too little you may have to replace the reverse side of a cushion with lining material).
5 When you are satisfied all is well, pin the calico pattern shapes along the fabric and cut out carefully. Label each piece, and mark the top in each case.
6 Unless a piece of furniture is unequal sided, pin the cover together wrong side out over the chair. Do the same with the cushion. When you have done this, you can measure the exact amount of piping cord you will need. Pipe all the seams, except for the ones to be tucked in. To do this, cut out bias strips for the corded piping, measuring about 7.5cm. (3in.) wide and joined together until the length required is obtained. Make up corded piping as shown on page 75, using the machine zipper foot.
7 Mark the position of the seamlines on the pinned-together cover, and pin gathers and darts roughly in place wherever they occur. Mark each end of any gathered area along a seam, such as round the front of the arms, or the curved top back of the chair.
8 Unpin the cover, Sew any gathering lines between the markers and any finished darts. Pin the corded piping stitch line exactly on the stitch line of a single thickness wherever required, with the cording lying inside the stitch line. Machine in place using the zipper foot close into the cording, and stretching the piping evenly along the material as you go, avoiding puckering or bumpiness in the cord.
9 Repin the gathered, darted and corded shapes together with care, and tack where pinned, leaving open the seams. Remove the pins and try the cover on the chair and cushion/s. Adjust carefully, with the openings over-lapped and pinned while you check the fit. When everything is fitted to your satisfaction, unpin the openings, remove the cover and machine the seams, using the zipper foot taken right into the cord.
10 Pin the Velcro or other fastening to the under- and over-laps of the seam opening, and pin, tack and machine in place. Turn narrow hems along the lower edges, and machine.
Check that all pins have been removed, and press.

Home sewing 17

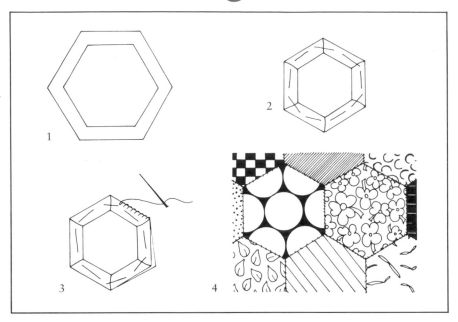

1   2

3   4

Patchwork

Patchwork is a practical and very beautiful way of using oddments of fabric. The patches are cut out following geometric shaped patterns called 'templates'. These templates are inexpensive and give you a perfect shape. They come in various basic shapes and sizes: the diamond; the square; the church window; the curved shell etc. Templates come in two parts: the smaller solid metal template is the replica of the finished patch and is used for cutting out the paper patch patterns. The larger 'window template' is for cutting out the fabric shape, and includes allowances for turning in the raw edges of the material. The window centre is the same size and shape as the matching metal template, and is transparent for centring the template over a design in the fabric. It is best to use similar types of material for a piece of patchwork, such as all cotton or all silk, all needlecord, or all velvet for even results, and easy cleaning.

Machined patchwork

The patches may be finely zig-zag stitched together instead of using hand oversewing, or may be tacked together, pressed, then machined along the joins from the right side using machine embroidery or zig-zag stitches.

Quilting

English quilting, the method given here, is lining and interlining material and stitching through all the layers in patterns. Sometimes quilting has added padding. It may also be corded and embroidered.

TRANSFERRING THE DESIGN: Measure and mark out the quilting design on the fabric right side, using tailor's chalk supplemented by tacking thread guidelines. Or using a tracing or your own design for a single motif, repeat this motif inside boxes, bands or diamond quilting lines, or as a free design.

    This can be transferred onto the lining and the quilting stitched from underneath, or when the three layers are tacked together, traced from below with tacking guidelines, then stitched from the right side. Best of all, punch small holes round the paper pattern of the design, and stencil through it onto the quilting surface with tailor's chalk. Complete the lines with chalk, then with tacking.

1 Place the metal template on brown paper and draw round it. Cut out the number of patches required. Centre the window template over a design in the material, and using tailor's chalk, draw round it. Cut out. Repeat for all the patches.

2 Pin the brown paper patterns onto the wrong side of the fabric shapes, equalising the seam allowance all round. Turn back the patch edges, press and tack to the paper.

3 Using a fine needle and thread, oversew two patches together right sides

facing along one edge. Repeat for other sides with fresh patches.

4 When complete, remove the tacking and brown paper patterns. Press. Line, and interline if wished or face the edges.

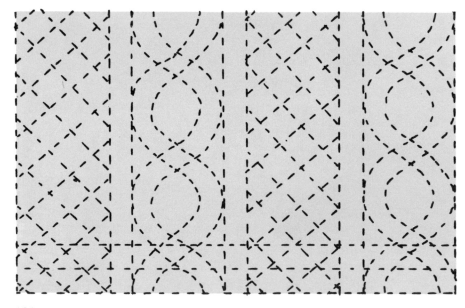

QUILTING: Cut out and pin the material to be quilted in layers, the quilting lines already marked on the right side, or underside of the lining, depending on the method chosen. Add wadding if wished, between the material and lining.

SEW: Hand sew with strong fine sewing thread and a fine strong needle. Sew with tiny running stitch, following the method for stab stitch, or with backstitch or chain stitch, through all layers following the design lines.

A padded quilt sewn by machine

1 Layers of quilting are tacked together: the cover, Terylene fleece padding and the lining. For unpadded quilting, flannelette, Winceyette or flannel are all suitable interlinings.

2 The fabric is measured and marked on the right side with the design chosen: squares, diamonds, bands, ornament, using tailor's chalk and a ruler. The layers are then placed together right side of lining and cover facing, wadding on top and pinned, tacked and machined together round the edges leaving an opening for turning right side out. Next the quilt is turned right side out ready for quilting and the design tacked round where marked.

3 The guidelines are followed by hand stitching through all layers, using running stitch, back stitch or chain stitch or:

4 FOR MACHINE QUILTING: Attach the quilting presser foot to the machine. The extended arm should be adjusted to the last stitch line to retain a parallel space between it and the present stitch line. Or use a zipper foot. You can use zig-zag or embroidery stitch lines as well as straight stitching.

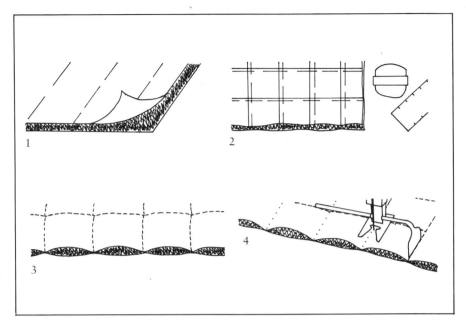

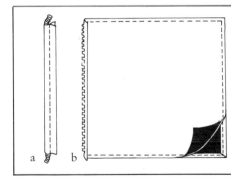

MAKING A CUSHION AND CUSHION COVER

Cushions are a discreet way of providing a room with an attractive flash of colour without committing to it in the room's permanent colour scheme. They are simple to make, and invaluable for using up odd pieces of material too large for the scrapbag, too small for clothes.

1 A basic cushion is made out of two matching shapes, possibly with a side panel, using strong mattress ticking or down-proof cotton cambric. Cotton sateen can be used for fleece.
Method: Make a paper pattern for the shapes plus seam allowances as before and cut out the front and back in the fabric chosen. Place the material shapes together, right sides facing, and pin and tack together round the sides, leaving an opening in the seam for turning the cushion right side out for stuffing. Remove the pins and machine. Remove the tacking. Press.

2 Turn the cover right side out. Stuff firmly with Terylene or Dacron fleece, and oversew the opening to close. Down should only be used in a downproof cover.

3 CUSHION COVER: Cut out two shapes to the same measurements as the cushion shapes with seam allowances. Sew any decoration onto the cushion front, on the right side at this stage. In the example, cotton print primrose petals and green leaves are appliquéd on black sateen.

4 Make corded piping to the length of the four sides of the cushion. (a) Stitch the corded piping round the four sides of the cushion cover front, raw edges matching, and corners mitred. Sew the piping in place using the zipper foot on the machine.

5 Place the cushion cover shapes together, right sides facing, and pin and tack them along three sides. Remove pins. (b) Machine close into the cording and remove tacking. Sew the zipper into the open side, open, with the tapes stitched to each edge. Turn right side out. Press. Pull the cushion cover onto the cushion; close zipper. (c)

121

Curtains

Sooner or later making some curtains, for a window, or a dressing table, or a shower, is almost certain to crop up, and you won't always want to have them made professionally. Fortunately, they are not difficult to make. Only large!

Unlined curtains

MEASURING: For any curtains, the first job will be to measure the window in order to calculate the required amount of curtain fabric, lining and curtain tape (if used). Take into account the length, the number of curtains, the fullness, the depth of hem turnings and ruffles, or of a plain pelmet and its interfacing.

The unlined curtains shown here are sill length, with the top hems forming a casing and hung on a spring rod, hooked on to metal eyelets, at either side of the window frame, with a ruffled frill instead of a pelmet, slotted through its hem casing on to a fixed rod across the top of the window.

Curtains like these are attractive made in cotton, sprigged, sheer, checked, or striped.

FOR MEASURING; Use a metre- or yardstick; a tape measure, notebook and pencil. Draw a rough sketch of the window, and standing on steps, hold up the metre- or yardstick to measure the length and width, taking the outside amounts to the distance you wish for the curtain's finished size – either inner or outer edge of the window aperture; or from the top of the sill, or longer, to the floor if wished.

Note these measurements beside your sketch. They will help the shop assistant work out how much material you will need for the curtains you have in mind. The amount will take into account:

(a) Curtain length plus hem and top and side turnings.

(b) Curtain width, the fullness related to the weight of the fabric, three or four times as wide for sheer, twice as wide for medium weight, one and a half times for heavy weight. The type of curtain tape chosen may affect the width required.

(c) The depth and width material needed for the pelmet or frill.

(d) Any extra for the pattern repeat, which could be as much as 64cm. to 77cm. (25in. to 30in.) deep.

(e) Any extra amount needed for drapes and swags and matching accessories.

(f) The amount of lining, if used.

All this added together and worked out in terms of the woven width of the fabric, to get the best value from the length. In addition, the amount and type of curtain tape required will need to be calculated. Though intended basically to finish the top hem of the curtains and provide loops for hooks needed to hang the curtain from the glide rail, it is also designed in a variety of styles for pleating or gathering the curtain folds decoratively and elegantly. (See maker's instructions.)

Any braid, fringe, curtain rings, pelmet interfacing, interlining, weights for heavy curtains, and pelmet press studs, can be bought at the same time.

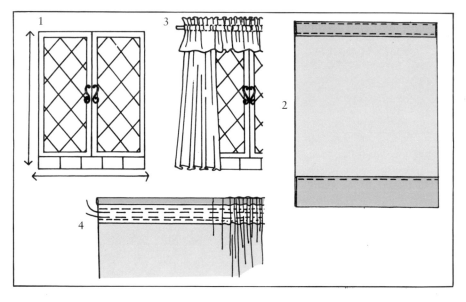

TO MAKE UNLINED CURTAINS: If the fabric is wide enough for a curtain to be cut from a single width, no seams are necessary. For extra fullness, another curtain width halved down the length, or used in full, depending on the fabric thickness, will need to be seamed to the first. Use plain or French seams.

1 Measure window; cut-out curtains.

2 Turn up a hem at the lower edge 6cm. (2½in.). Machine or slip hem. Make a 4cm (1½in.) hem at the top edge. Machine stitch close to both edges. (Vary this width depending on the type of rod or rail used, or if ruffled.)

3 FRILL: Turn, prepare and machine a 2cm. (¾in.) hem along the lower edge (or as desired) on a frill strip 2 to 2½ times the width of the window. Turn, prepare and machine an 8cm. (3in.) deep hem along the frill upper edge. Machine the hem close to the edge, and 4cm. (1½in.) above for the rod casing. Press.

4 Or sew on curtain tapes over a single hem turning.

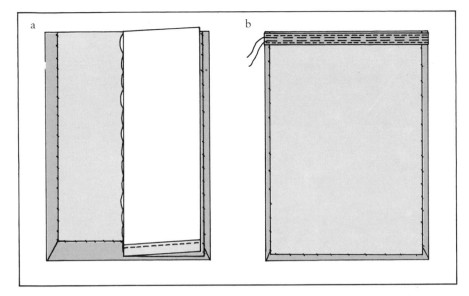

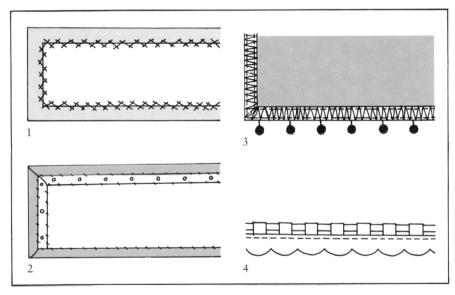

Lined curtains

Lined curtains are measured in the same way as unlined curtains, but with deeper hem allowances. Lining fabric, usually cotton sateen, is woven narrower than the curtain material, to allow for the sides of the curtain to be faced onto the wrong side a short distance at either side, for a good appearance. Ask about shrinkage, and the dye-fast qualities of the fabric when buying. These are important considerations.

TO MAKE LINED CURTAINS: Work out the length of curtains, including 5cm. (2in.) turning to go under the tape at the top, and a 7cm. to 8cm. (2½in. to 3in.) single hem turning at the lower edge. Cut number of widths of material (including half widths) required to make up the fullness. Cut lining about 5cm. (2in.) shorter, to fit 2cm. (1in.) inside the finished width.

Spread out a sheet, or cutting boards side by side, on the floor. Spread the curtain material out over it wrong side up. Pin and tack any widths to be joined together (take account of the direction of pile for velvet, remember), remove the pins and machine. Repeat for the lining.

Turn in the curtain sides onto the wrong side of the curtain to about 4cm. (1½in.). Slip hem.

Turn up hem at lower edge, mitred at corner, or with a neat, straight turning to form an L shape at the corner. Slip hem to curtain and at corner. Sew covered weights inside the hem if wished. Hem the lining too.

Spread the lining over the curtain, wrong sides facing, and smooth together (a). Turn in the right selvage of the lining and pin it to the curtain side turning, from the top down. Tack. Remove pins. Hem to the curtain where tacked. Remove the tacking.

Starting from the top, fold the lining onto the curtain wrong side for part of the way across. Smooth them together. Attach lining to curtain – invisibly by long stitches caught with small stitches between. Repeat for parallel stitch lines across curtain to other side.

Turn over the other lining selvage (b), and pin to the other turned-in side of the curtain. Tack and hem as before, about an inch from the edge. Make a single turning along the upper edge and sew on pleated tape along both edges, by hand or preferably machine. Draw strings to desired fullness. Turn up a 7cm. (3in.) seam at lower edge and slip hem lining to curtain.

Pelmet

1 Measure the pelmet strip plus turnings, and the interfacing: buckram, heavy duty canvas or non-woven interfacing. Turn pelmet edges onto interfacing. Pin. Tack. Remove pins. Catch or herringbone stitch in place.

2 Cut the lining to fit the pelmet, plus seam allowances. Turn in the raw edges, and pin, tack and hem to the pelmet all round. Sew press fastener pelmet or upholstery tape to the top and sides. (The other side of the fastening is tacked to the pelmet above the window.)

3 A pelmet edged with flat and bobble braid, machined in place.

4 A scalloped pelmet with faced loops strips, folded over and hemmed to the wrong side.

Cotton: Use silk, mercerised or cotton thread (C. = continental machine needle size).

Note: On Elna sewing machines 4 stitch length settings range from 6 to 20 to the inch, or from 2 to 8 to the cm.

Name	Description	Lining	Interfacing	Needles	Thread	Machine stitches to inch	Length in mm.
Batiste	Thin handkerchief cotton lawn. Used for robes, nighties, baby gowns, blouses.	Lawn, silk	Organdie, taffeta transparent Iron-on Vilene	Machine: 11 or C. 70 Hand: fine	50	12–15	1.7–2.1
Calico	Coarse, unbleached cream or white cotton. For jackets, trousers etc.	Usually unlined but sometimes lawn or taffeta	Firm Iron-on or medium Sew-in Vilene or taffeta	Machine: 14–16 C. 90–100 Hand: strong	20–36	6–10	2.5–4.3
Canvas	Plain woven fine to coarse. Used for sailing tops, beach shorts etc. Coarse canvas used for interfacing.	Usually unlined. Lawn for some skirts	Firm Iron-on or medium Sew-in Vilene	Machine: 14–16–18 C. 90–100–110 Hand: strong	20–40	6–10	2.5–4.3
Cheese-cloth	Fine, semi-sheer, crêpe-like cotton fabric. Pre-shrink. Also nylon cheesecloth.	Usually unlined. Lawn if any	Soft Iron-on Vilene or light Sew-in Vilene or cotton	Machine: 11 C. 70 Hand: fine	50	12–15	1.7or 2.1
Cotton	Crisp, plain woven matt fabric, usually washes well and is fairly inexpensive.	Usually unlined. Lawn if any	Soft Sew-in Vilene or soft Iron-on Vilene or taffeta	Machine: 14 C. 90 Hand: medium	40	10–12	2.1–2.5
Cotton gaberdine	Twill-woven close textured cloth.	Lawn, taffeta	Firm Iron-on or medium Sew-in Vilene	Machine: 14–16 C. 90–100 Hand: strong–medium	40	10–12	2.1–2.5
Cotton jersey	Fine stretch knit *usually stretch one way only*.	Usually unlined. Sometimes bonded	Superdrape Vilene	Machine: 14 C. 90 Hand: medium–fine	40	10–12	2.1–2.5
Cotton satin	Satin weave cotton with a dull sheen.	Lawn, taffeta	Soft Sew-in or Iron-on Vilene	Machine: 14 C. 90 Hand: fine–medium	40	10–12	2.1–2.5
Corduroy	Ribbed cotton velveteen. Hard-wearing. Various ribs, thickness.	Cotton, lawn, rayon, satin, taffeta or unlined	Heavy Sew-in Vilene	Machine: 14–16 coarse: 18 C. 90–100–110 Hand: medium or strong	20 to 40	6–10	2.5–4.3
Denim	Coarse jeans cotton with slight speckle. Finer silkier denim types.	Usually unlined but an adult's skirt may be lined	Firm Iron-on or medium Sew-in Vilene	Machine: 14–16 C. 90–100	36–40 cotton thread	6–10	2.5–4.3
Drill	Twill cotton.	Usually unlined. Possibly taffeta to line a woman's skirt	Firm Iron-on or medium Sew-in Vilene	Machine: 14–16 C. 90–100 Hand: medium or strong	36–40 cotton thread	6–10	2.5–4.3

Name	Description	Lining	Interfacing	Needles	Thread	Machine stitches to inch	Length in mm.
Flannelette (Wincey-ette)	Woven cotton fleecy-backed pyjama fabric.	Unlined	Usually none	Machine: 14 C. 90 Hand: fine to medium	36–40	8–10	2.1–4.3
Gingham	Medium cotton in popular check weave.	Unlined or lawn	Taffeta; or soft Iron-on Vilene; or medium Sew-in Vilene	Machine: 14 C. 90 Hand: fine to medium	40	10–12	2.1–2.5
Lace	Netted, fancy patterned or embroidered cotton, fine to coarse. Also other fibres. Crochet cotton lace: crochet look coarse lace.	Lawn; Jap silk; taffeta; organza	Organdie; taffeta; or transparent Iron-on Vilene	Machine: 11–14 C. 70–90 Hand: fine to medium	40–50 Coarse: cotton 36	10–12–15–20	1.3–1.7–2.1 2.5
Lawn	Fine plain woven cotton (and in other fibres).	Lawn; silk; taffeta	Taffeta; transparent Iron-on Vilene	Machine: 11 C. 70 Hand: fine	50	12–15	1.3–1.7
Madras	Indian plain woven cotton in dull dyed vegetable shades: blue, rust, brown, mustard, green. Typical multistripes and patterns. Not always crease resisting.	Unlined or cotton	Soft Iron-on Vilene or soft Sew-in Vilene; or taffeta	Machine: 11–14 C. 70–90 Hand: fine–medium	50 or 40	10–15	1.3–2.1
Muslin	Plain woven cotton, usually fine, and sheer. Dotted muslin is woven over with small spots.	Lawn	Transparent Iron-on Vilene; taffeta; organdie	Machine: 11 C. 70 Hand: fine	50	12–15	1.3–1.7
Needle-cord	Narrow rib very fine corduroy.	Usually unlined or lawn, cotton or taffeta	Medium Sew-in Vilene or taffeta	Machine: 14 C. 90 Hand: medium	40	10–12	2.1–2.5
Net	Fine net fabric. Choose flame-retardant.	Taffeta; satin	Organdie; transparent Iron-on Vilene	Machine: 11 C. 70 Hand: fine	50	12–15	1.7–2.1
Organdie	Fine, sheer cotton plain woven, matt, and crisp.	Lawn; Jap silk; taffeta; satin	Taffeta; transparent Iron-on or light Sew-in Vilene	Machine: 11 C. 70 Hand: fine	50	12–15	1.7–2.1
Piqué	Fine ribbed cotton, or with basket weave and other raised surface pattern. Crisp, fresh look.	Taffeta; lawn	Taffeta; soft Iron-on or soft Sew-in Vilene	Machine: 14 C. 90 Hand: medium	40	10–12	2.1–2.5
Poplin	Plain weave closely woven cotton with a smooth, slightly silky surface. Presses and handles well.	Lawn	Taffeta; soft Iron-on or soft Sew-in Vilene	Machine: 14 C. 90 Hand: medium	40	10–12	2.1–2.5

Name	Description	Lining	Interfacing	Needles	Thread	Machine stitches to inch	Length in mm.
Plush	Coarse, furry velvet, with brisk feel to the pile.	Crêpe de chine; satin; taffeta; cotton	Taffeta; medium Sew-in Vilene	Machine: 14–16 C. 90–100 Hand: medium to strong	36–40	6–10	2.5–4.3
Plissé	Fine plain woven cotton with crinkled bands, similar to seersucker.	Unlined or lawn	Taffeta; soft Iron-on or soft Sew-in Vilene	Machine: 14 C. 90 Hand: fine to medium	40	10–12	2.1–2.5
Quilting	Ready made cotton quilting fabric, printed or plain. In other fabrics and fibres, lined taffeta, satin, also nylon.	Cotton: flannel; flannelette; lawn	Medium Sew-in Vilene	Machine: 16 C. 100 Hand: medium to strong	20–36 cotton thread or mercerised 40	6–10	2.5–4.3
Sailcloth	Plain, strong rather stiff cotton.	Unlined or lawn, cotton. Quilting for anoraks.	Taffeta; or firm Iron-on or medium Sew-in Vilene	Machine: 16 C. 100 Hand: strong	20–36 cotton or button thread	6–10	2.5–4.3
Sateen	Satin weave cotton, strong with dull lustre.	Taffeta	Soft Sew-in or soft Iron-on Vilene	Machine: 14–16 C. 90–100 Hand: medium to strong	36–40	6–10	2.5–4.3
Seersucker	Fine crinkled cotton. Also in other fibres.	Unlined or lawn	Taffeta; soft Sew-in or soft Iron-on Vilene	Machine: 11–14 C. 70–90 Hand: fine–medium	50–40	12–15	1.7–2.1
Ticking	Tough closely woven cotton with navy or black stripes.	Unlined or lawn	Firm Iron-on or medium Sew-in Vilene	Machine: 16 C. 100 Hand: strong	36 cotton thread	6–10	2.5–4.3
Towelling	Woven (or* knitted terry) with loops over surface, varying in closeness. Single- or double-sided towelling.	Unlined	Medium Sew-in Vilene; calico	Machine: 16 C. 100 Hand: strong	36 cotton thread (or mercerised 40 for stretch terry)	6–10	2.5–4.3

*Knitted terry is usually made of synthetic or cotton and nylon mixtures. See synthetic materials.

Name	Description	Lining	Interfacing	Needles	Thread	Machine stitches to inch	Length in mm.
Twill	Closely woven fabric with an effect of diagonal fine ribbing in the weave.	Lawn; taffeta	Firm Iron-on or medium Sew-in Vilene; or taffeta	Machine: 14–16 C. 90–100 Hand: medium to strong	40 (36 cotton thread for coarse twill)	6–10	2.5–4.3
Voile	Sheer plain woven summer material. Usually cotton but in other fibres, such as Terylene or Dacron.	Lawn	Transparent Iron-on or light Sew-in Vilene; taffeta (cotton voile only)	Machine: 11 C. 70 Hand: fine	50	12–15	1.7–2.1

Name	Description	Lining	Interfacing	Needles	Thread	Machine stitches to inch	Length in mm.
Velveteen	Cotton pile rather non-lustrous velvet cloth.	Lawn; cotton; taffeta; satin; crêpe de chine; brocade	Taffeta; medium Sew-in Vilene	Machine: 14–16 C. 90–100 Hand: medium	36–40	6–10	2.5–4.3
Zephyr	Fine plain woven cotton rather like gingham, often multi-plaid checks.	Lawn; taffeta or unlined	Vilene; soft Sew-in or soft Iron-on; taffeta	Machine: 11–14 C. 70–90 Hand: fine to medium	40–50	12–15	1.7–2.1

Linen: Use mercerised cotton thread (C. = continental machine needle size).

Name	Description	Lining	Interfacing	Needles	Thread	Machine stitches to inch	Length in mm.
Damask	Fine, close woven linen with woven flower and other patterns.	Lawn; taffeta	Firm Iron-on or medium Sew-in Vilene; taffeta	Machine: 11–14 C. 70–90 Hand: fine or medium	40–50	12–15	1.7–2.1
Huckaback	With raised patterns in weave. Used for hand towels.	Lawn; taffeta	Firm Iron-on or medium Sew-in Vilene; taffeta	Machine: 11–14 C. 70–90	40–50	12–15	1.7–2.1
Linen	Plain woven fabric made from flax fibres. Often blended with other fibres. Matt. Fine to coarse. Many linen-type fabrics in other fibres.	Taffeta	Firm Iron-on or medium Sew-in Vilene; taffeta	Machine: 11–14 C. 70–90 Hand: fine to medium	40–50	10–12 or 12–15: fine linen	1.7–2.1 or 2.1–2.5
Slub	Linen woven with irregular knots and thicker parts in the plain weave.	Taffeta	Firm Iron-on or medium Sew-in Vilene; taffeta	Machine: 14 C. 90 Hand: medium–fine	40–50	10–12	2.1–2.5

Silk: Use silk or mercerised cotton thread (C. = continental machine needle size).

Name	Description	Lining	Interfacing	Needles	Thread	Machine stitches to inch	Length in mm.
*Brocade	Luxurious fabric with raised woven patterns, often with gold threads interwoven.	Jap silk or fine silk-satin	Light Sew-in Vilene; taffeta	Machine: 11 C. 70 Hand: fine	Silk thread	12–15	1.7–2.1

* For heavy brocade use needles, thread, stitch lengths a step larger, or more if needed and cotton or mercerised thread for cotton brocade.

Name	Description	Lining	Interfacing	Needles	Thread	Machine stitches to inch	Length in mm.
Chiffon	Diaphanous, soft, sheer material	Jap silk or imitation Jap silk	Transparent Iron-on Vilene (test first on synthetics); light Sew-in Vilene; taffeta; net	Machine: 9–11 C. 65–70 Hand: fine	50 or silk	15–20	1.3–1.7
Faille	Crosswise ribbed or corded silk.	Jap silk or imitation Jap silk	Soft Sew-in Vilene or taffeta	Machine: 11–14 C. 70–90 Hand: fine	50 or silk	12–15	17.–2.1
Jap silk	Light, simple, plain woven silk (for silk linings). Also known as China silk.	Unlined or organza	Light Sew-in Vilene; taffeta; organdie	Machine: 11 C. 70 Hand: fine	50 or silk	12–15	1.7–2.1

Name	Description	Lining	Interfacing	Needles	Thread	Machine stitches to inch	Length in mm.
Organza	Sheer, fine, floating silk with sheen. Extra lightweight.	Jap silk. Taffeta	Transparent Iron-on (test first); light Sew-in Vilene; taffeta; organdie	Machine: 11 C. 70 Hand: fine	50 or silk	15–20	1.3–1.7
Raw silk	Unbleached silk woven in rough state.	Jap silk or imitation Jap silk	Light Sew-in Vilene; taffeta	Machine: 11–14 C. 70–90 Hand: fine to medium–fine	40, 50 or silk	12–15	1.7–2.1
Shantung	Plain fine woven silk often with slub weave. Crisp but not naturally crease resisting. Imitations.	Jap silk or imitation Jap silk	Soft Sew-in Vilene or soft Iron-on Vilene (test first); taffeta	Machine: 11 C. 70 Hand: fine	40–50 or silk	12–15	1.7–2.1
Surah	Soft, twill woven silk, often striped or patterned. Man-made versions.	Jap silk, imitation Jap silk or fine taffeta	Soft Sew-in Vilene; soft Iron-on Vilene (test first); taffeta	Machine: 11–14 C. 70–90 Hand: fine to medium fine	40–50 or silk	12–15	1.7–2.1
Tie silk	Twill or rather close, thick silk.	Jap silk or imitation Jap silk	Soft Sew-in Vilene; soft Iron-on Vilene (test first); taffeta	Machine: 11–14 C. 70–90 Hand: medium–fine or fine	40–50 or silk	12–15	1.7–2.1
Tulle	Fine, gauze-like 'floaty' net veiling, often silk.	Organza; Jap silk or imitation Jap silk	Transparent Iron-on Vilene (test first); light Sew-in Vilene; taffeta	Machine: 9–11 C. 65–70 Hand: fine	60–50 or silk	15–20	1.3–1.7
Tussah or wild silk	Deep cream/beige colour rough silk made from silk spun by wild silk worms.	Jap silk; imitation Jap silk; or fine taffeta	Soft Sew-in Vilene; taffeta	Machine: 11–14 C. 70–90 Hand: fine to medium	40–50 or silk	12–15	1.7–2.7

Wool: Use mercerised cotton or silk thread (C. = continental machine needle size

* It is possible to iron-on Vilene for small areas of interfacing for most wool fabrics, but test on a spare piece of material first.

Name	Description	Lining	Interfacing	Needles	Thread	Machine stitches to inch	Length in mm.
Barathea	Finely woven wool with silky, granular surface.	Taffeta; crêpe de chine; lining satin; crêpe	Canvas; medium Sew-in; firm Iron-on Vilene	Machine: 14 C. 90 Hand: medium	40	10–12	2.1–2.5
Bouclé	Nubbly cloth with looped surface.	Line or underline with Jap silk taffeta; Bemberg; crêpe de chine	Medium Sew-in Vilene; taffeta	Machine: 14–16 C. 90–100 Hand: medium	40	10–12	2.1–2.5

Name	Description	Lining	Interfacing	Needles	Thread	Machine stitches to inch	Length in mm.
Broadcloth	Smooth cloth with slightly furry, silky nap.	Taffeta; crêpe-backed lining satin; brocade	Heavy Sew-in or firm Iron-on Vilene; canvas	Machine: 16 C. 90–100 Hand: medium strong	40	10–12	2.1–2.5
Camel hair and wool	A caramel colour fabric with camel hair blended in.	Taffeta; crêpe-backed lining satin	Heavy Sew-in or firm Iron-on Vilene: canvas	Machine: 14–16 C. 90–100 Hand: medium	40	10–12	2.1–2.5
Crêpe (wool)	Stretchy matt fabric with granular surface.	Jap silk; Bemberg; crêpe de chine; taffeta	Soft Sew-in or Superdrape Iron-on Vilene	Machine: 14 C. 90 Hand: fine to medium	40	10–12	2.1–2.5
Facecloth	Plain woven cloth with felt-like smooth surface.	Taffeta; Bemberg; Jap silk; silk; lining satin	Heavy Sew-in or firm Iron-on Vilene; canvas	Machine: 14–16 C. 90–100 Hand: medium	40	10–12	2.1–2.5
Flannel	Plain woven fabric, sometimes twill woven. Has slightly woolly look. Often grey. Worsted flannel has a firmer surface. (Also, traditional plain woven red or cream baby flannel, line with batiste or silk and fine sew.)	Taffeta; Bemberg	Medium Sew-in or heavy Sew-in Vilene depending on weight; or firm Iron-on Vilene	Machine: 14–16 C. 90–100 Hand: medium	40	10–12	2.1–2.5
Gaberdine	Twill woven wool with diagonal weave, firm surfaced, with a dull sheen.	Taffeta, imitation Jap silk	Heavy Sew-in or firm Iron-on Vilene	Machine: 14–16 C. 90–100 Hand: medium	40	10–12	2.1–2.5
Georgette	Sheer, matt stretchy fabric. Looks like a cross between chiffon and crêpe. Other fibres.	Jap silk; imitation Jap silk; crêpe de chine	Superdrape Iron-on Vilene or soft Sew-in Vilene; taffeta	Machine: 11–14 C. 70–90 Hand: fine	40–50 or silk	12–15	1.7–2.1
Jersey	Knitted fabric, in all fibres. Double jersey: double knit, stable fabric.	Crêpe; tricot	Superdrape Iron-on Vilene; Stretch tricot	Machine: 11–14 C. 70–90 Hand: fine to medium fine	40	12–15 Use a stretch stitch Heavy: 10	1.7–2.1 2.5
Mohair	Loose woven hair fabric from wool of Angora goat. Do not steam press. Dry iron. Can be woven or blended with other fabrics.	Taffeta, Jap silk or imitation Jap silk	Soft Sew-in Vilene; taffeta	Machine: 14 C. 90 Hand: medium	40 or silk	10–12	1.7–2.1
Serge	Crisp twill woven cloth with matt surface and slightly coarse, rough feel.	Taffeta; lining satin	Heavy Sew-in Vilene or firm Iron-on Vilene; canvas	Machine: 14–16 C. 90–100 Hand: medium or medium–strong	40	10–12	2.1–2.5

Name	Description	Lining	Interfacing	Needles	Thread	Machine stitches to inch	Length in mm.
Tweed	Woven woollen cloth, often blended with other fibres.	Crêpe de chine; crêpe; taffeta; lining satin	Heavy Sew-in or firm Iron-on Vilene; canvas; hair canvas	Machine: 14–16 C. 90–100 Hand: medium to strong	40	10–12	2.1–2.5
Twill wool cloth	Twill weave, with diagonal rib.	Taffeta; satin; crêpe de chine	Heavy Sew-in or firm Iron-on Vilene; canvas	Machine: 14–16 C. 90–100 Hand: medium to medium strong	40	10–12	2.1–2.5
Velour	Soft firm cloth, with a pile surface, almost like velvet nap.	Taffeta; satin; crêpe de chine	Heavy Sew-in or firm Iron-on Vilene; canvas	Machine: 14–16 C. 90–100 Hand: medium to medium strong	40	10–12	2.1–2.5
Viyella	Trade name for lightweight fine wool and cotton blend fabric.	Imitation Jap silk, taffeta	Soft Sew-in or soft Iron-on Vilene; taffeta	Machine: 14 C. 90 Hand: medium– fine	40	12–15	1.7–2.1
Worsted	Crisp, firm fine woollen fabric, with a smooth well-pressed look.	Taffeta	Medium or heavy Sew-in Vilene (depending on weight); firm Iron-on Vilene	Machine: 14–16 C. 90–100 Hand: medium	40	10–12	2.1–2.5

Types of tweed:

BIRDSEYE: Woven with a pattern of small claw-like shapes.
CHEVIOT: Twill weave plain or check wool.
DOG TOOTH: Irregular shape, repetitive check.
DONEGAL: Speckled and flecked pretty tweed black, white, brown or other colour mixtures.
HARRIS: Coarse, durable tweed. Often check or plain in browns, blues, greys. Use needle size 16–18 (100–110); strong thread and 6–10 st. (2.4–4.3mm.) to in. Hand-sewing needle: strong.
HERRINGBONE: Zig-zag chevron patterns in twill woven cloth.
HOPSACK: Plain woven wool tweed.
PEPPER AND SALT: Black and white speckled tweed.
PRINCE OF WALES CHECK: Showy plaid checks, but in black and white, brown and white etc., unlike colourful plaid.
SHEPHERD'S CHECK: Small gingham like check wool cloth often black and white, brown and white etc.

TATTERSALL CHECK: Horse blanket check of widely spaced single lines, such as black and mustard checks on a cream ground.

REVERSIBLE CLOTH: Wool woven double sided, perhaps plain on one side, check on the other. Use generous flat fell seams, and bind the edges with fold-over braid. Sew buttons on each side of the fabric, over one another . . . though this would mean reversing the buttonhole fastening to the 'man's' side on a woman's cape. Or use link buttons, or a braided flap fastening, detachable, to button onto both sides . . . in the reversible sense.

TARTAN: Traditional Highland red and green and blue and heather coloured multi-checks should be sewn according to the type of basic fabric construction, with special reference to matching the plaids at the seams.

Name	Description	Lining	Interfacing	Needles	Thread	Machine stitches to inch	Length in mm.

Rayon

* Some rayon frizzles up to nothing under a hot iron and synthetics are usually unsuited to the heat application required for fusing the fabrics together. If iron-on interfacing is used, test on a piece of the material first.

Name	Description	Lining	Interfacing	Needles	Thread	Machine stitches to inch	Length in mm.
Brushed rayon	Medium weight woven and slightly brushed fabric. Also tweed, cotton types. Easy to handle, care for, sew. Inexpensive. Ideal for sewing beginners.	Unlined or taffeta	Soft Sew-in Vilene: taffeta	Machine: 14 C. 90 Hand: medium	40	10–12	2.1–2.5
Crêpe	Slightly stretchy soft matt fabric, with a finely granular surface.	Imitation Jap silk; fine taffeta; silk	Superdrape Iron-on Vilene or soft Sew-in Vilene; taffeta	Machine: 11–14 C. 70–90 Hand: fine	40–50	12–15	1.7–2.1
Crêpe de chine	Has fine granular surface like crêpe, but is non-stretchy, and has a lustre like silk.	Taffeta; imitation Jap silk; silk	Taffeta; soft Sew-in Vilene	Machine: 11–14 C. 70–90 Hand: fine	40–50	12–15	1.7–2.1
Grosgrain	Crosswise corded rayon, fairly substantial medium weight silky fabric. Used for wedding outfits; evening skirts, formal wear.	Taffeta; imitation Jap silk	Medium Sew-in Vilene; taffeta; firm Iron-on Vilene (test first)	Machine: 14 C. 90 Hand: medium–fine	40	12–15	1.7–2.1
Moiré	Taffeta with a water mark running through it like woodgrain.	Taffeta	Soft Sew-in Vilene; soft Iron-on Vilene (test first); taffeta	Machine: 11 C. 70 Hand: fine	50	12–15	1.7–2.1
Moss crêpe	Similar to crêpe, but with a coarser, mossier granular surface, a heavier texture.	Imitation Jap silk; taffeta; silk	Superdrape Iron-on Vilene (test first); soft Sew-in Vilene; taffeta	Machine: 11 C. 70 Hand: fine	50	12–15	1.7–2.1
Ottoman	Rayon fabric with raised silk-like narrow cords across. In other fabrics.	Taffeta	Medium Sew-in Vilene; firm Iron-on Vilene (test first); taffeta	Machine: 14 C. 90 Hand: medium–fine	40	12–15	1.7–2.1
Satin	Shiny surface material, achieved by special satin weave. Various qualities from lining satin, through crêpe back satin, to duchesse stiff, rich satin.	Underline with organza; line with taffeta, silk	Vilene soft Sew-in or soft Iron-on (test first); taffeta	Machine: 11–14 C. 70–90 Hand: fine to medium–fine	50–40 or silk. Tack with silk.	12–15	1.7–2.1
Taffeta	Plain weave, crisp silky rayon used for lining. Better quality for evening gowns. Made of silk, nylon or polyester etc. Ribbed taffeta is known as 'Faille'. Paper taffeta is crisp and light as its name suggests.	Taffeta, satin, brocade, silk	Vilene soft Sew-in or soft Iron-on (test first); taffeta	Machine: 11–14 C. 70–90 Hand: fine to medium–fine	50–40 or silk	12–15	1.7–2.1

Name	Description	Lining	Interfacing	Needles	Thread	Machine stitches to inch	Length in mm.
Velvet	Well-known pile fabric. Crushed velvet has crushed surface look; cut velvet: raised designs on plain background. Sew with direction of pile upwards.	Taffeta, satin, brocade silk	Soft Sew-in Vilene or medium Sew-in Vilene depending on weight; taffeta	Machine: 11–14 C. 70–90 Hand: fine	50–40 or silk. Tack with silk	12–15	1.7–2.1
Metallic fabric such as gold or silver lamé. Also metallic knit fabric	Glittering metal or plastic threads woven or knitted in a wide range of fabrics, or combined with other material.	Underline if the fabric is scratchy. Face with lining material at hems, armholes. Cuffs and neck edges too. Otherwise line with rayon, polyester or Tricel taffeta, or Jap silk. Use tricot knit lining or underlining for metallic knit fabric	Soft Sew-in Vilene; taffeta	Machine: 11–14 C. 70–90 Hand: fine to medium. Change to a new needle often as metallic thread tends to blunt needles	50–40 synthetic thread	12–15	1.7–2.1
Bonded	Fabric laminated on the reverse side with knit or woven smooth material.	No lining necessary	Soft Sew-in Vilene or firm Sew-in Vilene depending on weight	Machine: 14–16 C. 90–100 Hand: medium–fine	Thread to suit fabric thickness		6–12 depending on material thickness (smaller stitch for finer fabrics) 2.5–4.3 mm. per stitch

See note about iron-on interfacing at beginning of *Rayon* section.

Synthetic Fabrics

The examples given in this list crop up frequently. If your synthetic fabric is not included, some similar material probably is. Fabrics made from the same type of original man-made fibres, and with the same construction are often somewhat alike, even if they have different trade names.

Sewing synthetic fabrics is in any case, not very different from sewing natural fabrics. Indeed they often look alike these days.

Apply the general advice for sewing a fabric, taking into account its construction . . . whether it is woven or knitted etc., the weight, i.e.: the thickness or thinness . . . the special problems of sewing knits, and use the appropriate synthetic sewing thread.

Follow the maker's instructions carefully with regard to iron-on non-woven interfacings. Some synthetic fabrics which are not normally ironed, or which need a cool iron, might not be suitable for this useful material. Test press first.

Name	Description	Lining	Interfacing	Needles	Thread	Machine stitches to inch	Length in mm.
Acrilan	Bulky acrylic. Woven medium weight.	Nylon, rayon or polyester; taffeta	Soft or medium Sew-in Vilene; synthetic taffeta	Machine: 14–16 C. 90–100 Hand: medium		10–12	2.1–2.5

Name	Description	Lining	Interfacing	Needles	Thread	Machine stitches to inch	Length in mm.
Acrilan Knit	Bulky knit material.	Unlined. If necessary use synthetic knit jersey lining or underlining	Superdrape Iron-on Vilene (but test first)	Machine: ball-point or extra sharp, new needle: 14; C.90 Hand: medium		12–15	1.7–2.1 Use stretch stitch if available
Courtelle	Acrylic, woven medium weight.	Nylon, polyester or rayon taffeta	Soft or medium Sew-in Vilene; synthetic taffeta	Machine: 14–16 C. 90–100 Hand: medium		10–12	2.1–2.5
Courtelle	Bulky acrylic knit.	Unlined, or if necessary, synthetic jersey for lining	Superdrape Iron-on Vilene (but test first)	Machine: ball-point or extra sharp new needle. 14; C. 90 Hand: medium		12–15	1.7–2.1 Use stretch stitch, if available
Crimplene	Polyester crimped jersey with a patterned surface and light silky-cotton knit texture.	None. If essential, use man-made lightweight jersey underlining	Vilene Superdrape Iron-on (but test first)	Machine: ball-point or extra sharp, new needle. 14; C. 90 Hand: fine–medium		12–15	1.7–2.1 Use stretch stitch if available
Dacron	Strong polyester fibre used in making fabrics and blends. Use synthetic thread, and the needle size, stitch length and machine stitch to go with the fabric.						
Nylon	Fine to medium woven nylon. Strong, easy care, slightly silky look fabric.	Nylon taffeta or nylon quilting for anoraks etc.	Vilene soft Sew-in; nylon taffeta	Machine: 11–14 C. 70–90 Hand: fine. Use very sharp		12–15	1.7–2.1
Nylon jersey	Medium weight soft, smooth surface, usually rather fine knit, if 100% nylon.	Usually unlined. If at all, combine with fine nylon jersey.	Vilene Superdrape Iron-on (but test first)	Machine: Ball-point or extra sharp new needle. 11–14; C. 70–90 Hand: fine to medium		12–15	1.7–2.1 Use a stretch stitch if available
Orlon knit	Acrylic bulky knit.	Unlined. If necessary, use fine man-made jersey for lining.	Vilene Iron-on Superdrape (but test first)	Machine: ball-point or extra sharp new needle. 14–16; C. 90–100 Hand: medium		12–15	1.7–2.1 Use a stretch stitch if available

Name	Description	Lining	Interfacing	Needles	Thread	Machine stitches to inch	Length in mm.
Qiana	Luxury man-made fabric of Qiana nylon is constructed in twills, satins, shantung, ottoman and silk-like materials.	Lining: polyester or rayon	Light Sew-in Vilene; polyester taffeta	Machine: 11 C. 70 Hand: fine	Polyester 50 Gütermann 100	12–15	1.7–2.1
Stretch Terry	Soft knit towelling in brilliant and subtle colours. Also plush velvet knit.	None	None as a rule: tape shoulder seams, also fitted waist seam	Machine: 11–14 C. 70–90 Use a ball-point or extra sharp new needle. Hand: fine to medium		12–15	1.7–2.1 Use a stretch stitch if available. Also roller presser foot or Even Feed foot.
Tricel	Tri-acetate; lightweight woven fabric, with scarf-silk look. Pleats well.	Nylon, Tricel or rayon taffeta	Light Sew-in Vilene; Tricel taffeta	Machine: 11 C. 70 Hand: fine		12–15	1.7–2.1
Tricel jersey	Lightweight jersey.	None. If necessary, lightweight tricot, or Tricel tricot	Superdrape Iron-on Vilene (but test first)	Machine: 11 C. 70 Hand: fine. Use a ball point or extra sharp new needle.		12–15	1.7–2.1 Use a stretch stitch, if available. Also the roller presser foot or Even Feed foot
Terylene	Woven lightweight lawn, chiffon. Strong, sheer, crease resisting. Or combined with cotton or wool.	Sheer: Terylene, otherwise Rayon or Tricel polyester taffeta	Vilene soft Sew-in or transparent Iron-on Vilene (test first)	Machine: 11 C. 70 Hand: fine. To 14 C. 90 for medium fabrics		Sheer: 15–20 Medium: 12–15	1.3–1.7 1.7–2.1
Terylene	Spun Terylene jersey, with a cotton jersey texture.	Unlined	Superdrape Iron-on Vilene (but test first)	Machine: 11–14 C. 70–90 Hand: fine. Use a ball-point, or extra sharp new needle		12–15	1.7–2.1 Use a stretch stitch and the roller presser foot or Even Feed foot.
Elasto-metric fibres in elastic fabrics	Stretch fabrics used in foundation garments, swimwear, elasticated parts of garments.	Usually unlined and not interfaced except with reinforcing stretch fabric		Machine: 11 C. 70 Hand: fine	Thread: elastic; synthetic 50	St. (stretch) 15–20	1.3–1.7 (Use a stretch stitch)

Linings & notions

Lining and underlining materials

BATISTE: Handkerchief fine cotton lawn for sheer cottons and some fine baby wear.

BEMBERG: Fine taffeta for dresses, skirts, suits, coats.

BONDING: Knit or woven fabric bonded on the reverse side of material, so no separate lining is needed.

BROCADE: Rayon, silk or satin for luxury fabrics such as velvet. Cotton brocade for velveteen, corduroy etc.

COTTON: For heavy cotton corduroy, cotton quilting and similar fabrics.

COTTON SATEEN: For men's wear and lining curtains.

CRÊPE: For jackets and coats. (Also satin-backed crêpe.)

CRÊPE DE CHINE: For skirts, jackets and coats. For bed quilts too.

FLANNEL: Traditional red or cream plain woven fine flannel, for lining or interlining coats, capes and some children's garments.

FLANNELETTE (or Winceyette): Fleecy backed or fleecy cotton for lining or interlining heavy duty coats such as reefer jackets, children's coats. Also for cotton quilts.

JAP SILK: Plain pure silk for silk, velvet, chiffon, fine wool and similar luxury fabrics.

IMITATION JAP SILK: Fine taffeta for dresses, skirts, jackets, coats. A good substitute for expensive pure silk.

LAWN: For cotton, voile and other sheer cotton fabrics, for corduroy and cotton quilting etc.

MILIUM: Insulated coat or jacket lining.

NYLON: For lining nylon and other man-made fabrics, and nylon quilting.

ORGANZA: For chiffon, silk, satin and similar luxury fabrics.

SATIN: Lining satin for dresses, skirts, jackets, coats. Also crêpe-backed satin, a softer version.

SILK: For silk, velvet, chiffon, lace and similar luxury fabrics. Also for fine wool.

TAFFETA: Widely used crisp lining fabric, in various types such as rayon, nylon, polyester, Tricel, Terylene. Suit the type to your main material.

TRICOT: Plain firm, close knit lining fabric, usually in man-made fibre, for lining Crimplene, jersey and other knitted fabrics.

WADDING: Terylene and other wadding sold by the metre for interlining coats, quilted anoraks and bed quilts.

WINCEYETTE: see flannelette.

Notions

NOTIONS are the items mentioned on the back of the pattern envelope, below the charts of material requirements. They are those indispensable sewing accessories, the buttons, zippers, tapes and trimmings so essential to dressmaking.

It is wise to buy all the pattern suggests before you leave the shop, or you may have to make a special trip later. Or to have a comprehensive supply at home, so that you always have the right size press fasteners, or a length of elastic when you need it. It is surprising how aggravatingly difficult it can be to find just the button or colour zipper you are looking for at short notice.

BELTING: This is the stiffening to go inside the covered belt. It can be tough corded ribbon, boned ribbon or grosgrain ribbon. Special belting is rubberised and very tough, or thin, stiff strip. Look for iron-on varieties too.

BUTTONS: Button size, believe it or not, is measured in lines . . . 40 lines to the 2.5cm. or inch. Thus a button said to be 80 lines wide is 5cm. (2in.) across. Try the covered button service from Singer Sewing Machine Shops and elsewhere. Covered buttons have special charm. Or cover your own with a re-usable, rustless button trim.

BUCKLES: Take the measurement across the buckle bar, slightly wider than your belt.

BIAS BINDING: Ready-made bias binding with the raw edges pressed in, comes in 12mm. (½in.), 25mm. (1in.) or 50mm. (2in.) widths.

BRAID: A run-down of some of the innumerable types of braid available is given on pages 94–95. It is basically flat, or doubled in half, and sold by length, from the roll.

ELASTIC: Elastic thread for shirring; general purpose elastic ranging from round hat elastic to wide strong flat elastic for waistbands. Plush covered and webbing elastic with one woven selvage is sold for underwear, and in broad, coloured and smartly striped versions for waistbands. Wide double selvage elastic for belts is also available.

HOOKS AND EYES: Range from tiny metal size 00 for fastening a collar band at the corner, to strong hooks and eyes, size 10, for waistband fastenings. In black or silver. Flat hooks and catches used for trousers' waistbands. Large sized corded hooks and eyes for fur coats etc.

HORSEHAIR BRAID: Fine horsehair braid for stiffening sheer hems.

IRON-ON: When you are faced with a repair in a hurry, or one that promises to be arduous, ask whether there is an iron-on alternative. Such as Vilene Wondaweb, for gluing up a hem, or Vilene Bondaweb for fusing two fabrics together. Try iron-on carpet tape, interfacing etc.

METAL EYELETS: Lacquered metal rings pressed into eyelet holes with eyelet pliers. Sold in kit form.

PINS: Pins must be rustless steel for dressmaking. Suit the pin size to the material thickness and durability or delicacy. Glass-headed pins are easy to see and pick up. Use brass silk pins for silks and velvet. A magnet is a boon for retrieving dropped pins.

PRESS FASTENERS: From tiny size to giant size in black and silver. Hammer on press fasteners too, for baby clothes; transparent plastic press fasteners; and press fastener tape for upholstery. Also in button form: 'Ginger Snaps' by Scovill Dritz.

RIBBON: From double satin baby ribbon, to wide velvet ribbon. By no means only for hair bows. Stitch brightly coloured satin ribbon over net for an inexpensive party dress.

TAPE: Ordinary cotton tape for apron strings; twill tape for reinforcing seams in knits, P.V.C. and fur. Seam tape, narrow double selvaged in many different colours, for covering raw edges when turning up hems.

TOGGLES: Wooden or plastic elongated knobs. For loop fastening attachments.

TRANSPARENT STICKY TAPE: Use two-side transparent sticky tape to help place a zipper, and for other sewing jobs. Sellotape, too, is constantly useful.

TRIMMING: Lace, broderie anglaise, organdie pleated edging, ready-made bows, sequin motifs, sew-on woolly lambs, embroidered anchors, swansdown feather edging, fake fur or fur trimming etc.

VELCRO: Ingenious tape with a furry appearance, with hooks on one surface and loops on the other which fasten together on impact.

ZIPPERS: Invisible lightweight, dress weight, skirt weight, etc.

Index

Glossary of sewing terms

A-line — A garment widening neatly, from a narrow top, in shape of an 'A'.

Bar tack — A short buttonhole-stitched thread chain to reinforce a vent in a seam, instead of an arrowhead or crow's foot tack. Also used instead of a metal eye in a hook and eye fastening.

Batik — A way of printing fabric by a process of waxing and dyeing.

Bolero — A short, Spanish jacket, usually with curved fronts.

Bouclé — Nubbly, loop-surfaced fabric.

Broderie anglaise — Eyelet embroidered fabric or trimming.

Buckram — Stiff, heavy-duty interfacing used for pelmets.

Cartridge pleats — Decorative parallel tube-like pleats, similar to cartridge holders in gun-belts. Unpressed.

Chevron — V-shaped pattern, formed by opposing bias stripes meeting exactly at a seam, or by a zig-zag design in the fabric.

Ciré — Shiny, slippery surface fabric, often silky fine knit.

Coat tab-hanger — A flat loop attached inside the neck edge of a garment at the centre back. Usually tape, a buttonhole-thread chain or made like a belt carrier, stitched down at each end.

Corded braid — Heavily frogged corded braid, richly ornamented and usually black, for edging velvet. Also corded braid buttons.

Dior pleat or slit — A finished opening in a centre back skirt seam, sometimes with an underlay attached to the skirt back-lining. To allow for movement in a narrow skirt.

Downproof — Fabric woven or treated so that no down, however fine, can escape. For pillows, duvets, cushions etc.

Epaulet sleeve — Sleeve set-in but with an attached shoulder yoke.

Fan pleating — An inverted pleat of concertina small pleats.

French cuff — Another name for a buttoned shirt cuff.

Gore — A shaped panel, as in a seamed skirt, where the narrow top widens gracefully at the hem, to form a fitted flared shape.

Grosgrain ribbon — Soft corded silk or rayon ribbon.

Gusset — An inset, shaped panel to allow for movement in a garment, usually stitched in where it might otherwise tear with the stress of wear, such as underarm on a kimono sleeve.

Heading — The name given to the frill allowance above a casing, as in a curtain.

Hessian — Plain woven coarse sacking-like cloth, used in furnishing, and for shopping bags etc.

Kapok — Cream coloured cotton-like fleece used for stuffing toys and cushions.

Kick pleats — Dapper little inverted pleats in a skirt to allow for movement, and as part of the design. Sometimes fan pleats.

Mandarin collar — Chinese style stand-up stiff collar, fastening at the front or side.

Moiré — Taffeta or similar fabric with a water mark effect.

Picot edge — A decorative edge to fine fabric made up of closely spaced tiny loops, as in the edge of lace trimming.

Pinking — Decorative zig-zag edge cut with pinking shears, as a seam finish, or for cutting out felt. Occasionally scalloping shears which are used for the same effect, but with tiny scallops.

Princess line: — A panelled garment with a fitted bodice and waistline, no waist seam, and a flared skirt.

Remnants — Short ends left over from bales of fabric, sold off cheaply.

Revers — Lapels of a blazer-shaped, tailored collar.

Scallops — Embroidered by drawing scallops on fabric, and buttonhole stitching-in crescents tapering into the ends, where the scallops link. Afterwards, the fabric outside the scallops is carefully trimmed away. See also *faced scallops*, page 21.

Seconds — Items, or fabric, with a slight imperfection, sold at a reduction in price on the perfect version.

Screen printing — Hand-printed fabric obtained by process of pressing the dye through a prepared silk screen, with very fresh, artistic effect.

Square neck facing — Made as for shaped facing and attached by same method. Clipped into corners of seam allowance, to turn square onto wrong side, and thus to lie flat.

Stock tie collar — A blouse collar with large ties, which are looped over one another to lie flat and be tucked into the waistband.

Stretch terry — A soft, knitted form of towelling used for baby garments.

Tie collar — A bias cut, stand-up interfaced collar, with interlined tie extensions (sometimes sheer, unlined) for loose front ties, or to tie into a neck bow.

Tie dye — Fabric dyed in sunburst style designs by knotting and tying in stones, then dyeing, sometimes in more than one colour.

Unpressed pleats — Fabric pleated, but not pressed into a crease, but with the pleats lying in soft folds.

Vicuna — Luxury wool obtained from the Latin American vicuna, an animal similar to a llama.

Personal measurement chart

RECORD YOUR PERSONAL MEASUREMENTS HERE, FOR QUICK REFERENCE AS YOU SEW

NAME: PATTERN SIZE:

BUST:

HIPS:

BACK WAIST LENGTH:

UNDERARM side seam to waist:

WAIST:

SHOULDER:

CHEST across below shoulder bones:

between waist and hips:

ARM outside arm shoulder to wrist with arm bent:

upper arm circumference:

wrist circumference:

SKIRT LENGTH *waist to hem*

short length:

knee length:

calf length:

maxi length:

ankle length:

floor length:

neck to hem

short length:

knee length:

calf length:

maxi length:

ankle length:

floor length:

WOMEN'S TROUSERS waist:

outside leg:

inside leg:

hips:

leg circumference:

thigh:

knee:

calf:

ankle:

basic width:

Trousers length can be taken from skirt length

FOR FURTHER DETAILS

see pages 31–33

CHILDREN *see page 115*

MEN *see page 116*

Shape of things to come

SEWING MACHINE OF THE FUTURE

The Singer Futura Electronic Sewing Machine has been evolved from a combination of skills and experience gained from over a century of building sewing machines, and more recently, from the company's work for the aerospace industry in the United States, when it moved into the electronic field.

The machine, fitted with transistors, is operated by a system of push buttons, which activate the electronic memory bank, potentially capable of storing five hundred and twelve stitch patterns.

An extremely flexible pre-set range of stitches and sewing jobs are available on the machine, with a wide range of overriding personal choice.

After selecting the stitch or sewing process required, a light pressure on the foot pedal instantly produces immaculate stitching. Plain sewing; embroidery; automatic buttonholes; perfect topstitching and many other sewing operations are instantaneously and effortlessly at your fingertips.

Electronic sewing in future will improve the ease, professionalism and accuracy of home sewing.

The epitome of *Sew Easy*

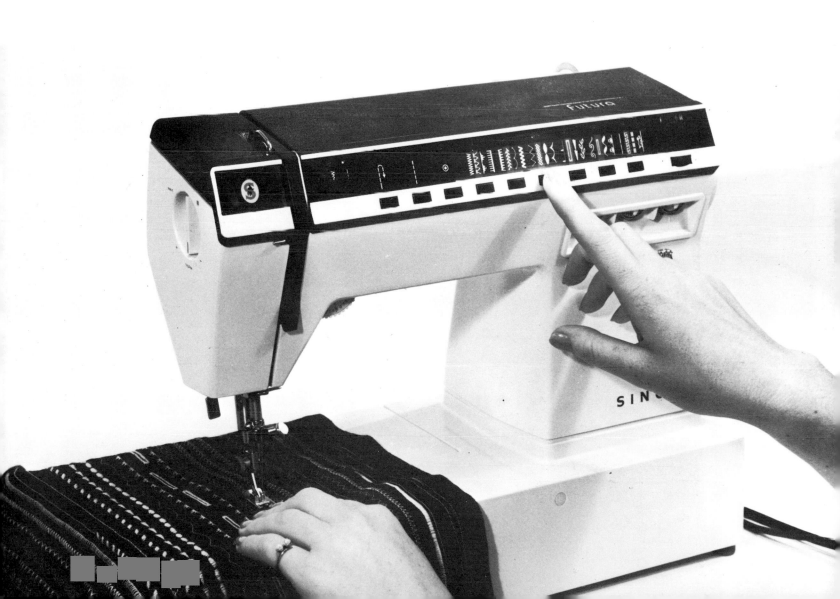

Acknowledgments

The author and publishers would like to thank the following firms for kind permission to reproduce copyright photographs and drawings and printed material; also thanks to the artists, designers and photographers who contributed to *Sew Easy*, Credits are given spread by spread.

Cover: Elna Sewing Machines Ltd. and A. E. Arthur Ltd.

1–5 *Drawing*, Arka Graphics

8 Sewing room corner: *photograph*, Nicholas Wegner

9 Dress forms: *left*, Diana; *right*, Twinfit, courtesy A. E. Arthur Ltd.

10 Work table: *Drawings*, Marian Appleton; Scovill Dritz Superboard; Arka Graphics

11 Ironing board: *photograph*, Nicholas Wegner; *drawing*, Marian Appleton

12 *Drawings*, Julia Hamlyn

13 Needles: *drawing*, Arka Graphics; needle threading: *drawings*, Julia Hamlyn/Arka Graphics

14–15 Thread: *drawing*, Julia Hamlyn; measuring tools: Marian Appleton

16 Weaves: Arka Graphics

18–19 *Drawings*, Marian Appleton

20 Bias binding: *facing drawings*, Julia Hamlyn

21 Mitred corner: Julia Hamlyn; scallops: Marian Appleton

22 Choice of sewing machines: *drawings*, Hand; Treadle: Julia Hamlyn; Electric: Marian Appleton

23 Chart picture of sewing machine parts: Arka Graphics; freely drawn from Singer Sewing Machine

24 *Drawings*, Julia Hamlyn

25 *Drawings*, Marian Appleton

26 *Drawings*, Julia Hamlyn, freely drawn from Singer Sewing Machine attachments

27 *Drawings*, Marian Appleton; Julia Hamlyn

28 Hand; treadle machine: *drawings*, Julia Hamlyn; electric: Marian Appleton

29 *Drawings*, Julia Hamlyn/Arka Graphics

30 Measuring cushion: *drawings*, Julia Hamlyn

31 Measuring yourself: *drawings*, Marian Appleton;

32 *Photographs*, Nicholas Wegner;

33 Chart: courtesy Vogue-Butterick Pattern Services Ltd. and the Pattern Manufacturer's Association

34 Trousers: *drawings*, Marian Appleton; chart: Julia Hamlyn

35 *Reproduction from pattern packet*: courtesy Butterick Patterns

36 Prepare for sewing: *Photograph*, Arka Graphics. *Sewing machine*: courtesy Elna Ltd.

37 *Photograph*, courtesy Butterick Patterns

38 Helen: *photograph*, Nicholas Wegner

39 *Pattern instructions sheets* reproduced by courtesy Butterick Patterns

40–41 *Drawings*, Julia Hamlyn/Arka Graphics

42–43 *Drawings*, Julia Hamlyn

44 Stripes: *drawings*, Marian Appleton; plaid: Julia Hamlyn

45 *Pattern charts* reproduced by courtesy of Butterick Patterns

46 *Drawing*, Julia Hamlyn

47 *Drawing*, Marian Appleton

48–49 *Drawings*, Julia Hamlyn/Arka Graphics

50 Clothes fit for a Palace: *photograph*, courtesy Vogue Patterns

51 Hat: *photograph*, courtesy of Butterick Patterns; Unit construction: *drawing*, Arka Graphics: courtesy Style Patterns.

52 Knit: *photograph*, courtesy of Butterick Patterns; velvet photograph: courtesy of Vogue Patterns

53 Fitting: *photograph*, Nicholas Wegner

54–55 *Drawings*, Julia Hamlyn

56–57 *Drawings*, Julia Hamlyn

58–59 *Drawings*, Julia Hamlyn. *Photograph*, courtesy of Vogue Patterns

60–61 *Drawings*, Julia Hamlyn. *Photograph*, courtesy of Butterick Patterns

62–63 Zipper: *photograph*, Arka Graphics; *drawings*, Julia Hamlyn

64–65 *Photograph*, courtesy of Butterick Patterns; *drawings*, Julia Hamlyn

66–67 Skirt marker: *photograph*, courtesy of Scovill Dritz Ltd.; *drawings*, Julia Hamlyn

68–69 *Drawings*, Julia Hamlyn

70–71 *Drawings*, Julia Hamlyn

72–73 *Drawings*, Julia Hamlyn

74–75 *Drawings*, Julia Hamlyn. *Photograph*, courtesy of Vogue Patterns

76 *Photograph*, courtesy of Butterick Patterns

77 *Drawings*, Julia Hamlyn

78–79 Patch pockets: *photograph*, courtesy of Butterick Patterns. *Drawings*, Julia Hamlyn

80–81 *Drawings*, Julia Hamlyn

82–83 *Drawings*, Julia Hamlyn; yoke-shaped facing: *drawing*, Arka Graphics

84–85 *Photograph*, courtesy of Butterick Patterns Ltd.; *drawings*, Julia Hamlyn; Arka Graphics

86–87 *Reprinted pattern on left*, courtesy of Vogue Patterns; frog fastening: *photograph*: right: courtesy of Butterick Patterns. *Drawings*, Julia Hamlyn

88 Pressing: *photograph*, Nicholas Wegner

89 Irons: *photograph*, courtesy of Hoover Ltd. Chart: courtesy of International Textile Care labelling Code Committee

90–91 *Photograph*, courtesy of Vogue Patterns; *drawings*, Julia Hamlyn

92–93 *Drawings*, Julia Hamlyn. *Photograph*, courtesy of Butterick Patterns

94–95 *Photographs*, courtesy of Butterick Patterns; *drawings*, Julia Hamlyn; Arka Graphics

96–97 *Photograph*, courtesy of Butterick Patterns; *drawings*, Julia Hamlyn

98–99 *Photograph*, courtesy of Butterick Patterns; *drawings*, Julia Hamlyn; Arka Graphics

100 *Drawings*, Julia Hamlyn/Arka Graphics; *photograph*, Fritz Wegner

101 *Photograph*, courtesy of Vogue Patterns

102–3 Smocking; shirring: *drawings*, Julia Hamlyn. Smocking stitches: Arka Graphics. *Photograph*, courtesy of Vogue Patterns

104–5 *Drawings*: Julia Hamlyn. Large belt: *drawing*, Arka Graphics

106–7 *Drawings*, Julia Hamlyn. *Photograph*, courtesy of Butterick Patterns.

108–9 *Photograph*, courtesy of Vogue Patterns. *Drawings*, Julia Hamlyn

110 *Photograph*, courtesy of Vogue Patterns

111 *Drawings*, Julia Hamlyn

112–13 *Photograph*: courtesy of Vogue Patterns; *drawings*, Julia Hamlyn; Arka Graphics

114–15 *Photograph*, courtesy of Butterick Patterns; *measurement chart* reproduced by courtesy of Vogue-Butterick Pattern Service.

116–17 *Photograph*: courtesy of Butterick Patterns; *drawings*, Julia Hamlyn

118–19 *Drawing*, Julia Hamlyn; loose cover armchair: Arka Graphics

120–1 *Drawings*, Julia Hamlyn

122–3 *Drawings*, Julia Hamlyn

143 Singer *Futura* Sewing Machine: *photograph*, courtesy: Singer (U.K.) Ltd.